W9-AVH-444

Pfeiffer
& COMPANY

THE 1992 ANNUAL: DEVELOPING HUMAN RESOURCES

(The Twenty-First Annual)

Edited by

J. WILLIAM PFEIFFER, Ph.D., J.D.

San Diego • Toronto • Amsterdam • Sydney

Copyright © 1992 by Pfeiffer & Company

Looseleaf ISBN: 0-88390-304-0
Paperbound ISBN: 0-88390-305-9
ISSN: 1046-333X

Library of Congress Catalog Card Number 86-643030

The materials that appear in this book *(except those for which reprint permission must be obtained from the primary sources)* may be freely reproduced for educational/training activities. There is no requirement to obtain special permission for such uses. We do, however, ask that the following statement appear on all reproductions:

Reproduced from
The 1992 Annual:
Developing Human Resources
J. William Pfeiffer, Editor
San Diego, California: Pfeiffer & Company, 1992

This permission statement is limited to the reproduction of materials for educational/training events. *Systematic or large-scale reproduction or distribution (more than one hundred copies)— or inclusion of items in publications for sale—may be done only with prior written permission.*

Printed in the United States of America

Published by

Pfeiffer & Company
8517 Production Avenue
San Diego, California 92121
619-578-5900
FAX (619) 578-2042

Pfeiffer & Company
International Publishers
4190 Fairview Street
Burlington, Ontario L7 L 4Y8 Canada
416-632-5832, FAX 416-333-5675

Pfeiffer & Company
Roggestraat 15
2153 GC Nieuw-Vennep
The Netherlands
31-2526-89840, FAX 31-2526-86885

Pfeiffer & Company
Ground Floor, 6-8 Thomas Street
Chatswood NSW 2067
Australia
61-2-415-1344, FAX 61-2-415-1051

This book is printed on acid-free, recycled stock that meets or exceeds
the minimum GPO and EPA specifications for recycled paper.

PREFACE

The contents of this *Annual*, the twenty-first volume in our series, attest to the fact that the field of human resource development (HRD)—which includes training, career development, personnel, management development, and organization development functions—is still thriving. The changes in the title of the *Annual* over the past twenty-one years reflect the evolution of HRD as well as the intention of Pfeiffer & Company to remain at the cutting edge of this field.

The central purpose of the *Annual* has always been to keep readers aware of and involved in the current developments in the field. Consequently, each year the contents of the *Annual* are selected and edited to reflect these developments as we at Pfeiffer & Company perceive them. For several years now the HRD function in most organizations has grown in terms of visibility and has exerted a stronger and more valuable influence in such efforts as strategic planning. The individual pieces selected for this *Annual* exemplify the depth of the field today. They not only serve as cause for optimism about the future of HRD; they also offer food for thought about the needs and requirements of that future.

In this year's *Annual*, the Lecturette, Theory and Practice, and Resources sections again are combined into a single Professional Development section. This format, initiated in 1984, allows greater flexibility in selection and facilitates a more coherent overview of what is occurring in the field of HRD.

In the Instrumentation section, Pfeiffer & Company intends to continue to publish practical measurement devices that are useful for trainers, consultants, and managers. Moreover, as has been the case in the last several *Annuals*, both the theoretical background for each instrument and practical suggestions for its administration and application are included. These features have been added to make the instruments easier to use and to increase their value to our readers. Those people who intend to submit instruments and other materials to the *Annual* are advised to take these standards into account.

There are several aspects of the *Annual* series that have remained consistent over the years. One is a continuing bias that the *Annual* be strongly user oriented, that everything in it be potentially useful to the professional trainers, consultants, and facilitators who read it. The content of this *Annual* focuses on increasing each reader's professional competence and, therefore, his or her impact on the field of HRD. In keeping with this objective, users are allowed to duplicate and modify materials from the *Annuals* for *educational and training* purposes, so long as the credit statement found on the copyright page of the particular volume is included on all copies. However, if Pfeiffer & Company materials are to be reproduced in publications for sale or are intended for large-scale distribution (more than one hundred copies in twelve months), *prior written permission* is required. Also, if a footnote indicates that the material is copyrighted by some source other than Pfeiffer & Company, no reproduction is allowed without the written permission of that designated copyright holder.

We at Pfeiffer & Company continue to solicit materials from our readers—especially materials with a clear organizational focus and those that reflect the changing nature of the HRD field. The success of the *Annual* as a clearing house for HRD professionals depends on the continual flow of materials from our readers. We encourage and welcome the submission of structured experiences, instruments, and articles, including both innovative methods and tried-and-true procedures. Our guidelines for contributors appear at the end of this year's Professional Development section and are available from the Editorial Department at the San Diego address listed on the copyright page of this volume. Submissions should be sent to the managing editor at the same address.

I want to express my appreciation to the dedicated people at Pfeiffer & Company who have produced this volume: Carol Nolde, project manager; Marian K. Prokop, editor; Mary Kitzmiller, managing editor; Jennifer O. Bryant, editor; Steffany N. Parker, editor; Judy Whalen, page compositor; Susan Odelson, page compositor; Paul Bond, graphic designer; and Heather Kennedy, graphic designer. Also, I am especially grateful to Dr. Beverly Byrum-Robinson, who has again reviewed all of our structured experiences from a facilitator's perspective and whose insightful recommendations have contributed significantly to the usefulness of these training designs. As always, I extend my deepest gratitude to our authors for their generosity in sharing their professional ideas, materials, and techniques so that HRD practitioners may benefit.

J. William Pfeiffer

San Diego, California
October, 1991

About Pfeiffer & Company

Pfeiffer & Company is engaged in publishing, training, and consulting in the field of human resource development (HRD). The organization has earned an international reputation as the leading source of practical publications that are immediately useful to today's facilitators, trainers, consultants, and managers. A distinct advantage of these publications is that they are designed by practicing professionals who are continually experimenting with new techniques. Thus, readers benefit from the fresh but thoughtful approach that underlies Pfeiffer & Company's experientially based materials, resources, books, workbooks, instruments, and tape-assisted learning programs. These materials are designed for the HRD practitioner who wants access to a broad range of training and intervention technologies as well as background in the field.

The wide audience that Pfeiffer & Company serves includes training and development professionals, internal and external consultants, managers and supervisors, team leaders, and those in the helping professions. For its clients and customers, Pfeiffer & Company offers a practical approach aimed at increasing people's effectiveness on an individual, group, and organizational basis.

TABLE OF CONTENTS

*See Structured Experience Categories, p. 5, for an explanation of numbering.

PROFESSIONAL DEVELOPMENT

GENERAL INTRODUCTION TO THE 1992 *ANNUAL*

The 1992 Annual: Developing Human Resources is the twenty-first volume in the *Annual* series. The series is a collection of practical and useful materials for human resource development (HRD) practitioners—materials written by and for professionals. As such, the series continues to provide a publication outlet for HRD professionals who wish to share their experiences, their viewpoints, and their procedures with their colleagues.

In accordance with the changes made in the *Annual* format in 1984, there are now three rather than five sections: Structured Experiences, Instrumentation, and Professional Development. The Professional Development section combines the Lecturettes, Theory and Practice, and Resources sections that appeared in the first twelve volumes of the series. Over the years, some of the distinctions among those three categories had become blurred; it also seemed that some of the materials in those sections would be more useful if placed elsewhere in the volume. The arrangement now used relates the published pieces more logically and conveniently and allows greater flexibility in meeting the needs and interests of HRD practitioners.

One feature of the individual *Annuals* in the series has remained consistent over the years: the quality of content. As has been the case with each volume, the materials for the 1992 *Annual* have been selected for their quality of conceptualization, applicability to the real-world concerns of HRD practitioners, relevance to today's HRD issues, clarity of presentation, and ability to provide readers with assistance in their own professional development. In addition to using these criteria for selecting valuable tools, we were also able to choose structured experiences that will create a high degree of enthusiasm among the participants and add a great deal of enjoyment to the learning process. As in the past several years, readers will notice a greater focus on organizational issues, which reflects the fact that a large number of our readers are organizationally based or are consultants and trainers for organizations. Thus, there is a need for more structured experiences that have organizational relevance or that can be used with intact groups, especially work teams. A description of the structured experiences selected for this volume is given in the "Introduction to the Structured Experiences Section."

The order of the structured experiences in the 1992 *Annual* is dictated by the categorization scheme of our *Structured Experience Kit* and the *Reference Guide to Handbooks and Annuals*. We believe that this order will prove to be logical and easy to use for our readers, particularly those who regularly use structured experiences in their work and who select them from the *Reference Guide* or the *Structured Experience Kit*.

The Instrumentation section of this *Annual* contains three new paper-and-pencil, instrumented-feedback inventories. These instruments are described in the "Introduction to the Instrumentation Section."

The Professional Development section is intended to assist readers of the *Annual* in their own professional development. The articles in the 1992 *Annual* cover a broad range of issues that confront HRD professionals today. These articles are described in the "Introduction to the Professional Development Section." The editor and the editorial staff continue to be pleased with the high quality of submitted materials. Nevertheless, just as we cannot publish every manuscript that is submitted, readers may find that not all of the works we include in the *Annual* are equally useful to them. We actively solicit feedback from our readers so that we may continue to select manuscripts that meet their needs.

Pfeiffer & Company follows the stylistic guidelines established by the American Psychological Association, particularly with regard to the use and format of references. Potential contributors to our publications may wish to purchase copies of the APA's *Publication Manual* from: Order Department, American Psychological Association, 1200 Seventeenth Street, N.W., Washington, DC 20036. Pfeiffer & Company also publishes guidelines for potential authors. These guidelines were revised in 1991, appear at the end of the Professional Development section of this *Annual*, and are also available from Pfeiffer & Company's Editorial Department.

Biographies of *Annual* authors are published at the end of each structured experience, instrument, and professional development article. In addition, at the end of each *Annual* is a list of contributors' names, affiliations, addresses, and telephone numbers. This information is intended to contribute to the "networking" function that is so valuable in the field of human resource development.

INTRODUCTION TO THE STRUCTURED EXPERIENCES SECTION

Training methods that stress experiential learning continue to grow in popularity. It has been widely acknowledged that adult-learning processes are different from those of younger learners and that vehicles for learning other than the traditional lecture need to be used in order to promote adult learning. Structured experiences are probably the most frequently used of the experiential-learning strategies.

Readers of past *Annuals* and those familiar with other Pfeiffer & Company publications will note that the structured experiences in the 1992 *Annual* are presented in an order that reflects their classification into categories, according to their focus and intent. A list of the six major categories and their subcategories can be found immediately following this introduction, and an explanation of the categorization scheme can be found in the "User's Guide" to the *Structured Experience Kit,* in the discussion beginning on page 25 of the *Reference Guide to Handbooks and Annuals* (1990 Edition), and in the "Introduction to the Structured Experiences Section" of the 1981 *Annual.*

The structured experiences in this *Annual* represent all six major categories: Personal, Communication, Group Characteristics, Group Task Behavior, Organizations, and Facilitating Learning. The first two structured experiences represent the Personal category. In "Coping Strategies" the participants identify thoughts, feelings, and behaviors that help and hinder in coping with stress; then they generate ways to reduce self-defeating reactions to stress and ways to enhance positive reactions that lead to successful outcomes. In the second activity, "Supporting Cast," the participants explore the characteristics of a support network and the roles that others plays in their lives; then they identify roles in their own support networks that need to be filled or enhanced and develop action plans to meet those needs.

The third structured experience, "Feedback Awareness," represents the Communication category. This activity, which is designed to be used with supervisors, offers principles and guidelines for giving and receiving feedback and allows the participants to practice using the guidelines.

The fourth activity, "The Good Leader," belongs to the Group Characteristics category and is designed to be used with leaders. It allows the participants to discuss and identify characteristics and behaviors that contribute to leader effectiveness and to consider the effects of various leader behaviors on group members and on task accomplishment.

The fifth, sixth, seventh, and eighth activities belong to the Group Task Behavior category. The fifth and sixth, "Group Calendar" and "Strengths and Needs," are intended for intact work groups and deal with group feedback. In "Group Calendar" the group members remember significant events from the past year, recognize and appreciate one another's achievements, and compare memories of significant work-related events. "Strengths and Needs" offers three work sheets that the group members complete and then share with one another: one that deals with the members' strengths, one through which the members state what they like about their jobs and what they would like to change, and one that deals with what the members need from one another. A highlight of this structured experience is complete instructions for a second, follow-up session for action planning.

In the seventh activity, "Whirlybird," the participants explore both intragroup collaboration and intergroup competition by constructing and "racing" whirlybirds, which are similar to pinwheels. In the eighth activity, a role play called "Zenoland," the participants experience the impact of cultural diversity and practice communicating and problem solving in a culturally diverse setting.

The ninth and tenth structured experiences are from the Organizations category. "Working at Our Company," which is designed to be used with an intact management or executive team, would be useful during strategic planning. In it the participants examine their personal and organizational values and explore the interaction between these two kinds of values. "Help Wanted," which is designed to be used with practicing and prospective consultants, allows the participants to practice collaborative problem solving in one-on-one consulting situations.

The last two of the twelve structured experiences represent the Facilitating Learning category. Both are designed for use with practicing or prospective facilitators. In "Good Workshops Don't Just Happen," the participants identify elements of facilitation that are vital to workshop effectiveness, harmful to workshop effectiveness, and neither vital nor harmful but reflective of facilitator style. In "Up Close and Personal with Dr. Maslow," the participants explore Maslow's (1970) theory of the hierarchy of needs as the basis for creating a positive learning climate in a training experience.

All structured experiences in this *Annual* include a description of the goals of the activity, the size of the group and/or subgroups that can be accommodated, the time required to do and *process*[1] the activity, the materials and handouts required, the physical setting, step-by-step instructions for facilitating the experiential task and discussion phases of the activity, and variations of the design that the facilitator might find useful. All of these activities are complete; the content of all handouts is provided.

REFERENCE

Maslow, A.H. (1970). *Motivation and personality* (2nd ed.). New York: Harper & Row.

[1] It would be redundant to print here a caveat for the use of structured experiences, but HRD professionals who are not experienced in the use of this training technology are strongly urged to read the "Introduction to the Structured Experiences Section" of the 1980 *Annual* or the "Introduction" to the *Reference Guide to Handbooks and Annuals* (1990 Edition). Both of these articles present the theory behind the experiential-learning cycle and explain the necessity of adequately completing each phase of the cycle in order to allow effective learning to occur.

STRUCTURED EXPERIENCE CATEGORIES

Numbers of Structured Experiences		Numbers of Structured Experiences	
1-24	Volume I, *Handbook*	281-292	1981 *Annual*
25-48	Volume II, *Handbook*	293-316	Volume VIII, *Handbook*
49-74	Volume III, *Handbook*	317-328	1982 *Annual*
75-86	1972 *Annual*	329-340	1983 *Annual*
87-100	1973 *Annual*	341-364	Volume IX, *Handbook*
101-124	Volume IV, *Handbook*	365-376	1984 *Annual*
125-136	1974 *Annual*	377-388	1985 *Annual*
137-148	1975 *Annual*	389-412	Volume X, *Handbook*
149-172	Volume V, *Handbook*	413-424	1986 *Annual*
173-184	1976 *Annual*	425-436	1987 *Annual*
185-196	1977 *Annual*	437-448	1988 *Annual*
197-220	Volume VI, *Handbook*	449-460	1989 *Annual*
221-232	1978 *Annual*	461-472	1990 *Annual*
233-244	1979 *Annual*	473-484	1991 *Annual*
245-268	Volume VII, *Handbook*	485-496	1992 *Annual*
269-280	1980 *Annual*		

485. COPING STRATEGIES: MANAGING STRESS SUCCESSFULLY

Goals

I. To offer the participants an opportunity to identify their own patterns of response to stressful situations.

II. To assist the participants in identifying thoughts, feelings, and behaviors that help and hinder in coping with stress.

III. To encourage the participants to generate alternatives for reducing their self-defeating reactions to stress and for enhancing the positive reactions that lead to successful outcomes.

Group Size

Two to six subgroups of three to five members each.

Time Required

Approximately one and one-half hours.

Materials

I. A copy of the Coping Strategies Work Sheet for each participant.

II. A pencil for each participant.

III. Blank paper for each subgroup (for the recorder's use).

IV. A newsprint flip chart and a felt-tipped marker.

V. Masking tape for posting newsprint.

Physical Setting

A room large enough so that the subgroups can work without disturbing one another. A table and chairs should be provided for each subgroup. If tables are not available, the facilitator should provide a portable writing surface for each participant.

Process

I. The facilitator announces the goals of the activity and distributes copies of the Coping Strategies Work Sheet and pencils. The facilitator asks each participant to think of two personal experiences of stress, one that he or she dealt with successfully and another that he or she did not handle well, and then to complete the work sheet accordingly. (Fifteen minutes.)

II. The participants are instructed to assemble into subgroups of three to five members each. The members of each subgroup are asked to discuss the contents of their work sheets and to identify *recurring patterns of perceptions, thoughts, feelings, behaviors, and resources* for successful experiences and unsuccessful experiences. The facilitator instructs each subgroup to select a recorder to record these patterns and to report them later to the total group. Each subgroup is given blank paper for the recorder's use. (Thirty minutes.)

III. While the subgroups are working, the facilitator prepares several sheets of newsprint, dividing each sheet into two columns, one with the heading "Successful Experience" and the other with the heading "Unsuccessful Experience." Periodically the facilitator informs the participants of the remaining time.

IV. After thirty minutes the facilitator reconvenes the total group and asks the recorders to take turns reporting the patterns that were identified. As the patterns are announced, the facilitator records each on newsprint under the appropriate heading. As each newsprint sheet is completed, it is posted. (Fifteen minutes.)

V. The facilitator leads a discussion based on the identified patterns of successful and unsuccessful experiences in coping with stress, asking the following questions:

1. What patterns of successful coping do you identify with or find particularly appealing?
2. How might you incorporate these patterns to a greater extent into your own style of coping with stress?
3. What patterns of unsuccessful coping do you particularly identify with?
4. What might you do to minimize the recurrence of these self-defeating patterns in your own reactions to stress?
5. What other resources (other people, techniques, and/or tools or equipment) might be useful to you as you strive to cope with stress more effectively?
6. What would be an appropriate first step for you to take in dealing with your next experience of stress?
7. What is it about any kind of stress that we most need to learn to deal with?

Variations

I. Copies of the work sheet may be distributed in advance so that the participants have more time to compose their responses.

II. If the total group is small, the facilitator may eliminate the use of subgroups and may record the patterns directly on newsprint.

III. The participants may be instructed to concentrate exclusively on either work-related stress or nonwork-related stress.

IV. The activity may be used to assist an intact work group in dealing with work-related stress. In this case the concluding discussion may be expanded by asking the participants to identify which elements in the work setting tend to alleviate or exacerbate stress, what action steps might be taken, who might take those steps, and by when. In addition, arrangements for a follow-up meeting should be made.

V. After Step V the participants may be asked (1) to complete individual action plans or (2) to role play a stressful situation using the strategies that they have learned.

Submitted by Anthony M. Gregory.

Anthony M. Gregory *is a senior partner and manager of CIVUN, one of the largest training and consulting firms in Israel. He also serves the Israeli Army as a psychologist assigned to the treatment of career army personnel and their families. In addition, Mr. Gregory published a training manual called* Parenting Styles *for the Ministry of Education in Israel.*

COPING STRATEGIES WORK SHEET

Successful Experience

1. Describe a situation in which you coped well with stress. (How did you perceive and/or assess the situation? What did you think was happening?)

2. What perceptions, thoughts, feelings, behaviors, and resources helped you to succeed in this situation?

3. How have you integrated these perceptions, thoughts, feelings, behaviors, and resources into your typical style of dealing with stress?

4. What other perceptions, thoughts, feelings, behaviors, and resources could you use in order to cope even better with stress?

Unsuccessful Experience

1. Describe a situation in which you did not cope well with stress. (How did you perceive and/or assess the situation? What did you think was happening?)

2. What perceptions, thoughts, feelings, and behaviors prevented you from dealing with this situation effectively?

3. As a result of this experience, what did you learn about coping with stress? What would (or did) you do differently the next time?

Comparison

Review your responses to the sections on "Successful Experience" and "Unsuccessful Experience." Describe the differences in how you perceived and handled the two situations.

486. SUPPORTING CAST: EXAMINING PERSONAL SUPPORT NETWORKS

Goals

I. To acquaint the participants with the characteristics of a supporting cast—the network of people who help a person to achieve his or her personal and professional goals.

II. To offer the participants an opportunity to explore the roles that others play in their lives.

III. To provide an opportunity for the participants to identify roles in their personal support networks that need to be filled or enhanced and to develop action plans to fill those needs.

Group Size

Up to ten triads. If the group does not divide evenly into triads, one or two groups of four may be formed.

Time Required

Approximately two hours.

Materials

I. A copy of the Supporting Cast Roles Sheet for each participant.

II. A copy of the Supporting Cast Tally Sheet for each participant.

III. A copy of the Supporting Cast Discussion Sheet for each participant.

IV. A copy of the Supporting Cast Action-Planning Sheet for each participant.

V. A pencil and a clipboard or other portable writing surface for each participant.

VI. A newsprint flip chart and a felt-tipped marker.

VII. Masking tape for posting newsprint.

Physical Setting

A room large enough so that the triads can work without disturbing one another. Movable chairs should be available.

Process

I. The facilitator tells the participants that this activity will offer them a way to examine their personal support networks and describes the goals of the activity. (Five minutes.)

II. Each of the participants is given a copy of the Supporting Cast Roles Sheet, a copy of the Supporting Cast Tally Sheet, a pencil, and a clipboard or other portable writing surface. The facilitator reviews the instructions and the role descriptions to ensure that the participants understand them before starting work. (Ten minutes.)

III. The participants are directed to work independently to complete the Supporting Cast Roles Sheet and the Supporting Cast Tally Sheet. (Twenty minutes.)

IV. The facilitator directs the participants to form triads.The facilitator distributes copies of the Supporting Cast Discussion Sheet and instructs the members of each subgroup to share with one another the results of identifying their individual supporting casts. (Thirty minutes.)

V. The facilitator distributes copies of the Supporting Cast Action-Planning Sheet and instructs the participants to work on it individually. (Ten minutes.)

VI. After the participants have had the opportunity to work individually on their action plans, the facilitator instructs them to confer with their triad partners and to elicit suggestions for action planning from one another. (Twenty minutes.)

VII. The total group is reassembled. The facilitator leads a group discussion based on the following questions:

1. What discoveries did you make in reviewing your responses? How did these discoveries affect you?
2. How many different people fill roles in your life? Did you expect the number to be larger or smaller? Why?
3. What particular roles seem well filled? What particular roles need support people? How do you account for that?
4. What needs do you see for finding additional people for your supporting cast? Why?
5. How easy or difficult will it be to effect the changes you want? What obstacles might you encounter? How can you ensure that you will take the steps that you have planned?

Variations

I. After Step VII the participants may redo the activity focusing on the roles that they see themselves playing in others' lives.

II. The facilitator may suggest that the participants concentrate on supporting casts either for professional or for personal goals.

III. Participants may make contracts with other members of their triads for following through on action planning.

Submitted by Marian K. Prokop. The supporting-cast roles are based on ideas developed in *Winning with People: Building Lifelong Professional and Personal Success Through the Supporting Cast Principle,* copyright © 1990 by Michael G. Zey, Ph.D., and reprinted with permission from Jeremy P. Tarcher, Inc., Los Angeles, CA.

***Marian K. Prokop** is an editor for Pfeiffer & Company in San Diego, California. Ms. Prokop previously worked as a writer/trainer for migrant education programs in New York and California. She has been a contributor to the* Annuals *and is one of the co-authors of* Pfeiffer's Official Frequent Flyer Guide, *co-published by Pfeiffer & Company, Bonus Books, and Frequent Publications in 1989.*

SUPPORTING CAST ROLES SHEET

Instructions: Following are descriptions of twelve supporting-cast roles[1] that others may play in your life. Read the descriptions and list the names of people who fill those roles for you. The same person's name may be listed as filling more than one role. For some roles, you may be able to list multiple names; for other roles, you may not be able to list any names. Fill in the Supporting Cast Roles Sheet as completely as possible.

1. *Advisors* bring information into your life, whether in personal or professional areas. They help you to establish personal priorities and to use informal networks to make progress toward your goals. In the space that follows, list the names of people in your life who give you information and progress reports about yourself:

2. *Catalysts* bring out the best in you. Their interactions with you enhance your creativity and energize you to accomplish more than you might accomplish alone. In the space that follows, list the names of people in your life who serve as sparkplugs for your thoughts and actions:

3. *Celebrators* cheer your successes with you. Celebrating reinforces your accomplishments and makes them more meaningful. In the space that follows, list the names of people in your life with whom you celebrate the good times:

[1] The supporting-cast roles are based on ideas developed in *Winning with People: Building Lifelong Professional and Personal Success Through the Supporting Cast Principle,* copyright © 1990 by Michael G. Zey, Ph.D., and reprinted with permission from Jeremy P. Tarcher, Inc., Los Angeles, CA.

4. *Cheerleaders* support and nurture you when times are tough. They provide short-term encouragement to help you through a particular crisis. In the space that follows, list the names of people in your life to whom you turn for emotional strength:

5. *Constructive critics* dare you to rethink your plans and to improve your ideas. Constructive critics also stimulate your creativity—as long as you can be open to new ways of looking at yourself. In the space that follows, list the names of people in your life who challenge your ideas and provide honest feedback:

6. *Contacts* represent your indirect links to success. They may not directly provide you with information or advice or leads, but they put you in contact with other people who can. In the space that follows, list the names of the people in your life who serve as contacts in your network:

7. *Esteem builders* help you to build a strong self-image. Because your success depends on what you think of yourself, esteem builders help you to believe that you can succeed and that you have a right to succeed. In the space that follows, list the names of people in your life who support and reinforce your self-image:

8. *Financiers* offer advice on making money, borrowing it, investing it, and saving it. Financiers might be friends or acquaintances, or they might be professional individuals or institutions, such as investment counselors or banks. In the space that follows, list the names of the people in your life who help you to manage your money and your entrepreneurial ideas:

9. *Public-relations specialists* advertise your accomplishments. They do "impression management" (Zey, 1990, p. 34), which is crucial to convincing others that you are accomplished and talented. In the space that follows, list the names of the people in your life who act on your behalf to spread the word about your abilities:

10. *Role models* may not even be people that you know personally. These are the people you want to emulate, the ones who model the values and behaviors that you want to live out in your life. In the space that follows, list the names of the people in your life whose successes you want to replicate:

11. *Sponsors* are people who help you to get ahead in your career. Typically they hold positions of power and influence and can help you to get raises and promotions. In the space that follows, list the names of the people in your life who back you and help you to "move up the ladder":

12. *Technical supporters* provide the kinds of services that are essential to everyday life. Such support might be in the form of a housekeeper, a day-care center, or a reliable repairperson—anyone whose work lets you get on with your career and life goals. In the space that follows, list the names of the people in your life who enable you to make the most of your time:

Reference

Zey, M.G. (1990). *Winning with people: Building lifelong professional and personal success through the supporting cast principle.* Los Angeles, CA: Jeremy P. Tarcher.

SUPPORTING CAST
TALLY SHEET

Instructions: List the people whose names appeared on the Supporting Cast Roles Sheet. Next to each name put a check mark indicating the role or roles each person plays in your life. Total the check marks in each column and row. You will have two totals: the number of support people in each role and the number of roles each support person plays.

Supporting Cast	Advisors	Catalysts	Celebrators	Cheerleaders	Constructive Critics	Contacts	Esteem Builders	Financiers	P.R. Specialists	Role Models	Sponsors	Technical Supporters	Totals
Totals													

SUPPORTING CAST DISCUSSION SHEET

Instructions: Within your subgroup, share your reactions to completing the Supporting Cast Roles Sheet. Use these sentence stems as guidelines.

1. The way I felt when I was completing the Supporting Cast Roles Sheet was...

2. The way I feel now that I have looked at the roles that others fill and do not fill in my life is...

3. Something else I am feeling is...

4. The areas that seem most important to me to address are...

5. What I have learned about my support network is...

SUPPORTING CAST
ACTION-PLANNING SHEET

Part I

Instructions: Identify one or more roles in your supporting cast that you want to expand. Respond to the sentence stems that follow and share your reactions with your partners.

Role ____

1. I would like more support in this role because...

2. In the past, this role was...

3. I give myself support in this role by...

4. People in my current support cast who could also fill this role are...

5. As I consider people I know or know of, some people who could fill this role are...

6. To find potential supporters, I could...

Role ______________________________

1. I would like more support in this role because...

2. In the past, this role was...

3. I give myself support in this role by...

4. People in my current support cast who could also fill this role are...

5. As I consider people I know or know of, some people who could fill this role are...

6. To find potential supporters, I could...

Role ____

1. I would like more support in this role because...

2. In the past, this role was...

3. I give myself support in this role by...

4. People in my current support cast who could also fill this role are...

5. As I consider people I know or know of, some people who could fill this role are...

6. To find potential supporters, I could...

Part II

Instructions: Reciprocity is an important part of building a supporting cast; strengthening your supporting cast depends in part on your willingness and your ability to function as part of someone else's supporting cast. Respond to the sentence stems that follow and share your reactions with your partners.

1. The skills I have that would be valuable in another person's supporting cast are...

2. I see myself as being good at filling the roles of...

3. I can find out what others want and need by...

4. I am willing to be part of someone's supporting cast when...

5. As part of my growth, I plan to contribute to the growth of others by...

487. FEEDBACK AWARENESS: SKILL BUILDING FOR SUPERVISORS

Goals

I. To enhance the participants' awareness of the impact of feedback.

II. To offer principles and guidelines for giving and receiving feedback.

III. To provide a vehicle for practice in giving and receiving feedback.

IV. To offer the participants an opportunity to discuss and identify feedback characteristics and techniques.

Group Size

Four to six subgroups of four participants each. This activity is designed for use with supervisors as participants.

Time Required

Two hours to two hours and fifteen minutes.

Materials

I. A copy of the Feedback Awareness Theory Sheet for each participant.

II. A copy of the Feedback Awareness Procedure Sheet for each participant.

III. Two copies of the Feedback Awareness Communication Sheet for each participant.

IV. Several sheets of blank paper and a pencil for each participant.

V. A clipboard or other portable writing surface for each participant.

VI. Five newsprint posters prepared in advance:

1. On the first poster:
    - The importance of feedback to supervisors and subordinates
    - The roles of the supervisor and the subordinate in the performance-feedback process

2. On the second poster:
    - Tips for eliciting quality feedback from a subordinate
    - Tips for discovering whether feedback given to a subordinate has been effective

3. On the third poster:

   Procedure

   - Brainstorm ideas. One partner records. (5 min.)
   - Choose best ideas. Other partner records. Monitor behavior. (10 min.)
   - Fill out Feedback Awareness Communication Sheet. (5 min.)
   - Share ideas with total group. (10 min.)
   - People in outer chairs switch places.
   - Repeat first four steps, using new topics. (30 min.)

4. On the fourth poster:

   Guidelines for Giving Feedback

   - Be objective.
   - Be specific.
   - Write about changeable behavior.
   - Describe how behavior affected you.

5. On the fifth poster:

   Guidelines for Receiving Feedback

   - Keep an open mind.
   - Listen. Do not interrupt, justify, explain.
   - Paraphrase the feedback.
   - If necessary, ask for example or explanation.

VII. A newsprint flip chart and a felt-tipped marker.

VIII. Masking tape for posting newsprint.

Physical Setting

A large room in which the subgroups can work without disturbing one another. There should be plenty of wall space for posting newsprint, and movable chairs must be provided.

During Step III the chairs for each four-member subgroup should be arranged in two dyads as shown in Figure 1. (When the subgroups have been assembled, each participant is seated directly opposite another.)

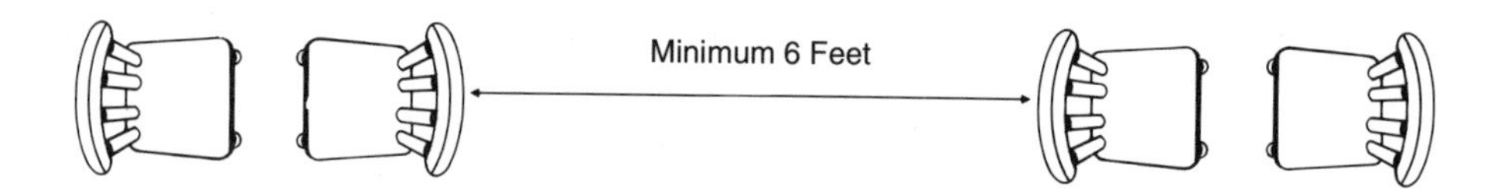

Figure 1. Arrangement of Chairs for One Subgroup

Process

I. The facilitator announces the goals of the activity, distributes copies of the theory sheet, and asks the participants to read this handout. (Ten minutes.)

II. The facilitator elicits and answers questions about the handout, clarifying the content as necessary. (Ten minutes.)

III. The participants are assembled into four-member subgroups, and each subgroup's chairs are arranged according to the configuration shown in Figure 1.

IV. The facilitator posts the first, third, fourth, and fifth prepared newsprint posters. *(See Materials, VI. Note that the second prepared newsprint poster is displayed later, after the participants have finished dealing with the topics on the first poster.)* Each participant is given a copy of the procedure sheet, two copies of the communication sheet, several sheets of blank paper, a pencil, and a clipboard or other portable writing surface. The facilitator reviews the content of both handouts while the participants follow on their copies and then elicits and answers questions about the content. (Ten to fifteen minutes.)

V. The facilitator instructs the participants to begin and then uses the steps described in the procedure sheet to guide the participants through the procedure. (One hour.)

VI. After the steps described in the procedure sheet have been completed, the participants are instructed to distribute their completed communication sheets to the partners whose names appear on those sheets and to clarify written comments as necessary. The participants are reminded to use the guidelines for giving and receiving feedback as they complete this step. (Ten to twenty minutes.)

VII. The facilitator reconvenes the total group and leads a discussion based on the following questions:

1. How did you feel when you wrote comments about other people's communication techniques?
2. How did you feel when you read the comments written about your own communication techniques?
3. On the basis of your experience during this activity, what barriers can you identify as interfering with the feedback process? What might be done to remove some of those barriers or to reduce their impact?
4. What have you learned about your own abilities to give and to receive feedback?
5. How might you improve your abilities to give and to receive feedback?
6. What will you do differently in the performance-feedback process in the future?

Variations

I. The facilitator may ask the participants to concentrate on either giving or receiving feedback.

II. After Step VII the participants may be asked to return to their subgroups. Within each subgroup two members role play a brief performance-feedback session while the remaining two members observe. Subsequently, the observers give feedback and all four members discuss the experience.

Submitted by Robert William Lucas.

Robert William Lucas *is the senior trainer at the National Headquarters of the American Automobile Association in Heathrow, Florida. He has over twenty years of experience in training, supervision, and management and has designed, developed, and delivered hundreds of training programs. He has published articles in a variety of publications on training, management, and customer service. Mr. Lucas is active in the American Society for Training and Development (ASTD) and currently serves on an advisory committee for the American Management Association. In 1988 he received the ASTD Award for Volunteer Services. He is also an adjunct faculty member at Seminole Community College in Sanford, Florida.*

FEEDBACK AWARENESS THEORY SHEET

The following statements describe the appropriate way to give feedback to a subordinate. As you read each, think about whether it reflects your own behavior.

1. *Before I give feedback, I consider whether to do so publicly or privately.* I praise people in front of peers or co-workers, but I reprimand in private.

2. *Before giving feedback, I check my impressions of the behavior with others, doing so in a way that does not threaten or incriminate.* I understand that misperceptions on my part can lead to giving ineffective feedback.

3. *I provide timely feedback.* I give feedback as soon as possible after the behavior has occurred so that it has maximum impact for my subordinate.

4. *I avoid surprising my subordinates with performance feedback.* I tell them that I intend to provide regular feedback on their performance, and then I follow through.

5. *I am objective in describing behavior.* I base my comments on observation, not on conjecture. I describe the behavior fully before I offer personal thoughts or feelings about it.

6. *I state specific details, not generalities.* I avoid comments like "You did a good job on the monthly report." Instead, I say things like "Your monthly report was clear and concise, and the graph you included gave an excellent illustration of the changing trend in production."

7. *I direct feedback at behaviors that my subordinates can change.* I realize that it is *not* helpful to comment on a subordinate's stutter, for example, whereas it *is* helpful to comment on a subordinate's need to improve writing skills.

8. *After describing the behavior, I tell my subordinate what I think and how I feel about that behavior, describing its impact on me.* I recognize that comments about personal thoughts and feelings help my subordinate to put the feedback in perspective.

9. *After giving feedback, I verify that my subordinate has understood my message as I intended it.* I listen carefully to what my subordinate has heard; if the message has been misunderstood, I clarify as necessary.

10. *After I have given negative feedback, I give my subordinate time to make the desired change while I monitor the behavior in question.* I avoid constant negative feedback on a particular behavior because it is counterproductive and harmful. If the behavior improves, I praise my subordinate; if it does not improve, I consider performance-counseling alternatives.

FEEDBACK AWARENESS
PROCEDURE SHEET

Procedure

1. You and your partner spend five minutes brainstorming ideas about the two topics listed on newsprint. One of you records ideas.
2. The two of you spend ten minutes discussing the brainstormed ideas and choosing the best ones. The other partner (the one who did not write previously) records final ideas. As you work, each of you monitors the other's use of the techniques listed on the Feedback Awareness Communication Sheet. Two minutes before the end of the discussion period, the facilitator announces the remaining time. Two minutes later you are told to stop working.
3. Each of you writes his or her name and the partner's name on one copy of the Feedback Awareness Communication Sheet and spends five minutes writing brief comments about the partner's communication techniques. Each strives to write feedback according to the "Guidelines for Giving Feedback" on this sheet. (Your facilitator will post these guidelines in abbreviated form for your convenience.) Until instructed otherwise, each of you keeps the completed communication sheet.
4. After five minutes the facilitator asks you to stop writing. The person who recorded final ideas shares them with the total group when instructed to do so. The other subgroups also share their ideas. As ideas are presented, the facilitator records them on newsprint, displays them, and leads a brief discussion about them.
5. The two people in the outer chairs (see the illustration below) switch places so that everyone has a new partner. The facilitator displays another newsprint poster with two new topics.

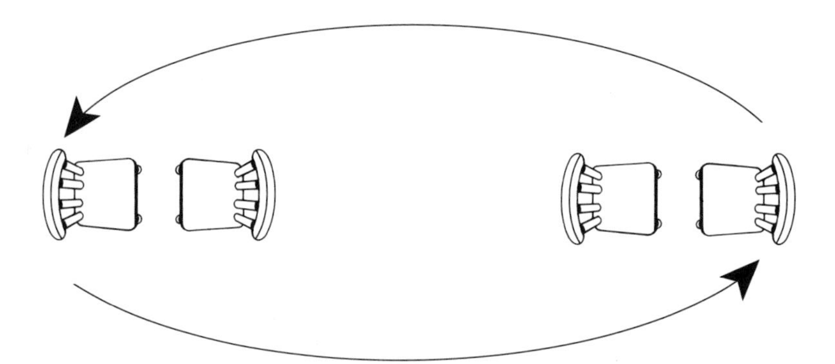

6. Steps 1 through 4 are completed again, this time centering on the new topics.

Guidelines for Giving Feedback

- Be objective in describing the behavior.
- State specific details, not generalities.
- Deal only with changeable behavior.
- Describe the impact of the behavior on you.

Guidelines for Receiving Feedback

- Keep an open mind; be willing to hear ways to improve.
- Listen without interrupting, justifying, or explaining.
- Paraphrase the feedback so that the person who gave it can determine whether you understood the intended message.
- If you do not understand, ask for an example or further explanation.

FEEDBACK AWARENESS COMMUNICATION SHEET

Instructions: Write your name and your partner's name in the blanks below. Answer the six questions, jotting down any specifics that might be useful to your partner. Then describe your partner's communication strengths and areas for development.

Your Name ______________________________

Your Partner's Name ______________________________

During the conversation, did your partner:

1. Use clear language?

2. Speak at a rate that you could easily follow and comprehend?

3. Use specific rather than general terms?

4. Avoid jargon?

5. Periodically verify that you understood?

6. Maintain good eye contact?

Communication Strengths:

Communication Areas for Development:

488. THE GOOD LEADER: IDENTIFYING EFFECTIVE BEHAVIORS

Goals

I. To provide the participants with an opportunity to explore different views of leadership.

II. To offer the participants an opportunity to discuss and identify the characteristics and behaviors that contribute to a leader's effectiveness.

III. To encourage the participants to consider how leadership evolves in a group and the effects of various leadership behaviors on group members and task accomplishment.

Group Size

Four subgroups of five to seven participants each. This activity has been designed for use with leaders as participants.

Time Required

Approximately two hours and fifteen minutes.

Materials

I. A copy of The Good Leader Theory Sheet for each participant.

II. Four copies of The Good Leader Observer Sheet (one for each subgroup's observer).

III. A pencil for each subgroup's observer.

IV. A clipboard or other portable writing surface for each subgroup's observer.

V. A newsprint flip chart and a felt-tipped marker for each subgroup.

VI. A newsprint flip chart and a felt-tipped marker for the facilitator's use.

VII. Five rolls of masking tape for posting newsprint (one roll for each subgroup and one for the facilitator).

Physical Setting

A room that is large enough to allow the subgroups to complete their assignments without disturbing one another. Movable chairs should be provided, and plenty of wall space should be available for posting newsprint.

Process

I. The facilitator announces the goals of the activity, asks the participants to form subgroups of five to seven members each, and gives each subgroup a newsprint flip chart, a felt-tipped marker, and a roll of masking tape.

II. The facilitator states that the members of each subgroup will be discussing and listing *characteristics and behaviors that contribute to a leader's effectiveness.* As this topic is announced, the facilitator writes it on newsprint, posts the sheet of newsprint, and displays it so that all subgroups can see it.

III. The facilitator goes on to explain that the members of each subgroup will brainstorm characteristics and behaviors and then discuss the brainstormed items until they achieve consensus on a final list. Each subgroup is instructed to select an observer as well as a recorder. The facilitator explains the functions of these two people: The observer will observe the activity, make notes on what is observed, and later share those notes with the subgroup; the recorder will record the subgroup members' ideas on newsprint. The facilitator also announces that a newsprint copy of each subgroup's consensus list will be collected at the end of the discussion period.

IV. Each observer is given a copy of the observer sheet, a pencil, and a clipboard or other portable writing surface and is asked to follow the instructions on the sheet.

V. The facilitator states that the subgroups have twenty minutes in which to complete their task and then asks them to begin.

VI. After twenty minutes the facilitator calls time and collects the newsprint lists, explaining that the lists will be displayed and discussed later. Then each participant is given a copy of the theory sheet and is asked to read this sheet. (Ten minutes.)

VII. The subgroups are instructed to spend twenty minutes discussing the posted topic again, following the same procedure, but to compose new lists, this time considering information from the theory sheet as well as their own experience and ideas. The facilitator emphasizes that the subgroups are simply to *consider* the theory-sheet information and that they need not accept it or incorporate it into their lists unless they choose to do so.

VIII. After twenty minutes the facilitator calls time, collects the new lists, and reassembles the total group. All of the original lists are posted, and then all of the new lists are posted. (The facilitator leaves some wall space between the two sets of lists so that they appear distinctly separate.)

IX. The facilitator leads a discussion of the two sets of lists, helping the participants to construct a final list of characteristics and behaviors that contribute to a leader's effectiveness. (Note: The participants may not be able to reach consensus about which items to include in the final list. In this case the facilitator may use a majority vote or another means to determine the components of the final list. Regardless of the method chosen to construct the final list, it is important that the facilitator acknowledge the legitimacy of different viewpoints about what constitutes leader effectiveness.) The final list is recorded on newsprint and displayed prominently. (Twenty minutes.)

X. The facilitator announces that the observers will take turns sharing their observations with the total group and that while the participants listen they are to compare these reports with the final list of leader characteristics and behaviors. After all observers have shared, the facilitator invites the participants to comment on their reactions and on the comparisons they made. (Twenty to thirty minutes.)

XI. The facilitator leads a concluding discussion by asking questions such as these:

1. What were your reactions to generating the first list in your subgroup? What were your reactions to generating the second list? What were your reactions when we worked as a total group to construct the final list?
2. What do your reactions suggest to you about your view of a good leader?
3. What have you learned about identifying effective leader characteristics and behaviors? What have you learned about practicing those characteristics and behaviors?
4. How would you now define effective leadership in terms of results?
5. What is one new leader behavior that you intend to practice in your position?

Variations

I. The activity may be shortened by eliminating the first discussion procedure (Step V) and/or the role of the observers.

II. The activity may be used with an intact work group by having the members focus first on effective leader behaviors that are currently displayed in their group. After the theory sheet has been introduced, if the group's second list is appreciably different from the first, the members may be asked to speculate about how the group's work results might be affected by the leader behaviors described in the theory sheet. In contrast, if the group's second list is not appreciably different from the first, the members may be asked to discuss how their group is currently using the theory-sheet behaviors, why these behaviors work, and what results are achieved by using these behaviors.

III. After the final step, the participants may be asked to devise action plans for adopting the new leader behaviors that they want to use.

IV. For the first discussion procedure, the facilitator may distribute copies of a theory sheet that is opposite in view from the one used in the second discussion procedure.

Submitted by Gerry Carline.

Gerry Carline *is an organizational-effectiveness consultant with his own consulting firm, OE Training and Development Associates in Saskatchewan. He specializes in large-systems change, focusing on strategic management in a total-quality context, and has consulted with a variety of organizations across Canada and throughout the Caribbean. He has also developed and delivered a number of training seminars on consulting skills, communications, strategic planning, and leadership.*

THE GOOD LEADER THEORY SHEET[1]

Chapter 9: A Good Group

...When leaders become superstars, the teacher outshines the teaching.

Also, very few superstars are down-to-earth.... Before long they get carried away with themselves. They then fly off center and crash.

The wise leader settles for good work and then lets others have the floor. The leader does not take all the credit for what happens and has no need for fame. A moderate ego demonstrates wisdom.

Chapter 11: The Group Field

Pay attention to silence. What is happening when nothing is happening in the group? That is the group field....

People's speech and actions are figural events. They give the group form and content.

The silence and empty spaces, on the other hand, reveal the group's essential mood, the context for everything that happens....

Chapter 17: Like a Midwife

The wise leader does not intervene unnecessarily. The leader's presence is felt, but often the group runs itself....

Remember that you are facilitating another person's process. It is not your process. Do not intrude....

If you do not trust a person's process, that person will not trust you.

Imagine that you are a midwife. You are assisting at someone else's birth. Do good without show or fuss. Facilitate what is happening rather than what you think ought to be happening. If you must take the lead, lead so that the mother is helped, yet still free and in charge.

When a baby is born, the mother will say: we did it ourselves.

Chapter 26: Center and Ground

The leader who is centered and grounded can work with erratic people and critical group situations without harm.

Being centered means having the ability to recover one's balance even in the midst of action. A centered person is not subject to passing whims or sudden excitements.

Being grounded means being down-to-earth, having gravity or weight. I know where I stand, and I know what I stand for: that is ground.

---

[1] These excerpts have been reprinted with permission from *The Tao of Leadership* by John Heider. Copyright 1985 by Humanics Limited, Atlanta, Georgia, USA.

The centered and grounded leader has stability and a sense of self.

One who is not stable can easily get carried away by the intensity of leadership and make mistakes of judgment....

Chapter 31: Harsh Interventions

There are times when it seems as if one must intervene powerfully, suddenly, and even harshly. The wise leader does this only when all else fails.

As a rule, the leader feels more wholesome when the group process is flowing freely and unfolding naturally, when delicate facilitations far outnumber harsh interventions. Harsh interventions are a warning that the leader may be uncentered or have an emotional attachment to whatever is happening....

Even if harsh interventions succeed brilliantly, there is no cause for celebration.... Someone's process has been violated.

Later on, the person whose process has been violated may well become less open and more defended....

Making people do what you think they ought to do does not lead toward clarity and consciousness. While they may do what you tell them to do at the time, they will cringe inwardly, grow confused, and plot revenge.

That is why your victory is actually a failure.

Chapter 43: Gentle Interventions

Gentle interventions, if they are clear, overcome rigid resistances.

If gentleness fails, try yielding or stepping back altogether. When the leader yields, resistances relax.

Generally speaking, the leader's consciousness sheds more light on what is happening than any number of interventions or explanations. But few leaders realize how much how little will do.

Chapter 60: Don't Stir Things Up

Run the group delicately, as if you were cooking small fish.

As much as possible, allow the group process to emerge naturally....

If you stir things up, you will release forces before their time and under unwarranted pressure. These forces may be emotions which belong to other people or places. They may be unspecific or chaotic energies which, in response to your pressure, strike out and hit any available target.

These forces are real. They do exist in the group. But do not push. Allow them to come out when they are ready.

When hidden issues and emotions emerge naturally, they resolve themselves naturally....

Chapter 81: The Reward

It is more important to tell the simple, blunt truth than it is to say things that sound good. The group is not a contest of eloquence.

It is more important to act in behalf of everyone than it is to win arguments. The group is not a debating society.

It is more important to react wisely to what is happening than it is to be able to explain everything in terms of certain theories. The group is not a final examination for a college course.

The wise leader is not collecting a string of successes. The leader is helping others to find their own success.... Sharing success with others is very successful.

The single principle behind all creation teaches us that true benefit blesses everyone and diminishes no one.

THE GOOD LEADER OBSERVER SHEET

Instructions: Your subgroup is about to complete a two-part assignment. During the first part, the members will be discussing and identifying leadership characteristics and behaviors. During the second part, they will read a theory sheet on this topic and then complete the same task, this time using the content of the theory sheet as well as their own experience and ideas.

While the members work, jot down answers to the following questions. Later you will be asked to share the questions and your answers with the members of your subgroup. Until then *do not share the content of this sheet with anyone.*

Part 1: First Discussion

1. How does leadership of the subgroup evolve?

2. How would you describe the leadership that emerges? How does the leadership that emerges compare with the subgroup's list of characteristics and behaviors?

3. How do the members respond to that leadership?

4. How does the leadership influence the successful accomplishment of the task?

Part 2: Second Discussion (After Theory Sheet)

1. Compare the subgroup leadership during the first discussion with the leadership during the second discussion. What similarities do you see? What are the differences?

2. What are the similarities and differences in the members' responses to the subgroup leadership?

3. What are the similarities and differences in the accomplishment of the task?

489. GROUP CALENDAR: CELEBRATING SIGNIFICANT EVENTS

Goals

I. To offer the participants a nonthreatening method of getting to know one another better.

II. To give the participants the opportunity to remember significant work-related events that took place during the past year and to recognize and appreciate one another's achievements.

III. To allow the participants to compare memories of significant work-related events.

Group Size

All members of an intact work group. If there are more than eight participants, the facilitator will need to establish subgroups for processing (see Steps VI and VII).

Time Required

One hour to one hour and fifteen minutes.

Materials

I. A pad of 3" x 3" Post-it™ notes for each participant.

II. A pencil for each participant.

III. A newsprint flip chart and a felt-tipped marker.

IV. Masking tape for posting newsprint.

Physical Setting

A room with enough wall space for displaying three sheets of newsprint side by side. The participants should be seated so that they can view the sheets of newsprint without difficulty.

Process

I. The facilitator explains the goals of the activity.

II. The facilitator posts three newsprint sheets side by side and divides each sheet into quadrants with a felt-tipped marker. The facilitator then writes the name of a month in each quadrant, thus creating a calendar (see Figure 1).

Jan.	Feb.	May	June	Sept.	Oct.
March	April	July	Aug.	Nov.	Dec.

Figure 1. Arrangement of Calendar Pages

III. The participants are instructed to think back on the past year and to reflect privately about significant *work-related* events that have affected them personally and/or their work group. The facilitator explains that "significant work-related events" may include projects, promotions, group or task-force accomplishments, unexpected changes, changing jobs or positions, and so on.

IV. While the participants are reflecting, the facilitator distributes pads of Post-it™ notes and pencils. Each participant is instructed to select three or four significant events and to write a brief description of each event on a separate Post-it™ note, including the month in which the event occurred. The following examples are given:

- "Finished policy report (with Bill)" (April);
- "Fred retired—worked with us for six years" (November); and
- "Customer signed six-month contract for our services" (December).

(Ten minutes.)

V. The participants are instructed to place their notes on the appropriate months of the posted calendar. The facilitator then groups notes listing similar events together and separates dissimilar events visually, as illustrated in Figure 2.

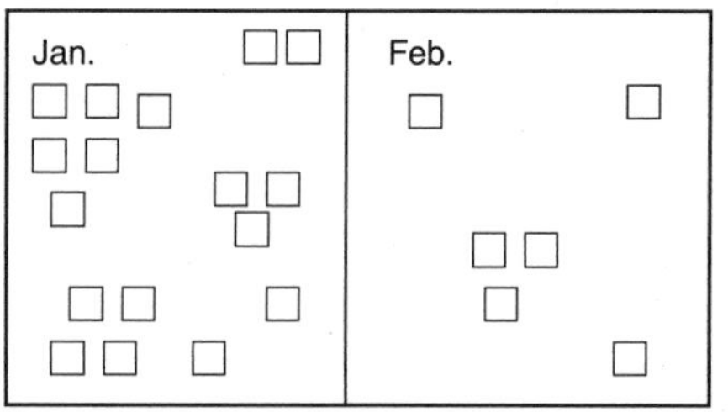

Figure 2. Sample Placement of Notes on Group Calendar

VI. The facilitator reads each note aloud to the group, comments on any similarities among notes, inquires about emotions attached to each event, and calls the participants' attention to areas on the calendar in which notes are bunched together or spread apart. The facilitator also mentions any events that are remembered as taking place at different times of the year or that various people remember as happening differently and asks the participants to comment on these discrepancies. (Fifteen to twenty-five minutes.)

VII. The facilitator leads a discussion of the group's progress in the past year, asking group members to recognize one another's accomplishments, to talk about sad or happy times during the year, and to discuss times during which their team functioned above or below normal capacity. The following questions are helpful:

1. What is your reaction to sharing this experience as a group? How did you feel while discussing your group calendar?
2. How would you describe your group in the last year? What phrase captures the group's progress?
3. What were the highs? What were the lows? How did those highs and lows affect the group?
4. As a result of this experience, what have you learned about the group and about one another?
5. How can you use what you have learned to enhance relationships and productivity in the group?

Variations

I. The activity may be used as an icebreaker in a team-building workshop.

II. If the work group is exceptionally large, the facilitator may limit the number of items that each participant may place on the calendar. Alternatively, the facilitator may choose not to set limits and to have the participants mill around the calendar and review the items silently. Afterward, the facilitator leads a processing discussion, asking the participants to find common, significant themes in the posted items.

III. The participants may be allowed to submit one or more personal events along with the work-related events.

IV. If the facilitator is an internal consultant or is acquainted with the work group, he or she may add personal items to the calendar and discuss them with the group.

V. The facilitator may ask the participants to identify major events that affected the entire organization during the year (such as a company takeover, a hiring freeze, a recession, and so on). The participants may be instructed to post such events on the calendar or on a separate newsprint sheet above the calendar. The facilitator then leads a discussion of how people respond to more "global" happenings and crises.

VI. The facilitator may ask the participants to imagine their group calendar one year from now. The participants may be asked to envision the coming year and to note one or two highlights that they would like to look back on. This activity can help group members to prioritize objectives and goals, to request support from one another, or simply to get a sense of the pace of the year to come.

VII. The activity may be closed with the facilitator's asking each participant to write a description of one planned vacation—including month and destination—on a Post-it™ note and to post the vacation notes on the calendar. A calendar full of vacations can help the participants to view the coming year as a time of fun and excitement.

Submitted by Marc B. Sokol and Douglas A. Cohen.

Marc B. Sokol, Ph.D., *is a management and organization development specialist at AT&T Bell Laboratories in Short Hills, New Jersey. He received his doctorate in industrial and organizational psychology from the University of Maryland in College Park. He is an adjunct faculty member of the Psychology Department at Rutgers University and of the Graduate Program of Management at Polytechnic University.*

Douglas A. Cohen *is an organization effectiveness consultant at AT&T Bell Laboratories. He received his master's degree in applied behavioral science from the Leadership Institute of Seattle and now consults with executives and managers and their teams throughout AT&T. His purpose in his work is to influence and reshape the thinking of client systems to incorporate the principles and skills of organizational learning.*

490. STRENGTHS AND NEEDS: USING FEEDBACK FOR GROUP DEVELOPMENT

Goals

I. To provide an opportunity for the participants to give one another feedback about the strengths they bring to their work group.

II. To offer the participants a chance to identify what they like on the job and what they would like to change and then to share this information with one another.

III. To provide a structure through which the participants can express what they need from one another.

IV. To provide an opportunity for the participants to do action planning based on their strengths, likes, items they would like to change, and needs.

Group Size

All members of an intact work group.

Time Required

This activity is conducted in two sessions. Session 1, sharing feedback, requires two to three and one-half hours, depending on the size of the work group. Session 2, action planning based on the information shared in the first session, requires approximately three hours.

Materials

Session 1

I. For each participant, enough copies of Strengths and Needs Work Sheet A to equal the number of other participants. (For example, if there are six participants, each participant receives five copies of the work sheet.)

II. One copy of Strengths and Needs Work Sheet B for each participant.

III. For each participant, enough copies of Strengths and Needs Work Sheet C to equal the number of other participants.

IV. One copy of the Strengths and Needs Sample Planning Chart for each participant.

V. A pencil for each participant.

VI. A clipboard or other portable writing surface for each participant.

VII. A newsprint poster prepared in advance with the following content:

Guidelines for Receiving Feedback

- Listen to feedback; do not discount, debate, analyze it.
- If you don't understand, ask for clarification/examples.
- Paraphrase feedback. Verify that you heard correctly.
- If you wish, thank the person who gave feedback.

VIII. Masking tape for posting newsprint.

Session 2

I. Each participant's poster-sized planning chart (prepared in advance and brought to the session by each participant).

II. Each participant's notes about (1) how he or she can capitalize more on personal strengths and likes and (2) what he or she might be able to do about desired changes and about meeting others' expressed needs (prepared in advance and brought to the session by each participant).

III. A copy of the Strengths and Needs Action-Planning Guide for each participant plus a supply of extra copies in case the participants want them.

IV. A large supply of blank paper (enough so that each participant can have at least ten sheets if desired).

V. A pencil for each participant.

VI. A clipboard or other portable writing surface for each participant.

VII. The newsprint poster on guidelines for receiving feedback (prepared for the first session).

VIII. A newsprint flip chart and several colors of felt-tipped markers.

IX. Masking tape for posting newsprint.

Physical Setting

For Session 1, a room with movable chairs placed in a circle. The circle should be close to the wall on which the facilitator plans to display the newsprint poster (see Materials, Session 1, VII).

For Session 2, a room with movable chairs and plenty of wall space for posting newsprint. It is preferable, but not essential, to have a table on which the participants can work to complete their strengths poster (see Process, Session 2, Step X).

Process

Session 1

I. The facilitator explains that the activity will be conducted in two sessions: In the first session the participants will give one another feedback about their strengths as group members, educate one another about what they like and what they would like to change on the job, and state what they need from one another; in the second session the participants will do action planning based on information shared during the previous session. The facilitator explains that by sharing this information and acting on it, the participants can strengthen their group and further its development. (Five minutes.)

II. Each participant is given the appropriate number of copies of Strengths and Needs Work Sheet A, a pencil, and a clipboard or other portable writing surface and is asked to read the instructions on the work sheet. Subsequently, the facilitator reviews the instructions and elicits and answers questions about them. (Five minutes.)

III. Each participant is instructed to complete one copy of the work sheet for every member of the team except himself or herself. (Ten to fifteen minutes.)

IV. After all participants have completed their copies of work sheet A, the facilitator explains that each group member will take a turn at receiving feedback and that the maximum time each person has for giving feedback is one minute. The facilitator posts the prepared newsprint sheet of guidelines for receiving feedback, reviews these guidelines with the participants, and elicits and answers questions. These guidelines remain posted throughout the session. (Five minutes.)

V. The facilitator asks for a volunteer to receive feedback. (If no participant volunteers, the facilitator selects one and explains that the remaining members will take turns in clockwise order.) After all feedback statements have been read aloud and clarified to the feedback recipient's satisfaction, the facilitator instructs those who read statements to give their sheets to the feedback recipient. Then the facilitator either asks for another volunteer or selects the person who is next in clockwise order. The feedback procedure is repeated until all participants have received feedback.

VI. The facilitator distributes copies of Strengths and Needs Work Sheet B and asks the participants to complete this sheet according to the instructions. (Ten minutes.)

VII. After the participants have completed work sheet B, they are told that they are to take turns reading their work sheets aloud to the group. The facilitator emphasizes that while one member is reading, the others are to listen carefully; afterward the listeners may ask questions for clarification. Then the facilitator asks for a volunteer or selects a participant to begin, and the procedure continues until all participants have taken a turn.

VIII. Each participant is given the appropriate number of copies of Strengths and Needs Work Sheet C and is asked to read the instructions. Then the facilitator reviews the instructions and elicits and answers questions about them. (Five minutes.)

IX. The facilitator instructs each participant to complete one copy of the work sheet for every member of the team except himself or herself. (Fifteen to twenty minutes.)

X. After all participants have completed their copies of work sheet C, the facilitator explains that each group member will take a turn at receiving feedback about what the other members need from him or her and that the maximum time each person has for giving feedback is one minute. The facilitator then briefly reviews the posted guidelines for receiving feedback. (Five minutes.)

XI. The facilitator asks for a volunteer to receive feedback. (If no participant volunteers, the facilitator selects one and asks that the remaining members take their turns in clockwise order.) After all feedback statements have been read aloud and clarified to the feedback recipient's satisfaction, the facilitator instructs those who read statements to give their sheets to the feedback recipient. Then the facilitator either asks for a second volunteer or selects the person who is next in clockwise order. This procedure is repeated until all participants have received feedback. *(Note: This step can produce a great deal of affect, so the facilitator needs to be prepared to intervene appropriately.)*

XII. The facilitator leads a discussion based on these questions:

1. How did you feel when you gave feedback to your fellow group members? How did you feel when you received feedback?
2. What did you discover about what your fellow group members like on the job? What did you discover about what they would change?
3. What strengths are represented in this group? How do those strengths benefit the group? How do they benefit the organization?
4. How is it beneficial for group members to talk about what they like on the job, what they would change, and what they need from one another?
5. What have you learned about yourself as a member of this group?
6. What have you learned about your fellow group members that helps you understand better what you need from them?
7. What have you learned about the feedback process?
8. What have you learned about the connection among people's strengths, what they like on the job, what they would change, and what others need from them?
9. How can you use what you have learned to enhance the productivity or cohesiveness of the group?

XIII. The facilitator makes arrangements for the second session, again explaining that the purpose of that session is to do action planning based on the information just shared. The facilitator gives each participant a copy of the Strengths and Needs Sample Planning Chart; explains that the chart offers a way to display information from completed copies of work sheets A, B, and C; and asks each participant to prepare a similar chart in poster (newsprint) size for the action-planning session. In addition, each participant is instructed to spend some time thinking and making notes about (1) how he or she can capitalize more on personal strengths and likes and (2) what he or she might be able to do about desired changes and about meeting others' expressed needs. The facilitator emphasizes that each participant is to bring the prepared planning chart and the notes to the action-planning session.

Session 2

I. The facilitator asks each participant to post his or her poster-sized planning chart.

II. The facilitator displays the newsprint poster on guidelines for receiving feedback and reviews the content with the participants, urging them to follow these guidelines during the session. This poster remains on display throughout the session. (Five minutes.)

III. The facilitator distributes blank paper, pencils, and clipboards or other portable writing surfaces. The participants are instructed to circulate around the room, reading one another's planning charts. The facilitator encourages the participants to jot down notes about agreements they would like to make with one another and any other ideas that occur to them. (Twenty to thirty minutes.)

IV. The facilitator reassembles the group and invites the participants to share their reactions and the contents of their notes. As ideas are expressed, the facilitator records highlights on newsprint, posts the newsprint, and displays it for the remainder of the session. (Fifteen to twenty minutes.)

V. The facilitator leads a brief discussion about patterns, similarities, and differences in the planning charts and the implications for the group. (Ten minutes.)

VI. The participants are asked to spend ten minutes making arrangements to meet with one another during the next hour for the purpose of making agreements and planning whatever action they wish. (Ten minutes.)

VII. The facilitator gives each participant a copy of the Strengths and Needs Action-Planning Guide and several sheets of blank paper, announcing that extra copies of the guide and extra blank paper are available if the participants need them. The facilitator briefly reviews the action-planning steps, explaining how they fit into the action-planning process, and ensures that the participants understand the procedure they are to follow with their partners. (Ten minutes.)

VIII. The facilitator instructs the participants to spend the next hour meeting with partners to make agreements and to plan action. As the participants work, the facilitator monitors their activity, announces the remaining time at intervals, and provides assistance if needed. (One hour.)

IX. The facilitator announces the end of the planning time, reassembles the total group, and encourages the participants to make arrangements later to do any planning that they did not have time to complete during the session. The participants are invited to share some of their one-sentence summaries of the agreements they have reached. As the participants share, the facilitator records highlights on newsprint. (Ten minutes.)

X. The facilitator gives the participants a sheet of newsprint and several different colors of felt-tipped markers and asks them to make a poster that celebrates the strengths of their group. (Ten to fifteen minutes.)

XI. After the poster has been completed, the facilitator posts it and invites the participants to share their reactions to making the poster. Afterward the facilitator congratulates the participants on their work during the two sessions and encourages them to keep their poster and to display it in their usual meeting room or elsewhere to remind them of the strengths in the group.

Variations

I. The entire activity may be completed as a one-day team-building intervention. In this case one of two approaches may be taken after Session 1, Step XII: (1) The homework assignments from Step XIII may be omitted, and the participants may be asked to work from their completed handouts; or (2) the facilitator may ask the participants to complete the homework assignments in the group setting and then proceed with action planning. Because either of these two alternatives increases the time required for Session 2, the facilitator may want to omit Step V from Session 2 and make any other time adjustments necessary.

II. The facilitator or the group leader may collect all completed work sheets, create a planning chart for each participant, assemble the resulting charts into a handout, and distribute copies of the handout for use during Session 2.

III. With a team in which some trust has already been built through team-building activities, the structured experience may be shortened by using only work sheets A and C. With a team in which no team-building activities have been used, the structured experience may be shortened by using only work sheets A and B.

Submitted by Terri Burchett.

Terri Burchett *is an organization and management development specialist at Tucson Medical Center, Tucson, Arizona. Her responsibilities include facilitating team-building activities and conducting strategic-planning retreats within the health-care system. She coordinates and instructs management classes for the 2,700 employees who work for the system of clinics and long-term care facilities in eastern and southern Arizona. Ms. Burchett has served on the board of the Old Pueblo Chapter of the American Society for Training and Development for two years and is board president of a health-care clinic in southern Tucson that serves low-income and homeless populations. She has published several articles on team building and management development in periodicals such as* Personnel Journal.

STRENGTHS AND NEEDS
WORK SHEET A

Instructions: Fill out one of these sheets for every other member of your group. Write your name in the "From" blank and the name of the person who is to receive the feedback in the "To" blank. Then spend a couple of minutes writing a *brief but specific* completion to the statement that follows. Use only the space provided; do not write lengthy paragraphs. Give examples if they would be helpful in explaining what you mean.

Later you will read your statement aloud, clarify your meaning if asked, and then give this sheet to the person.

Here are two sample statements:

- *An area of strength that you bring to the group is* your willingness to help any co-worker who needs it. I really appreciated it when you offered to help me proofread the minutes of the department meeting last week, and Alice told me she was grateful when you volunteered to make copies of those minutes.
- *An area of strength that you bring to the group is* your writing ability. When any of us can't find the right word to use in a letter or report, we can turn to you for suggestions.

From __________________________

To ____________________________

An area of strength that you bring to the group is:

STRENGTHS AND NEEDS
WORK SHEET B

Instructions: Consider the different aspects of your job: task assignments, relationships with co-workers, equipment, systems, procedures, policies, and so on. Then read and complete the following statements, being as specific as you can but using only the space provided.

When you are considering what you *like* about your job, think about what you find satisfying, motivating, or challenging in a positive sense.

When you are considering what you *would like to change,* think about what you find dissatisfying, demotivating, or stressful.

Later you will read this sheet aloud, clarifying your meaning if asked.

Here are two sample statements:

- *What I like about my job is* (1) the large variety of tasks, (2) flexible hours, (3) long-term projects that I can be in charge of and really sink my teeth into, and (4) the opportunity to be mentored by people I respect and admire.
- *What I would like to change about my job is* (1) the amount of time I spend making copies at the copying machine, (2) the frantic pace at deadline time, (3) the lack of privacy and the noise in my office, and (4) the unreliable phone system.

What I like about my job is:

What I would like to change about my job is:

STRENGTHS AND NEEDS
WORK SHEET C

Instructions: Fill out one of these sheets for every other group member. Write your name in the "From" blank and the name of the person who is to receive the feedback in the "To" blank. Then spend a couple of minutes completing the statement that follows.

Be specific in describing how you would like the person to act and under what circumstances, but do not write lengthy paragraphs; use only the space provided. If you wish, you may explain why you need what you are asking for and/or how the person would benefit by giving you what you need.

Later you will read your statement aloud, clarify your meaning if asked, and then give this sheet to the person.

Here are two sample statements:

- *What I need most from you is* to get me the new-product descriptions three weeks before the deadline for advertising copy instead of only a week before. Having three weeks to write the copy would mean I wouldn't have to drop everything and race to meet the deadline.
- *What I need most from you is* to give me some space when you see that I'm upset. It usually takes me at least fifteen minutes to calm down enough to talk about what's bothering me. After some cooling-off time I can be more appreciative of your comments and your concern.

From ______________________________

To ________________________________

What I need most from you is:

STRENGTHS AND NEEDS SAMPLE PLANNING CHART

CHRIS

Strengths	Likes	Desired Changes	Others' Needs
Writing ability Cheerful disposition Willingness to help Understanding of statistics Knowledge of company procedures	Variety of tasks Flexible hours Long-term projects Being mentored	Too much time spent at copying machine Frantic pace at deadline time Lack of privacy and noise in office Unreliable phone system	Submit monthly reports sooner (Fred) Keep voice down when talking on phone (Karen) Give more feedback (Lee) Assist in writing product descriptions (Dale) Devise a handout on customer-service guidelines (Pat)

STRENGTHS AND NEEDS ACTION-PLANNING GUIDE

Action-Planning Steps

1. Define current situation.
2. Define desired change.
3. Describe how success will look or feel.
4. List steps to take.
5. Decide who will take steps.
6. List kinds of help/resources/approval needed.
7. List names of people who might help, provide resources, approve action.
8. Decide who will seek help, resources, approval.
9. Determine a deadline for each step.
10. Arrange to meet periodically to assess progress.

Procedure to Follow with Your Partner

1. Share ideas and suggestions.
2. Plan action.
3. Get feedback from each other about whether planned action would meet needs.
4. Negotiate as necessary.
5. Come to agreement about action to be taken.
6. Use any or all of the above action-planning steps, jotting down whatever information seems pertinent.
7. Summarize what you plan to do in a single sentence.

491. WHIRLYBIRD: EXAMINING COMPETITION AND COLLABORATION

Goals

I. To offer the participants an opportunity to experience and explore both intragroup collaboration and intergroup competition.

II. To encourage the participants' creativity.

III. To facilitate team building within individual subgroups through the completion of a collaborative task.

Group Size

Three to six subgroups of three to five members each.

Time Required

One hour and fifteen to thirty minutes.

Materials

I. A copy of the Whirlybird Assembly Instructions for each participant.

II. A pencil for each participant.

III. Assorted paper: newsprint, card stock, tissue, bond, glossy, wrapping, and so on (enough so that each subgroup can experiment more than once with each type of paper).

IV. A ruler for each subgroup, plus several extra rulers to be displayed on the supply table.

V. A pair of scissors for each subgroup, plus several extra pairs to be displayed on the supply table.

VI. A roll of transparent tape for each subgroup, plus several extra rolls to be displayed on the supply table.

VII. Several different colors of felt-tipped markers for each subgroup.

VIII. A stopwatch for timing the drop of each whirlybird. (The stopwatch may or may not be necessary, depending on the method of competition chosen. See Step IV.)

Physical Setting

A large room in which each subgroup can work comfortably. A table and movable chairs should be provided for each subgroup. In addition, there should be a table on which to display the paper and extra supplies. The setting should include access to an open stairwell or other elevated area to serve as the site from which whirlybirds will be dropped.

Process

I. The facilitator asks the participants to assemble into subgroups of approximately equal size (three to five members each), and each subgroup is asked to be seated at one of the tables.

II. Each subgroup is given a ruler, a pair of scissors, a roll of transparent tape, several different colors of felt-tipped markers, and enough copies of the Whirlybird Assembly Instructions and pencils to accommodate all subgroup members.

III. The facilitator explains that the subgroups will be using the distributed materials and the paper and extra materials on the supply table to construct whirlybirds, that at the end of the construction period the subgroups will drop their whirlybirds from the "drop site," and that the subgroup whose whirlybird takes the longest time to drop to the floor will win the competition. The subgroups are encouraged (1) to experiment with paper and design modifications (different wing lengths, different numbers of wings, different weights, and other modifications), (2) to test the various models they construct before selecting one for competition, and (3) to decorate their competition models with colorful designs if they wish. The facilitator tells the subgroups that they have forty-five minutes to come up with competition models and then asks them to begin; several times during the construction period the facilitator reminds the participants of the remaining time.

IV. After forty-five minutes the facilitator calls time and announces the beginning of the competition at the drop site. The competition may take any of several forms (chosen by the facilitator or by the participants): for example, a single race with all subgroups competing at once, a "best of five" series for each subgroup, or several "heats" after which the two best-timed whirlybirds compete against each other. Ultimately, the subgroup whose whirlybird has the longest drop time is declared the winner. (Ten to fifteen minutes.)

V. The facilitator reassembles the total group and leads a concluding discussion by asking the following questions:

1. How do you feel about your subgroup right now? Would you describe your subgroup as a team? If so, how?

2. How would you describe the way in which you and the other members of your subgroup worked together as you constructed your whirlybird?

What were some indications of creativity in your subgroup? Of collaboration? Of competition?

3. How did you feel about the other members of your subgroup during the construction period? How do you account for those feelings?
4. How did you feel during the competition? How did you feel about the other subgroups?
5. On the basis of this experience, how would you define the "good news" and the "bad news" about collaborative efforts? How would you define the "good news" and the "bad news" about competition? Which of the two—collaboration or competition—is more likely to lead to a "team" feeling and why?
6. What have you learned about collaboration and competition that you can apply at work? What is one thing that you might do differently in the future?

Variations

I. Different kinds of winners may be declared, for example, the subgroup with the most colorful whirlybird or the subgroup with the greatest number of design modifications.

II. Individual participants may be instructed to build their own designs; subsequently the individuals join subgroups to collaborate with others.

III. The subgroups may be set up to operate in different ways (one subgroup with an assigned leader, another with the members assigned to different construction items, another whose members work individually before they work together, and so on). Afterward the facilitator processes how these differences affected the competition.

Submitted by Gary Gemmill and Gary Wagenheim.

***Gary Gemmill, Ph.D.**, is a professor of organizational behavior in the School of Management at Syracuse University. During the past twenty-five years, he has worked as an organizational consultant to the top management of national and international organizations in the areas of leadership, team development, and intergroup relations. He has published numerous articles on the psychodynamics of small-group behavior in such journals as* Human Relations, Small Group Research, Small Group Behavior, Psychological Reports, *and* Consultation. *Currently, he is writing a book on the psychodynamics of small groups within organizations. He periodically conducts weekend workshops for groups in addition to his university and committee work.*

Gary Wagenheim *is an assistant professor in the Department of Organizational Leadership and Supervision in the School of Technology at Purdue University. Mr. Wagenheim owned and operated a chain of retail clothing stores prior to his appointment at Purdue. His research interests include leadership and small-group behavior.*

WHIRLYBIRD ASSEMBLY INSTRUCTIONS

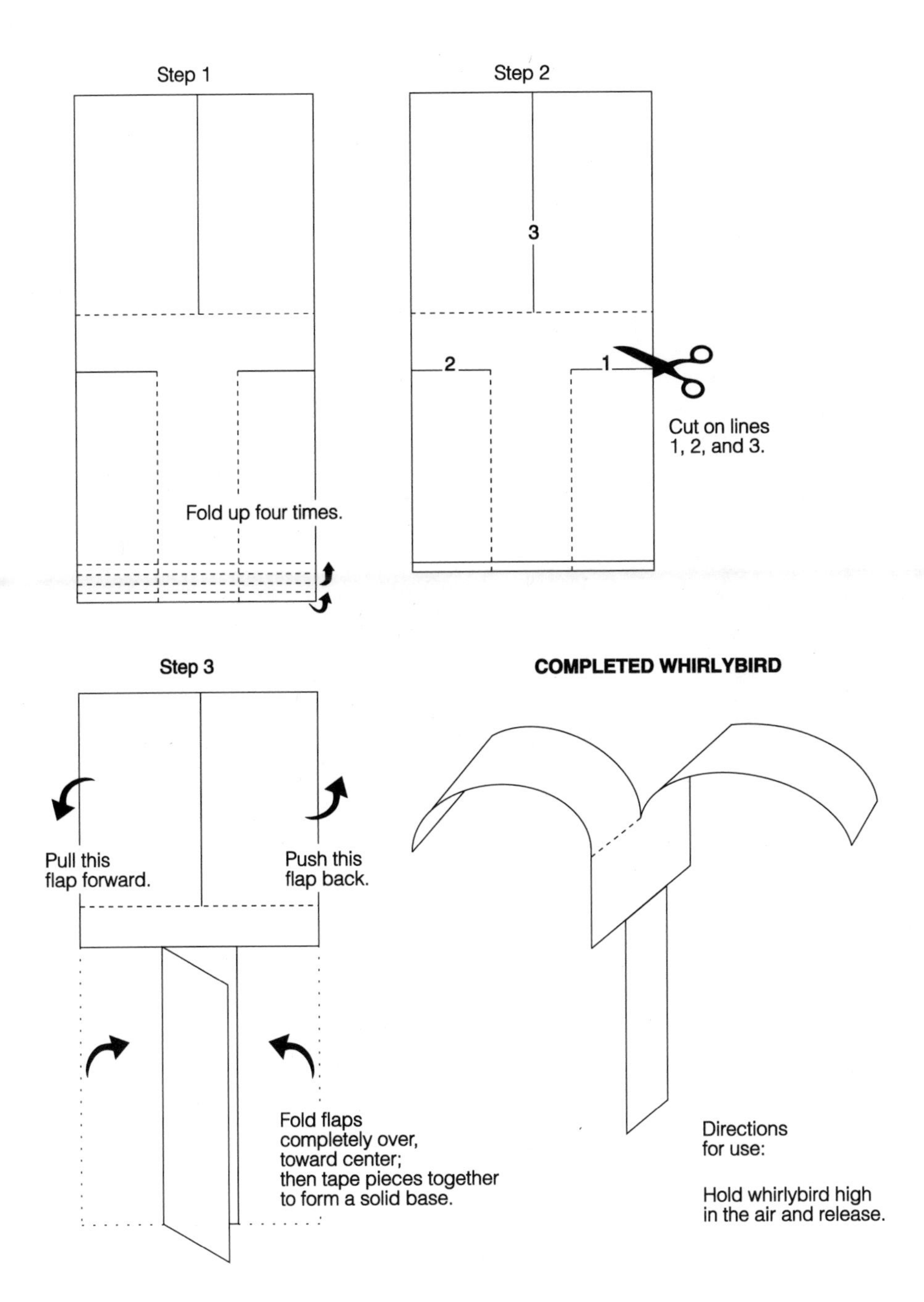

492. ZENOLAND: MANAGING CULTURE CLASH

Goals

I. To encourage the participants to consider the impact of cultural diversity on interactions among people.

II. To foster the participants' awareness of and sensitivity to cultural attitudes and behaviors that are different from their own.

III. To provide an opportunity for the participants to practice communicating and problem solving in a culturally diverse setting.

Group Size

Four subgroups of five to seven participants each.

Time Required

Approximately two hours and forty-five minutes.

Materials

I. A copy of the Zenoland Situation Sheet for each participant.

II. A copy of Zenoland Role Sheet A: The International Aid Team for each participant assigned to that team.

III. A copy of Zenoland Role Sheet B: The Province Chief and Staff for each participant assigned to that team.

IV. A copy of Zenoland Role Sheet C: The All-Seasons Team and the Minister of the Interior for each participant assigned to that team.

V. A copy of Zenoland Role Sheet D: The Press Team for each participant assigned to that team.

VI. A copy of the Zenoland Observer Sheet for each observer. (All but five participants observe the representatives' meeting that takes place during Step VII.)

VII. Five name tags completed as follows:

1. One labeled "International Aid Leader";
2. One labeled "Province Chief";
3. One labeled "Minister of the Interior";
4. One labeled "All-Seasons Vice President"; and
5. One labeled "Senior Correspondent."

VIII. Several sheets of blank paper and a pencil for each participant.

Physical Setting

A large room that allows the subgroups to conduct separate meetings without disturbing one another. Movable chairs must be provided. It is preferable to have a movable table for each subgroup; if tables are not available, the facilitator should provide a clipboard or other portable writing surface for each participant.

After the participants have finished their subgroup work, the tables must be moved aside and the chairs placed in a group-on-group configuration.[1] The five subgroup representatives sit in the inner circle, with the remaining participants seated in the outer circle so that they can observe the interactions of the role players during the meeting.

Process

I. The facilitator announces that the participants are about to participate in a role play that will point out the complexity of issues connected with cultural diversity in a group.

II. The participants are assembled into four subgroups of five to seven members each. One subgroup is designated A, one is designated B, one C, and one D.

III. Each participant is given a copy of the Zenoland Situation Sheet and is asked to read this handout. (Five minutes.)

IV. Materials are distributed to the subgroups:

1. Subgroup A receives enough copies of role sheet A to accommodate all members, blank paper and pencils for all members, and the name tag labeled "International Aid Leader."
2. Subgroup B receives role sheet B, blank paper and pencils, and the name tag labeled "Province Chief."
3. Subgroup C receives role sheet C, blank paper and pencils, and the name tags labeled "All-Seasons Vice President" and "Minister of the Interior."
4. Subgroup D receives role sheet D, blank paper and pencils, and the name tag labeled "Senior Correspondent."

V. The facilitator asks the subgroups to read their role sheets, to assign the representatives' roles as indicated on those sheets, and to give the name tags to the representatives to wear throughout the activity. (Ten minutes.)

VI. The facilitator announces that the subgroups have one hour to plan for the representatives' meeting discussed in their role sheets, emphasizes the

---

[1] A group-on-group configuration consists of two groups of participants: One group forms a circle and actively participates in an activity; the other group forms a circle around the first group and observes the first group's activity.

importance of maintaining roles, and then asks the subgroups to begin. While the subgroups work, the facilitator periodically apprises the participants of the remaining time and consults with the subgroups if asked.

VII. After one hour the facilitator calls time and instructs the participants to rearrange the furniture for the representatives' meeting. Each observer (every participant who does not play a role in the meeting) is given a copy of the observer sheet and is asked to follow the instructions on the sheet. The facilitator announces that the meeting participants have forty-five minutes to meet their objective and then asks the minister of the interior to begin the meeting.

VIII. After forty-five minutes the facilitator stops the role play and leads a discussion based on the observers' observations and the meeting participants' reactions. (Fifteen minutes.)

IX. The facilitator asks the following concluding questions:

1. What was it like to interact with people from different cultures?
2. What have you learned about cultural diversity among members of a group?
3. What experiences have you had in interacting with co-workers from cultures that are different from your own? What happens when we expect a person from a different culture to behave as we do? What happens when we attempt to understand the behavior of culturally different co-workers in terms of *their* cultures instead of our own?
4. It is predicted that the work force will become increasingly diverse in the years to come. As a result, what changes can we expect in organizations?
5. What are the disadvantages of a culturally diverse work environment? What are the advantages?
6. How might a more diverse work force affect you personally? What can you do to foster positive relationships at work with people from cultures that are different from your own?

Variations

I. The facilitator may assign participants to subgroups in order to ensure some degree of diversity (in gender, culture, regional background, or other elements) within subgroups. If this option is chosen, the facilitator may wish to ask one member of each subgroup to observe the subgroup's process, answer work-sheet questions about the subgroup's treatment of its own cultural diversity, and report observations to the subgroup before the conclusion of the planning session. The following questions, adapted from those in the observer sheet, may be used on the work sheet:

1. How would you describe the members' awareness of the cultural diversity within the subgroup?

2. How does that level of awareness affect the members' problem-solving ability?
3. How does it affect their communication patterns?
4. What effect does it have on their decision making?

Subsequently, each subgroup can incorporate the observer's feedback into final preparations for the representatives' meeting.

II. Prior to conducting the activity, the facilitator may ask individual participants to research specific cultures and then to incorporate their research into their roles during the activity. For example, a participant assigned to the International Aid Team may be asked to research American feminism and subsequently to play the role of an American feminist.

III. If there are more participants than can be accommodated by the four subgroups, the facilitator may devise another role sheet for a fifth subgroup consisting of the president of Zenoland and his or her cabinet. The goal of the fifth subgroup might be to unify the different factions represented in the meeting and to further the economic development of Zenoland. Also, the president might be from a different province, where the religious influence is not a factor. (The president would participate in the representatives' meeting.)

Submitted by Josephine Lobasz-Mavromatis.

Josephine Lobasz-Mavromatis *is an associate professor at the Institute of Public Service International at the University of Connecticut, where she teaches courses in human resource management. She also designs programs and study tours for international managers, develops and facilitates cross-cultural workshops, and advises and consults on internationally related activities for individuals and organizations. She is a member of the Board of Directors of the World Affairs Council Inc. of Connecticut and is an active member of the Society of International Education Training and Research and the American Society for Training and Development. Her articles on international business opportunities have appeared in the* Connecticut Business Journal.

ZENOLAND
SITUATION SHEET

Zenoland, a small country bordered on the south and east by the Green Sea, is experiencing economic problems. The three main industries—raising livestock, fishing, and copper mining—are not able to support the country adequately.

In an effort to boost the ailing economy, the government of Zenoland is beginning to promote tourism. Although the whole country boasts marvelous scenery, the area along the Green Sea is being most heavily promoted because its climate is so desirable and its beaches are spectacularly beautiful.

Three months ago the southern part of Zenoland experienced a severe earthquake. An agency known as International Aid, based in the United States, dispatched a team of medical personnel, social workers, construction engineers, and other technicians to assist in caring for the injured and homeless and in redeveloping the region. The team is stationed in the province of Isol by the Green Sea, where the greatest damage occurred. The team members' help has proved so valuable that two weeks ago the province chief of Isol asked them to stay an extra six months to assist in stabilizing the area.

The people of Isol, unlike Zenolanders from some of the other provinces, live by very strict religious rules. In accordance with these rules, men's and women's activities are segregated and women's activities are extremely limited. For example, the women of Isol rarely enter the Green Sea, and when they do they are fully clothed and accompanied by other women.

Last week Miss Bach, a Canadian nurse from the International Aid team, went swimming alone at the Green Sea in Isol. When she arrived at the beach, she removed her clothing, revealing a two-piece bathing suit. Some young fishermen were repairing nets nearby and began to shout in the native language of Zenoland. When she walked to the water's edge, they came closer and began to throw rocks at her. She ran into the sea and they followed her, repeatedly striking her with their fists. She nearly drowned in the surf before she was rescued and revived by tourists who saw what was happening from a bus and stopped to help.

Isol is in an uproar over this incident: The members of the International Aid team are upset; many local people are demanding that the team leave the country; and visiting foreign journalists are clamoring for further information. Meanwhile, Isol still needs help in its rebuilding efforts. The president of Zenoland has asked the minister of the interior to convene a meeting today to determine what to do to resolve the situation. The participants in the meeting will be the *minister of the interior;* the *province chief of Isol;* the *vice president of All-Seasons, Inc.,* a development company that plans to build a resort here in Isol, on the Green Sea; the *senior correspondent* from the group of visiting foreign journalists; and the *leader of the International Aid team.* The president has said that by the end of the meeting the participants must arrive at a consensus decision about what to do to resolve the situation.

ZENOLAND ROLE SHEET A: THE INTERNATIONAL AID TEAM

Note: One team member must assume the role of the team leader.

You are a member of the team sent by International Aid to help the people of Isol after the earthquake. During your stay you have come to love Isol; the people are warm and courageous, and the climate and scenery are wonderful. After living through the initial horror of the earthquake, all of you were looking forward to the next six months—until the attack on Miss Bach.

Miss Bach took a day's leave to swim at the Green Sea. As she related, the incident happened after she removed her skirt and blouse, revealing her two-piece bathing suit. Suddenly the fishermen nearby began to shout. Miss Bach does not understand the native language of Zenoland; after gazing at them a moment and being unable to figure out what was the matter, she lay down her towel and her book and started walking toward the water. At that point some of the fishermen ran toward her. Initially she thought they might be warning her of danger—perhaps a shark—but then they began to throw rocks at her. She panicked and ran into the sea, but they followed her and continued their attack with their fists. Finally she was rescued by tourists who were riding by the area in a bus and demanded that the bus driver stop so that they could help. A number of the tourists chased the fishermen away while others revived Miss Bach. Subsequently, the tourists returned Miss Bach to the team quarters, where she has been recuperating ever since. The driver of the tour bus, who speaks the native language, told you and the other members of your team what one of the fishermen had said: that the nurse was evil; that she had no clothing and was a temptress sent by the devil; that she must not be allowed to continue to minister to any sick or injured people of Zenoland; and that if she continued to live in the team quarters, then all who lived there must also be devils.

You and the other team members are very upset. Your idyllic life at Isol has become a nightmare. A number of native people raise their fists and shout as they pass your quarters; others are avoiding you. You have heard that some are suggesting it is time for the team to go home, despite the fact that there is still much work to be done.

Later your leader will be attending the meeting to determine what should be done about this situation. The other members of your team have been invited to attend the meeting, but they will not be allowed to participate. Now your team must come up with two solutions—a first choice and an alternative—that your leader can present during the upcoming meeting. When devising solutions, remember your objectives: (1) to convince the other meeting participants to allow your team to continue its much-needed work and (2) to ensure the team members' safety for the rest of their time in Isol.

ZENOLAND ROLE SHEET B: THE PROVINCE CHIEF AND STAFF

Note: One team member must assume the role of the province chief.

Your team consists of the province chief of Isol and the chief's staff. All of you are active in running the province.

Today there will be a meeting to determine what should be done about the unfortunate situation involving the young nurse from the International Aid team. Although your entire team has been invited to attend, only the province chief will participate in the meeting.

You know that the fishermen who are accused of attacking the nurse are good, religious young men. You and the other members of your team have reviewed their written reports, which state that the fishermen had never seen such a display of immodesty as the one the nurse engaged in. It is clear that she provoked them. Several of the fishermen returned to the site later and demonstrated against "the devils"—the young nurse and her colleagues. Isol is in an uproar. In fact, many native people are demanding not only that the team from International Aid leave but also that fences be put up to keep foreigners away from the beaches.

Another dimension of this problem is that the minister of the interior is working with the vice president of All-Seasons to develop Isol into a resort area. Even before the incident with the nurse, you were uneasy about the proposed resort. Now the incident has convinced you that morals in Isol will deteriorate if a resort is built. Surely other foreigners who visit will behave as badly as the nurse did—perhaps even worse. Also, you are aware that Zenolanders from other provinces do not share Isol's morals and are more than willing to have this incident highlighted further in the media. Therefore, you were especially distressed when you learned that the senior correspondent from a group of foreign journalists will be attending the upcoming meeting.

You cannot understand why the nurse would have done what she did. Everyone knows that a lady should not go into the sea unless she is fully clothed and in the company of other ladies. In fact, very few Zenolanders—men or women—swim in the sea. Primarily the local people use the sea for fishing or medicinal purposes. (It is said that some aches and skin disorders can be alleviated with sea water.)

Before this incident the team members from International Aid had been so helpful that the province chief asked them to stay for an extra six months. Now, however, you are beginning to wonder about the wisdom of that decision. If the team stays, its presence may do more harm than good.

Now your team must come up with two solutions—a first choice and an alternative—that the province chief can present during the upcoming meeting. When devising solutions, remember your objectives: (1) to convince the other meeting participants that the resort must not be built, (2) to keep the foreign journalists from writing about the incident, and (3) to ensure the continuance of earthquake relief in some form.

ZENOLAND ROLE SHEET C:
THE ALL-SEASONS TEAM AND THE MINISTER OF THE INTERIOR

Note: One team member must assume the role of the minister of the interior, who will conduct the meeting discussed in the situation sheet; another must assume the role of the vice president.

The minister of the interior is entering into a venture-capital arrangement with All-Seasons, Inc., the development company that you and your fellow team members represent. Although it is based in Atlantic City, New Jersey, All-Seasons owns and operates profitable luxury resorts and casinos not only in Atlantic City but also at the Côte d'Azur, France; at Chiang Mai, Thailand; and along the Bosporus in Turkey. According to the terms of this arrangement, All-Seasons will open a resort and casino here in the province of Isol, on the Green Sea. Research of the area indicates that its warm waters, lush vegetation, and beautiful beaches will lure tourists from all over the world.

You and your fellow team members are in the process of finalizing the plans for the resort. But a message yesterday from Mr. Xerxes, publisher of *The Zenoland Times,* the local newspaper, warned that the attack on the nurse from the International Aid team may have jeopardized the resort project. Unfortunately, the research on Isol did not reveal the strict religious rules and social customs that are now coming to light. (Even the minister of the interior, who is from another province characterized by a vastly different lifestyle, did not understand how fervently the people of Isol feel about their customs.) If the local fishermen are this upset about one woman in a two-piece bathing suit, how will they react when the beaches are covered with female tourists, similarly clad? And how will they feel about the casino?

On a positive note, the senior press correspondent is a friend of the minister of the interior, so this person may prove to be an ally during the upcoming meeting. You are anxious to protect All-Seasons' investment in the proposed resort. The resort could be an economic boon not only to All-Seasons but also to the minister and to Zenoland itself.

Now your team must come up with two viable solutions—a first choice and an alternative—that the minister of the interior and the All-Seasons vice president can present during the upcoming meeting. (The other members of your team have been invited to attend, but they will not be allowed to participate.) When devising solutions, remember your objectives: (1) to convince the other meeting participants that the resort and casino should be built and (2) to find some way to protect the resort's guests from being persecuted by the people of Isol.

ZENOLAND ROLE SHEET D: THE PRESS TEAM

Note: One team member must assume the role of the senior correspondent.

As members of the international press, you and the other members of your team have been invited to Zenoland by the Zenoland Development Council, a division of the Ministry of the Interior, to meet important people in the government and to tour several sites that are being considered for development for various industries, including tourism. Your original itinerary for today included the site of a proposed resort to be built here in Isol, on the Green Sea, by All-Seasons, Inc., an Atlantic City-based development company.

At a local coffee shop last night, you and your fellow journalists heard the story of the attack on the nurse. All of you are anxious to interview those involved and to file stories. You also heard that today there will be a meeting to determine what should be done about this situation. Late last night you and your fellow journalists requested that your team's senior correspondent, who enjoys a long-standing friendship with the minister of the interior, be allowed to participate in the meeting. Shortly thereafter your request was granted.

If it were not for this friendship, the senior correspondent's participation would never have been approved. The correspondent had to agree that the meeting would be "off the record" and that the minister of the interior could review the resulting news story before publication. Clearly, this entire situation is extremely delicate and must be handled with great finesse on the part of the correspondent. It is important to get a good, accurate story without antagonizing the minister of the interior.

You and your fellow journalists are getting together before the meeting to decide (1) what information and clarification of the situation you need in order to write about the incident and its implications and (2) how the senior correspondent should behave during the meeting to increase the likelihood of getting a good story.

ZENOLAND
OBSERVER SHEET

Instructions: Your task is to observe the meeting attended by the minister of the interior, the province chief of Isol, the vice president of All-Seasons, the senior correspondent, and the leader of the International Aid team. As you observe, think about and/or jot down answers to the following questions. Later your facilitator will invite you and the other observers to share observations with the total group.

1. How would you describe the level of awareness of cultural diversity among the meeting participants?

2. What impact does that level of awareness have on their problem-solving ability? on their communication patterns? on their decision making?

3. How are the representatives acknowledging and accommodating cultural differences? How are they working to transcend those differences and to find a mutually beneficial solution?

4. What are the representatives doing that interferes with finding a mutually beneficial solution? (What seems to be getting in the way?)

493. WORKING AT OUR COMPANY: CLARIFYING ORGANIZATIONAL VALUES

Goals

I. To offer the participants an opportunity to examine and to discuss their personal and organizational values.

II. To encourage the participants to explore the interaction of personal and organizational values.

III. To enhance the participants' effectiveness as team members.

Group Size

All members of an intact management or executive team.

Time Required

Approximately two hours.

Materials

I. A copy of the Working at Our Company Instruction Sheet 1, prepared in advance on newsprint.

II. A copy of the Working at Our Company Instruction Sheet 2, prepared in advance on newsprint.

III. A copy of the Working at Our Company Theory Sheet for the facilitator.

IV. Several sheets of blank paper and a pencil for each participant.

V. A clipboard or other portable writing surface for each participant.

VI. A newsprint flip chart and a felt-tipped marker for the facilitator's use.

VII. Masking tape for posting newsprint.

Physical Setting

A room large enough for the participants to work comfortably.

Process

I. The facilitator explains the goals of the activity. (Five minutes.)

II. After posting the first newsprint sheet, Working at Our Company Instruction Sheet 1, the facilitator distributes paper, pencils, and portable writing surfaces. The participants then are directed to work individually to develop their responses. (Five minutes.)

III. The second newsprint sheet, Working at Our Company Instruction Sheet 2, is posted. Again each participant is instructed to work individually to develop his or her responses. (Five minutes.)

IV. The facilitator presents a lecturette on personal and organizational values, using the Working at Our Company Theory Sheet as a framework. (Ten minutes.)

V. The participants are polled about their responses to the Working at Our Company Instruction Sheet 1. The organizational actions that instilled a sense of pride in the participants are listed in the left column of a newsprint sheet labeled "Prouds." The facilitator then leads a discussion about these actions and the reasons that they make the participants feel proud. The reasons are listed in the right column of the newsprint sheet labeled "Values." *(Note: It may be necessary to probe the participants' responses to uncover the underlying values. A reason is usually an explanation, whereas a value usually can be expressed in a single word.)* (Fifteen minutes.)

VI. The participants are polled as to the organizational actions about which they feel uncomfortable. These responses are listed in the left column of another newsprint sheet labeled "Sources of Discomfort." The facilitator leads a discussion about the reasons that these actions make the participants uncomfortable, with the intent of eliciting the underlying values that were violated. These values are listed in the right column of the newsprint sheet labeled "Values." *(Note: This portion of the activity can raise considerable negative affect; it is important to allow ample time to resolve these feelings.)* (Thirty to forty minutes.)

VII. Posting a new sheet of newsprint, the facilitator asks the participants to review the organizational actions that they listed as "Prouds" and "Sources of Discomfort." The facilitator notes that people observing organizational actions do not always agree about the reasons behind those actions. The participants are asked to brainstorm other values that the actions they listed might imply, using questions such as "What assumptions might employees make about the values underlying this action or decision?" or "What might an outside observer conclude about the values of this organization?" These responses are listed on the newsprint sheet. (Fifteen to twenty minutes.)

VIII. The facilitator leads a concluding discussion based on the following questions:

1. What do your organization's actions imply about your organization's values?

2. How important is it to you to make your values clear in the decisions you make for this organization? Why? What have you learned about the importance of values to individuals and organizations?

3. What happens when organizational and personal values conflict?

4. How can you communicate your values to employees and to customers?
5. How might you alter your decision-making process so that your organizational decisions better reflect the personal values of this team of managers or executives?

Variations

I. The group may continue to develop a values statement for the organization that can be distributed to other employees for comments and suggestions.

II. The activity may be limited to those actions and decisions that create pride.

III. This activity may be used with a top-management group and a nonmanagerial group. Subsequently, the two sets of results are compared in a joint meeting.

IV. The activity may begin by having participants make a list of their own personal values.

Submitted by Leonard D. Goodstein.

Leonard D. Goodstein, Ph.D., *is a consulting psychologist based in Washington, D.C., as well as a senior vice president for Pfeiffer & Company. After more than thirty years as an academic, he joined Pfeiffer & Company (then University Associates) as president and later chairman of the board. Subsequently, he served as chief executive officer of the American Psychological Association. Currently he consults with multinational organizations, specializing in organizational and executive development as well as strategic planning. He is a frequent contributor to the professional literature, including the* Annuals *and is one of the co-authors of* Shaping Strategic Planning: Frogs, Dragons, Bees, and Turkey Tails, *co-published by Pfeiffer & Company and Scott, Foresman in 1989.*

WORKING AT OUR COMPANY
INSTRUCTION SHEET 1

Consider your career with this company. Identify two or three organizational actions, policies, or programs that have instilled a sense of pride in you about working here. What was it about these actions, policies, or programs that influenced you to feel this way?

Make some notes about these items so that you can discuss them with the total group.

WORKING AT OUR COMPANY
INSTRUCTION SHEET 2

Consider your career with this company. Identify two or three organizational actions, policies, or programs about which you feel uncomfortable. What was it about these actions, policies, or programs that influenced you to feel this way?

Make some notes about these items so that you can discuss them with the total group.

WORKING AT OUR COMPANY THEORY SHEET

Values, according to *The Random House College Dictionary,* are those "ideals, customs, or institutions that arouse an emotional response, for or against them, in a given society or a given person." Generally a value can be captured in one or two words. Some examples of values a person might hold are love, family, freedom, honesty, education, financial security, safety, health, equal rights, intelligence, fame, success, charity, perseverance, respect, and so on.

Just as each person holds a unique set of values, each organization also holds a unique set of values. Examples of organizational values might include teamwork, profitability, customer service, creativity, harmony, quality, technology, and so on. Within an organization, the personal values of individual employees may agree or conflict with those of other employees, or they may agree or conflict with the values of the organization.

An individual has personal values long before he or she experiences organizational values. An employee may have difficulty being comfortable, happy, or productive when the actions of the organization are incongruent with his or her values. Organizational *actions* reflect organizational values, just as personal *actions* reflect personal values. Certain behaviors evoke pride or distress because of their degree of consistency with values. This is true for personal as well as organizational behaviors.

Most people can name their core personal values. However, if an organization does not establish and publish its values, people are left to infer them from organizational actions. Also, if an organization acts in a way that is inconsistent with published values, people become confused.

For example, suppose that the management of an organization decides to purchase new state-of-the-art equipment for its Southwest division. If the organization does not establish and announce the values behind this decision, an employee might infer any one of a number of reasons, conclusions, and values, including the following:

Presumed Reason	Conclusion	Inferred Values
The company must be planning to consolidate its operations in the Southwest division.	Employees in other divisions are going to be laid off.	Profitability; disregard for human resources
The Southwest division must be doing well, and management hopes to use it as a model division.	Our division can strive to do well and to be the next to get the new equipment.	Quality; employee motivation
The Southwest division must be lagging behind, and management hopes that the new equipment will boost production.	Machines are taking jobs away from people in this company.	Technology; productivity
The new equipment will make it possible to move toward self-directed work teams.	This company cares about its employees.	Teamwork; employee satisfaction

Now suppose that the organization's management makes the announcement about the equipment changes in this way: "The old equipment in the Southwest division required chemicals that were a potential hazard to employees and to the community. Newer equipment uses the same process that we use in our other divisions and therefore does not require potentially hazardous chemicals." The announcement might then continue in one of the following ways:

1. "Because our company values being environmentally responsible, we are proud to announce the purchase of new, state-of-the-art equipment for our Southwest division."
2. "Because our company values protecting its investors from lawsuits, we have decided to purchase new, state-of-the-art equipment for our Southwest division."

Either announcement clearly defines and publishes to employees and customers where the managers of the organization stand and what they value. It is vital to do this defining and publishing of values and to use values to make decisions and to explain why decisions are made. Until an organization operates from an awareness of its values, employees will continue to make assumptions about what the organization values, and the practical aspects of doing business may be adversely affected.

Reference

The Random House college dictionary. (1988). New York: Random House.

494. HELP WANTED: COLLABORATIVE PROBLEM SOLVING FOR CONSULTANTS

Goals

I. To offer the participants an opportunity to practice collaborative problem solving in one-on-one consulting situations and to receive feedback on their efforts.

II. To assist the participants in identifying which consultant behaviors are effective in collaborative problem solving and which are not effective.

Group Size

Four to six subgroups of four participants each. This activity has been designed for use with practicing and prospective consultants.

Time Required

Approximately two and one-half hours.

Materials

I. A set of Help Wanted Employee Role Sheets 1 through 4 for each subgroup (a different role sheet for each subgroup member).

II. One copy of the Help Wanted Consultant Sheet for each participant.

III. Two copies of the Help Wanted Observer Sheet for each participant.

IV. Several sheets of blank paper and a pencil for each participant.

V. A clipboard or other portable writing surface for each participant.

VI. A newsprint flip chart and a felt-tipped marker.

VII. Masking tape for posting newsprint.

Physical Setting

A room large enough so that the subgroups can conduct role plays without disturbing one another. Movable chairs should be provided.

Process

I. The facilitator announces the goals of the activity.

II. After instructing the participants to assemble into subgroups of four members each, the facilitator explains the role-play process: In each subgroup there are four roles—employee, human resource consultant, and two observers. The subgroup members will conduct four different role plays, taking turns in roles so that each participant plays the employee once, the consultant once, and an observer twice. After each role play the observers will share their observations with the role players, concentrating on giving feedback to the consultant; then all four members will discuss the experience, including what the consultant might have done differently.

III. A set of employee role sheets is distributed to each subgroup in such a way that each member receives a different sheet. The facilitator then gives each participant the remaining materials: one consultant sheet, two observer sheets, blank paper and a pencil, and a clipboard or other portable writing surface.

IV. The facilitator asks the participants to spend ten minutes reading the three handouts and jotting down notes about how to play their employee roles. The participants are cautioned not to share the contents of their employee role sheets.

V. Each subgroup is instructed to decide which two members will participate in the first role play as employee and consultant.

VI. The facilitator asks the subgroups to spend ten minutes conducting their role plays, with the observers listening closely and filling out their observer sheets.

VII. After ten minutes the facilitator stops the role plays and asks the subgroups to spend fifteen minutes on feedback and discussion.

VIII. The facilitator asks the members of each subgroup to spend five minutes preparing for the next role play by determining who will assume which roles and by reviewing the appropriate handouts.

IX. Steps VI through VIII are repeated three times so that each participant has a chance to play the role of consultant and to receive feedback. (One and one-half hours.)

X. The facilitator reconvenes the total group and leads a discussion based on these questions:

1. How productive were the various role plays in terms of solving the employee problems?
2. What elements did the most-productive role plays have in common? What elements did the least-productive role plays have in common?
3. What have you learned about the skills that are necessary for effective consultation in collaborative problem-solving efforts?
4. What is one thing that you will do differently in future collaborative problem-solving efforts as a result of participating in this activity?

During this discussion the facilitator records effective elements and consultant behaviors on newsprint and posts the newsprint prominently.

Variations

I. To save time, the facilitator may form triads instead of subgroups of four and may use three of the four role sheets.

II. Prior to conducting the activity, the facilitator may ask the participants to contribute ideas for employee role sheets involving employee problems that they have personally encountered and/or been confronted with. Subsequently, the facilitator writes new role sheets based on those problems and uses the new handouts during the activity.

III. The participants may be asked to use the effective consultant behaviors generated during Step X to create a checklist to assess their own behaviors in future collaborative problem-solving efforts.

Submitted by Carol Nolde.

***Carol Nolde** is a developmental senior editor for Pfeiffer & Company. In this capacity she evaluates, develops, compiles, writes, and edits various kinds of HRD publications and assists authors in the developmental process. She has taught high school English and has been an editor for Hallmark Cards, Inc., in Kansas City, Missouri, and for Control Data Corporation in La Jolla, California. Carol has been with Pfeiffer & Company for twelve years and has been the project manager of the* Annual *for the last five years.*

HELP WANTED
EMPLOYEE ROLE SHEET 1

"My Boss Is Driving Me Crazy"

You have been with your company for seventeen years. You have been promoted four times and have been in your present job, which you love, for five years. You have a solid record of glowing performance appraisals from three previous supervisors. Now you are the most senior person in your department, and your co-workers often look to you for guidance.

Things were great until your old boss resigned and your new boss came on the scene two months ago. During his first day on the job, the new boss called a meeting with the members of your department and announced that one of the reasons he was hired was to come up with ways to increase profit. You know that profit is down, but, like most of your co-workers, you feel that this situation is attributable to an economic recession; things should pick up in a few months, once the national economy recovers. Your new boss, on the other hand, has other ideas. He believes that you and your co-workers should address the company's financial situation by trying new systems and processes to boost productivity. He seems ready to dump all of the old systems—many of which you personally designed—in favor of new approaches.

The new boss frequently quotes statistics and academic studies to back up his ideas, but he never cites examples from his own experience in the corporate world. That is probably because he has so little experience. He recently earned his M.B.A. from Harvard, and this is his first full-time job. You do not have a college degree, but you have certainly proved yourself on the job. How can he possibly know more than you do about how to manage your work?

Now everything you do comes under his scrutiny; you are continually justifying the way you do things. Twice you have tried talking with him privately about this problem. You told him that your basic philosophy is "If it isn't broken, don't fix it." On both of these occasions, although he was extremely polite, he said that you were "resistant" and "behind the times."

The job you love is in jeopardy, and you have no idea what to do next. Consequently, you have made an appointment with the company's human resource consultant. Maybe the consultant can help you come up with a way to save your job and your sanity.

HELP WANTED
EMPLOYEE ROLE SHEET 2

"I Can't Get What I Need to Do My Job"

Each month you must prepare a report on the previous month's foreign sales. On the fifteenth of the month, you must give copies of the completed report to each of the company's top executives, who then review the report and use it as the centerpiece of a monthly meeting at which they determine future marketing directions.

Your report is based on a monthly printout of foreign sales. Once you have the printout, you analyze sales and then write the report, making recommendations based on your analysis. The process of reviewing the information and writing the report takes about one and one-half days, so you need the printout at least two full days before the report is due.

Terry in Data Processing is responsible for giving you the printout. You used to be able to count on Terry to get the printout to you on time. But six months ago the company installed a new computer system, and since then Terry has been late with the printout every month. Most of the time you receive the printout only one working day before your report is due, which means you have to stay up half the night writing. Also, although you have not received any negative feedback about your recent reports, you know that you have not had enough time to do your best work on them.

You have talked with Terry about this problem several times, emphasizing how important the report is, how long it takes you to prepare the report, and how grateful you would be if you received the printout on time. Terry always apologizes, saying that once all of the bugs are worked out of the new system you will receive your reports on time. However, Terry cannot say when the bugs will disappear, so you do not know how much longer this situation will go on. You have also talked to your own manager, who says that he sympathizes with how difficult the situation is, that he appreciates your patience and all the overtime you have put into preparing your reports, but that there is nothing he can do.

This situation must change. For a full week before the report is due every month, you are a nervous wreck. Today you are going to see the company's human resource consultant, who may be able to help you come up with a solution to the problem.

HELP WANTED
EMPLOYEE ROLE SHEET 3

"I Can't Take the Stress"

Eight months ago you were an order taker when the higher-paid position of troubleshooter became available. You applied for this position and got it.

As troubleshooter, you are the person who has to rectify the situation when something goes wrong with a customer's order. You spent your first month in the position attending customer-service training and learning the ropes. But all your training did not prepare you for the stress of this job.

All day long you receive customer calls and letters. The message is always the same, regardless of whether the customer is genial or angry: "Fix this NOW." Many customers seem genuinely desperate. You are always behind in your work; there is so much to do, and all of it needs to be done instantly. You cannot even enjoy your lunch break in peace unless you leave the premises; your co-workers, who cover for you during lunch, interrupt you with questions about how to handle the various situations that arise. Even after you go home at night, you cannot stop thinking about all the work you did not finish during the day and about what tomorrow might bring. Your spouse is expressing frustration, saying that you are distracted and unapproachable since you took the new job; even your children seem to stay away from you as much as possible, apparently fearing that you will snap at them.

Although the extra money has been nice, you have begun to think that it is not worth what you have to go through on this job. You have talked with your manager about this problem on three occasions. The first couple of times she tried to reassure you by saying that you are still learning the job, that you are doing fine so far, and that with time the work will seem easier. On the third occasion, you brought her a brochure you found for a two-day stress-management workshop offsite and asked if the company would pay for you to attend. She said that the company could not afford to send you to the workshop now due to poor cash flow but that maybe she could send you in six months or so.

You know that you cannot last another six months with things as they are now. You must do something about your stress level as soon as possible. Consequently, you have decided to talk with the company's human resource consultant, who may be able to help you come up with a solution to the problem.

HELP WANTED
EMPLOYEE ROLE SHEET 4

"My Co-Worker Won't Cooperate"

Two months ago you and a co-worker, Chris, were assigned to work together on an important project. Your assignment was to gather and analyze data, agree on recommendations based on the data, and present those recommendations to your manager in a written report. You have only a week left until the project deadline, and you are afraid you will not make it.

In the beginning things went well. Chris was great at research—thorough and precise. Whenever you became bored with the research process, you dropped out and Chris willingly kept going, seemingly tirelessly. The trouble started when Chris could not let go of the analysis phase.

Your approach to work is very different from Chris's. You look at the facts, weigh them, make your decision, and act on it. You do not have the patience for a lot of research, but once the data are accessible you are ready to move. Chris, on the other hand, is wonderful at uncovering information but needs to analyze every piece of data from every conceivable angle before making a decision.

You were ready with your own recommendations a week ago, and you tried without success to convince Chris that they are sound. In frustration you started writing the report by yourself and then dropped by Chris's office to announce what you were doing. Chris protested indignantly that you were ignoring the mandate of the assignment by writing your own personal opinions. You said that missing the deadline would also be ignoring the mandate. Chris replied that there was plenty of time left and that writing prematurely would result in a "shoddy end product." You asked when Chris would be ready to help with the writing, and Chris said, "I'm not sure. I can't say until I've checked a few more details." At that point you threw up your hands and left Chris's office.

You thought about ignoring Chris and finishing the report, but you know that Chris is a much better writer than you and would be able to polish the report in a way that you never could. But will Chris ever be ready to write?

It is a matter of pride with you that you never complain about your colleagues, so you have not talked with your manager about this problem. When she has asked about your progress, you have made vague comments like "It's coming along."

Now you have decided to talk with the company's human resource consultant, who may be able to help you solve the problem and complete the report on time.

HELP WANTED
CONSULTANT SHEET

Instructions: Your task is to conduct a collaborative problem-solving session. You have no authority to change the situation; instead, your purpose is *to help the employee empower himself or herself to resolve the problem.* Here are some questions that might be useful during the conversation:

1. What is the situation now? Who is involved in the problem? What has each person, including you, done to contribute to the problem?

2. If the situation were changed to your complete satisfaction, what would that perfect situation look/sound/feel like? How would you know when you had what you wanted?

3. What have you tried so far in your attempts to solve the problem? What else could you try? Which facets or elements of the problem are in your control? Which are out of your control? Whose help do you need?

4. What can you do to close the gap between the current situation and the desired situation? What steps can you take? What will your first step be?

HELP WANTED OBSERVER SHEET

Instructions: During the role play, observe the interactions of the employee and the consultant and write answers to the following questions. Later you will share your questions and answers with the other members of your subgroup.

1. What behaviors (verbal and nonverbal) is the consultant using?

2. Which consultant behaviors contribute to problem resolution?

3. Which consultant behaviors seem to get in the way of problem resolution?

4. On a scale of 1 to 10, how productive is the role play in terms of solving the employee's problem?

495. GOOD WORKSHOPS DON'T JUST HAPPEN: DEVELOPING FACILITATION SKILLS

Goals

I. To assist the participants in identifying elements of facilitation that are (1) vital to workshop effectiveness, (2) harmful to workshop effectiveness, and (3) reflective of style (rather than vital or harmful).

II. To offer the participants an opportunity to consider and discuss facilitation practices, techniques, and styles.

Group Size

As many as twenty participants who are practicing or prospective group facilitators.

Time Required

Approximately two hours.

Materials

I. A set of fifty-two 4" x 6" index cards, each containing one of the fifty-two numbered statements on the Good Workshops Don't Just Happen Statement List.

II. A copy of the Good Workshops Don't Just Happen Suggested-Response Sheet for each participant plus one copy for the facilitator's use.

Physical Setting

A room large enough so that the participants can move about freely to confer with one another. Movable chairs should be available as well as a table on which the facilitator can place spare cards (see Steps II and III).

Process

I. The facilitator introduces the goals of the activity.

II. The facilitator explains that each participant is about to receive the same number of index cards and that each card bears a statement about facilitating a workshop. The facilitator distributes the prepared cards, leaving the extras on the table. (For example, if there are eighteen participants, each is given two cards, and the sixteen remaining cards are placed on the table.)

III. The participants are told to read their cards and to judge whether or not each card statement describes *an element that contributes to the effectiveness of a workshop*. The facilitator explains that for the next few minutes the participants will be able to keep their cards or to trade them, one for one, with other participants, in order to obtain statements representing elements that contribute the most to workshop effectiveness. The facilitator also explains that a participant may choose one of the extra cards on the table, discarding another card in exchange and leaving it on the table.

IV. After five or six minutes, the facilitator announces that the participants have one more minute to complete the trading process. After another minute the facilitator calls time and asks the participants to be seated.

V. The facilitator asks for volunteers to share card statements that represent elements they consider *vital* to an effective workshop and to explain why these elements are vital. Before the sharing begins, the facilitator stipulates that after each statement is shared and explained, the listening participants will be invited to respond by agreeing or disagreeing and then stating why; subsequently, the facilitator will read the "suggested response" to that statement from the Good Workshops Don't Just Happen Suggested-Response Sheet. (Twenty minutes.)

VI. Volunteers are asked to share card statements that represent elements they consider *harmful* to workshop effectiveness and to explain why these elements are harmful. The facilitator again stipulates that the listening participants will be invited to agree or disagree with each assessment and that afterward the "suggested response" will be read. (Fifteen minutes.)

VII. The facilitator asks volunteers to share card statements that *reflect facilitator style* (rather than elements that are vital or harmful) and to state whether these styles reflect their personal preferences. The participants are again informed that the listeners will be invited to comment on each shared statement and that subsequently the facilitator will read the "suggested response" for that statement. (Twenty minutes.)

VIII. The facilitator leads a discussion about the cards that were left on the table after the trading process, asking the participants to classify the statements as *vital to workshop effectiveness*, *harmful to workshop effectiveness*, or *reflective of facilitator style*. After the participants have shared their opinions of each statement, the facilitator reads the "suggested response." (Thirty minutes.)

IX. The facilitator leads a concluding discussion based on these questions:

1. What insights have you gained about your own style of facilitation? What is the difference between a matter of style and an element that is vital to workshop effectiveness?

2. What conclusions can you draw about the elements that are vital to an effective workshop? What conclusions can you draw about elements that are harmful?

3. How might you use some of the facilitation strategies that we have discussed? What is one thing that you can do in your next workshop to make it more effective?

X. Each participant is given a copy of the Good Workshops Don't Just Happen Suggested-Response Sheet and is encouraged to keep it and to discuss its contents with colleagues in the future.

Variations

I. The participants may be divided into three subgroups, each of which is assigned the task of trading for one of the three categories of cards (vital, harmful, or reflective of style). After the trading period, each subgroup is asked to prepare a brief presentation on its cards, citing reasons that those cards were chosen for that category.

II. The facilitator may introduce the activity by asking the participants to discuss the best and worst workshops they have ever attended or facilitated and the elements and/or critical incidents that characterized those workshops.

Submitted by Kathleen Kreis.

Kathleen Kreis, Ed.D., *is the director of English for the Buffalo Public Schools in Buffalo, New York. She frequently facilitates workshops for organizations on subjects such as communication, employee motivation, prevention of burnout, writing, and the Enneagram personality theory. She previously served as a lecturer in the Department of Organization, Administration, and Policy in the State University of New York at Buffalo. Her articles have been published in periodicals such as* The Executive Educator, American Journal of Nursing, *and* The Canadian Administrator.

GOOD WORKSHOPS DON'T JUST HAPPEN STATEMENT LIST

1. I include both total-group and subgroup activities.
2. I offer to clarify any points that I make, asking again and again if I have been clear.
3. When I know that I need to make a workshop presentation, I develop a script in advance and then follow it during the workshop.
4. I keep participants from digressing and make sure that they stick to the topic at hand.
5. I feel comfortable about stopping at any time for participant questions.
6. I delay the start of a workshop until most of the participants have arrived.
7. I urge every participant to speak, to offer his or her opinion.
8. I prepare written plans for any workshop that I facilitate.
9. I begin a workshop on time and end on time, no matter what.
10. I limit the number of times that a participant speaks so that no one dominates.
11. I believe in group confidentiality: what is said in the group stays in the group.
12. I avoid philosophical debates with participants who disagree with the premise of the workshop.
13. I entertain questions only at designated times so that the flow of the workshop is not interrupted.
14. I provide frequent breaks for participants—at least one break every one and one-half hours.
15. I dress as I think most participants will dress.
16. When participants are engaged in lengthy or loud side conversations that are off the topic, I call their attention back to the group.
17. I try to keep the workshop agenda flexible enough to include concerns brought up by participants.
18. I try to respect every participant's opinions, even if they are totally different from mine.

19. When planning a workshop, I review participant evaluations of previous workshops that I have facilitated on the same subject.

20. I dress up when I facilitate a workshop.

21. I overplan for every workshop that I facilitate—just in case.

22. I consider participant laughter to be a positive sign, indicating that participants are relaxed and that the workshop is going well.

23. I ask participants to raise their hands and be recognized before they speak.

24. After I facilitate a workshop, I debrief with fellow facilitators.

25. I avoid training jargon and try to use a vocabulary that will be easily understood by all participants.

26. At the beginning of a workshop, I share the agenda with the participants, telling them what to expect.

27. Before asking participants to "sign up" as volunteers for an activity, I always explain what the volunteers will be asked to do.

28. When planning a workshop, I expect it to go well.

29. The facilitator should do most of the talking at a workshop.

30. Before I facilitate a workshop, I prioritize the agenda items, determining what I *must* accomplish and what I *might* include.

31. The most important aspect of a workshop is the opportunity for people to meet and share.

32. Spontaneity is an important aspect of every workshop; I plan and prepare as little as possible and let the rest just happen.

33. It is important to distribute handouts that participants can keep.

34. No participant should be forced to speak.

35. I like to control the way in which participants learn during a workshop.

36. A workshop facilitator is like a teacher.

37. I insist on a comfortable workshop environment with movable chairs.

38. Participants should have fun in a workshop.

39. During a workshop I freely share my own experiences and opinions.
40. I thank individual participants each time they offer comments to the group.
41. During a workshop I never talk about myself and only share my opinions when asked.
42. The most important aspect of a workshop is the opportunity for participants to gain confidence and to enhance their self-esteem.
43. I accomplish every item on my workshop agenda, even if I must accelerate my pace to do so.
44. I ignore participants who are engaged in side conversations that are off the topic.
45. The facilitator makes the difference in whether a workshop succeeds or fails.
46. When planning a workshop, I worry about all the things that could go wrong.
47. I include a variety of activities for the participants, including light as well as heavy topics.
48. When I know that I need to make a workshop presentation, I practice in advance.
49. When planning a workshop, I provide participants with something to hear, something to see, and something to do.
50. The most important aspect of a workshop is the new information that participants learn.
51. I point out similarities and differences in points of view from participant to participant.
52. I like to stand at a lectern and have the participants' chairs arranged in front of me in theater style.

GOOD WORKSHOPS DON'T JUST HAPPEN SUGGESTED-RESPONSE SHEET

1. I include both total-group and subgroup activities.

   Reflective of style. Learning can take place with either total-group or subgroup activities.

2. I offer to clarify any points that I make, asking again and again if I have been clear.

   Harmful. The first part of the statement—"I offer to clarify any points that I make"—is vital to workshop effectiveness. However, the second part of the statement—"asking again and again if I have been clear"—negates the positive effect of seeking to clarify.

3. When I know that I need to make a workshop presentation, I develop a script in advance and then follow it during the workshop.

   Harmful. Following a script slavishly may indicate inflexibility as well as inadequate familiarity with the material.

4. I keep participants from digressing and make sure that they stick to the topic at hand.

   Reflective of style. However, too much digression can be harmful.

5. I feel comfortable about stopping at any time for participant questions.

   Vital. Unanswered questions may keep participants from learning the next step of a process or skill.

6. I delay the start of a workshop until most of the participants have arrived.

   Harmful. Although some people might say that this practice is a matter of style, it is important to remember that delaying in this fashion punishes the participants who have arrived on time.

7. I urge every participant to speak, to offer his or her opinion.

   Harmful. This practice may be seen as applying too much pressure. Participants should be *encouraged* to speak, but not addressed individually and *urged.*

8. I prepare written plans for any workshop that I facilitate.

   Vital. Guidelines for activities, discussions, and so on are essential.

9. I begin a workshop on time and end on time, no matter what.

   Harmful. The phrase "no matter what" indicates inflexibility.

10. I limit the number of times that a participant speaks so that no one dominates.

    Harmful. Some might say that this approach is a style issue; but determining how many times any participant will be allowed to speak and adhering to such a limitation may squelch participation, creativity, and enthusiasm.

11. I believe in group confidentiality: what is said in the group stays in the group.

    Vital. If confidentiality is not ensured, a safe learning environment cannot be created and maintained.

12. I avoid philosophical debates with participants who disagree with the premise of the workshop.

    Vital. Such debates are not resolvable, and they waste the time of those who accept the workshop premise.

13. I entertain questions only at designated times so that the flow of the workshop is not interrupted.

    Harmful. Some might say that this issue is stylistic, arguing that participants can keep lists of their questions to ask at a later time; however, many participants will not ask their questions under these circumstances.

14. I provide frequent breaks for participants—at least one break every one and one-half hours.

    Vital. Breaks allow participants a chance to refresh themselves, to recover from the intensity of learning experiences, to become better acquainted with one another, to network, and to continue their learning on an informal basis.

15. I dress as I think most participants will dress.

    Reflective of style. Because of their own individual expectations, participants may or may not respond positively to the facilitator's imitating their style of dress. Also, this issue may or may not be governed by the dress code of a sponsoring organization.

16. When participants are engaged in lengthy or loud side conversations that are off the topic, I call their attention back to the group.

    Reflective of style. The issue of side conversation has to be dealt with carefully. Some facilitators believe that asking participants to discontinue side conversations is inappropriate because the intervention may feel punitive to the participants. However, side conversations that are lengthy or loud may distract or annoy the participants who are trying to listen to the facilitator or to another participant who has the floor. In this case the facilitator must exercise tact in drawing the conversing participants back to the group. A comment such as "We'd be happy to hear from everyone, but let's do it one at a time" is a tactful way to address the situation.

17. I try to keep the workshop agenda flexible enough to include concerns brought up by participants.

    Vital. The participants' concerns represent a significant opportunity for learning and for resolving issues related to the training agenda; they may experience frustration and resentment if they are not allowed to deal with their concerns.

18. I try to respect every participant's opinions, even if they are totally different from mine.

    Vital. If the participants are to have a positive learning experience, they must feel valued, not denigrated.

19. When planning a workshop, I review participant evaluations of previous workshops that I have facilitated on the same subject.

    Reflective of style. This practice is a good idea but not essential to workshop effectiveness.

20. I dress up when I facilitate a workshop.

    Reflective of style. See the comments on Item 15.

21. I overplan for every workshop that I facilitate—just in case.

    Harmful. This attitude may set up an attitude of worry on the part of the facilitator. A more productive attitude would be reflected in the statement "I plan many options for conveying information."

22. I consider participant laughter to be a positive sign, indicating that participants are relaxed and that the workshop is going well.

    Reflective of style. Some facilitators choose to incorporate humor into a workshop or to foster it, and some do not. Laughter is not an issue related to the effectiveness of training. Participants may be having a positive learning experience without laughing; on the other hand, they may be relaxed, laughing, and having a good time without learning.

23. I ask participants to raise their hands and be recognized before they speak.

    Harmful. Participants may feel that this practice is too regimented.

24. After I facilitate a workshop, I debrief with fellow facilitators.

    Vital. Consulting with peers is an excellent way to learn, to share, and to improve one's techniques.

25. I avoid training jargon and try to use a vocabulary that will be easily understood by all participants.

    Vital. The use of uncommon words or jargon may annoy the participants and/or interfere with their learning.

26. At the beginning of a workshop, I share the agenda with the participants, telling them what to expect.

    Vital. Sharing expectations at the beginning promotes trust, commitment, and participation. On the other hand, springing surprises on the participants diminishes the learning environment.

27. Before asking participants to "sign up" as volunteers for an activity, I always explain what the volunteers will be asked to do.

    Vital. See the comments on Item 26.

28. When planning a workshop, I expect it to go well.

    Vital. Remember the power of the self-fulfilling prophecy and positive self-talk.

29. The facilitator should do most of the talking at a workshop.

    Harmful. The facilitator is not the only source of useful, pertinent information at any workshop.

30. Before I facilitate a workshop, I prioritize the agenda items, determining what I *must* accomplish and what I *might* include.

    Vital. This approach to planning means that all of the essential subject matter will be included in the workshop.

31. The most important aspect of a workshop is the opportunity for people to meet and share.

    Reflective of style. This issue is partially dependent on the purpose and the subject matter of the workshop. The participants' ideas are always a valuable resource, but they are not necessarily the most important one.

32. Spontaneity is an important aspect of every workshop; I plan and prepare as little as possible and let the rest just happen.

    Harmful. Flexibility is important, and spontaneity may be valuable in certain kinds of workshops; but failing to plan and prepare carefully may lead to disaster.

33. It is important to distribute handouts that participants can keep.

    Reflective of style. Some participants appreciate something tangible to keep and to refer to later. If participants are expected to apply training concepts on the job, as is the case with skills training, handouts may be particularly useful as reinforcement of learning.

34. No participant should be forced to speak.

    Vital. Coercion undermines learning.

35. I like to control the way in which participants learn during a workshop.

    Harmful. Participants have different styles of learning, and all styles need to be respected.

36. A workshop facilitator is like a teacher.

    Reflective of style. However, an effective facilitator is not like a teacher who only lectures and maintains rigid expectations about learning and about participant behavior.

37. I insist on a comfortable workshop environment with movable chairs.

    Reflective of style. Such an environment may simply be unavailable. At some point, though, discomfort interferes with learning.

38. Participants should have fun in a workshop.

    Reflective of style. Fun is not essential for learning, but for some participants it may reinforce learning.

39. During a workshop I freely share my own experiences and opinions.

    Reflective of style. Productive learning can take place with or without personal sharing on the part of the facilitator. Some participants expect the facilitator to share personal information, whereas others learn more if they do not rely on the facilitator's opinion. It is important, though, that personal opinions be presented as just that—opinions; presenting them as "truth" undermines the facilitator's credibility.

40. I thank individual participants each time they offer comments to the group.

    Reflective of style. It is important to acknowledge participant contributions, but thanking every participant for every comment may be cloying.

41. During a workshop I never talk about myself and only share my opinions when asked.

    Reflective of style. Some facilitators believe that sharing information about themselves personalizes the learning experience for participants; others do not feel that such sharing is necessary.

42. The most important aspect of a workshop is the opportunity for participants to gain confidence and to enhance their self-esteem.

    Reflective of style. With certain kinds of skills training, confidence and self-esteem may be important components.

43. I accomplish every item on my workshop agenda, even if I must accelerate my pace to do so.

    Reflective of style. Completing the agenda may or may not be important, and accelerating the pace may or may not diminish the learning experience.

44. I ignore participants who are engaged in side conversations that are off the topic.

    Reflective of style. Some facilitators invite such participants to join in one way or another; some ignore this behavior. It is difficult for the facilitator to be certain that a side conversation is off the topic.

45. The facilitator makes the difference in whether a workshop succeeds or fails.

    Harmful. This attitude can lead to assuming too much responsibility and burning out.

46. When planning a workshop, I worry about all the things that could go wrong.

    Harmful. The self-fulfilling prophecy could turn this attitude into reality.

47. I include a variety of activities for the participants, including light as well as heavy topics.

    Reflective of style. It is possible that the subject matter of the training or the issue at hand is inherently heavy. In this situation including some light material might be perceived either as welcome relief or as totally inappropriate.

48. When I know that I need to make a workshop presentation, I practice in advance.

    Reflective of style. Some facilitators cannot feel confident about giving presentations unless they have practiced; others feel confident without practicing.

49. When planning a workshop, I provide participants with something to hear, something to see, and something to do.

    Vital. Participants need to be actively engaged in the learning experience.

50. The most important aspect of a workshop is the new information that participants learn.

    Reflective of style. Other elements may take precedence over new information, particularly in interpersonal or skills training. (For example, gaining confidence and self-esteem or sharing with other participants may be more critical than absorbing new information.) However, most facilitators would agree that if some learning does not take place—whether that learning could be described as "new information" or as something else—then the workshop is a failure.

51. I point out similarities and differences in points of view from participant to participant.

    Reflective of style. Pointing out similarities in points of view highlights themes in the workshop; pointing out differences highlights potential avenues of growth. However, participants can be encouraged to discover similarities and differences on their own. It is also possible that participants can learn without considering similarities and differences, although many facilitators consider this to be an important part of learning.

52. I like to stand at a lectern and have the participants' chairs arranged in front of me in theater style.

    Reflective of style. Some facilitators believe that this kind of seating arrangement sets up a barrier between the facilitator and the participants.

496. UP CLOSE AND PERSONAL WITH DR. MASLOW: DESIGNING TRAINING TO MEET TRAINEES' NEEDS

Goals

I. To explore Abraham Maslow's (1970) theory of the hierarchy of needs as the basis for creating a positive learning climate in a training experience.

II. To present a format for designing a training module.

III. To offer the participants an opportunity to practice designing and presenting a training module that meets trainees' needs.

Group Size

Four subgroups of four to eight members each. This activity is designed for use with practicing and prospective trainers as participants.

Time Required

Approximately three hours.

Materials

I. A copy of the Up Close and Personal with Dr. Maslow Theory Sheet for each participant.

II. A copy of the Up Close and Personal with Dr. Maslow Resource Sheet for each participant.

III. Four newsprint signs prepared in advance, each listing one of the following questions:

1. What methods or techniques can a trainer use to satisfy trainees' needs for *safety?*
2. What methods or techniques can a trainer use to satisfy trainees' needs for *belonging?*
3. What methods or techniques can a trainer use to satisfy trainees' needs for enhancing *self-esteem?*
4. What methods or techniques can a trainer use to satisfy trainees' needs for *self-actualization?*

IV. Four newsprint flip charts with easels.

V. Four felt-tipped markers.

VI. Four rolls of masking tape for posting newsprint.

Physical Setting

A room large enough so that the subgroups can work without disturbing one another. Plenty of wall space should be available for posting newsprint. Movable chairs should be provided.

Process

I. The facilitator introduces the activity by stating that Abraham Maslow's (1970) theory of the hierarchy of needs can serve as the basis for creating a positive learning climate during a training experience. Each participant is given a copy of the Up Close and Personal with Dr. Maslow Theory Sheet and is asked to read this sheet. (Five minutes.)

II. The facilitator leads a discussion on the contents of the theory sheet, eliciting and answering questions as necessary. (Ten minutes.)

III. The facilitator posts the prepared newsprint signs in four separate corners of the room and places a newsprint flip chart, an easel, and a felt-tipped marker next to each sign. The participants are assembled into four subgroups of four to eight members each. Each subgroup is instructed to be seated next to one of the four posted signs.

IV. Each subgroup is instructed to spend three minutes brainstorming as many answers as possible to the question listed on the newsprint sign posted in its corner. The facilitator asks each subgroup to select a recorder to write the subgroup's ideas on the newsprint flip chart displayed on the easel *(not on the posted newsprint sign)*.

V. After three minutes the facilitator calls time and asks each subgroup to turn over the newsprint sheets it has filled so that a blank sheet is displayed on the easel. Then each subgroup is instructed to move clockwise to the next posted sign and to repeat the brainstorming procedure explained in Step IV.

VI. Step V is repeated twice more so that each subgroup completes the brainstorming procedure for every sign. After the fourth brainstorming period, the subgroups are instructed to remain where they are.

VII. The facilitator distributes copies of the resource sheet and asks the participants to read this sheet. (Five minutes.)

VIII. The facilitator reviews the content of the resource sheet and answers any questions that the participants may have. (Ten minutes.)

IX. Each subgroup is instructed to spend forty-five minutes designing and organizing a ten-minute training module on the information generated in that corner. The facilitator explains the particulars of the task:

1. Each training module should be designed and presented in such a way that it meets as many of the needs in Maslow's hierarchy as possible.
2. Any newsprint information, generated by any subgroup, may be used.
3. Each subgroup member must have a role in the presentation.
4. Visual aids may be used.
5. Each presentation must follow the guidelines on the resource sheet.

The facilitator encourages the subgroups to be creative and to vary their instructional strategies, gives each subgroup a roll of masking tape for posting newsprint, and then asks the subgroups to begin. While the subgroups work, the facilitator monitors their progress, periodically advises them of the remaining time, and provides assistance if asked.

X. After forty-five minutes the facilitator calls time and asks the subgroups to take turns making their presentations, beginning with the subgroup assigned to safety needs and progressing through Maslow's hierarchy in order. Before each subgroup begins its presentation, the facilitator asks the remaining participants to move their chairs so that they can see the members of that subgroup. After each presentation the facilitator leads a brief discussion and critique of that training module (based on the content of the resource sheet), assessing which needs were met by the module and how they were met. The facilitator ensures that each critique ends on a positive note. (One hour.)

XI. The facilitator leads a concluding discussion by asking these questions:

1. What is your reaction to developing and presenting a training module in accordance with the guidelines on the resource sheet? How was this experience different from other experiences you have had in developing and presenting training?
2. What similarities did you find in the ways in which information was conveyed in the presentations?
3. What have you learned about the relationship between Maslow's hierarchy of needs and the creation of a positive learning climate? What have you learned about using those needs to design and present a training module?
4. How will you apply what you have learned to training that you conduct in the future?

Variations

I. When clarifying the task, the facilitator may stipulate that each presentation must meet the need(s) about which it presents information.

II. The participants may be asked to develop action plans for upcoming training events, incorporating what they have learned.

III. To shorten the activity, the facilitator may ask the members of each subgroup to answer only one of the posted questions and then to stay in that corner and to develop a module based on the information that they have just generated.

IV. The subgroups may be asked to follow the guidelines on the resource sheet to develop a single activity instead of a training module. Each subgroup may be instructed to show how the activity meets the need to which the subgroup was assigned.

Reference

Maslow, A.H. (1970). *Motivation and personality* (2nd ed.). New York: Harper & Row.

Submitted by Bonnie Jameson.

***Bonnie Jameson** is a private consultant who works as a designer, trainer, and facilitator in human resource development. Her focus is on the development of the individual, the group, and the organization. As the lead trainer of the MANAGE program for the United Way of America in the San Francisco area, she trains in all aspects of not-for-profit management, including planning, change, and problem solving. Ms. Jameson also lectures on leadership, assertiveness, and management in the Nursing and Business Departments at California State University at Hayward.*

UP CLOSE AND PERSONAL WITH DR. MASLOW THEORY SHEET

Abraham Maslow's (1970) theory of the hierarchy of needs (Figure 1) is generally accepted as part of the foundation of the field of human resource development. The human needs that comprise the hierarchy—physiological, safety, belonging, self-esteem, and self-actualization—are the primary motivators that, if satisfied, will help individuals to understand themselves and, in turn, to understand others. Maslow believed that people meet these needs in ascending order from most basic for survival, represented at the bottom of the triangle in Figure 1, to least basic, represented at the top of the triangle. For example, a person usually meets most of his or her physiological needs before safety needs become a concern; physiological and safety needs are usually met before belonging needs become a concern; and so on.

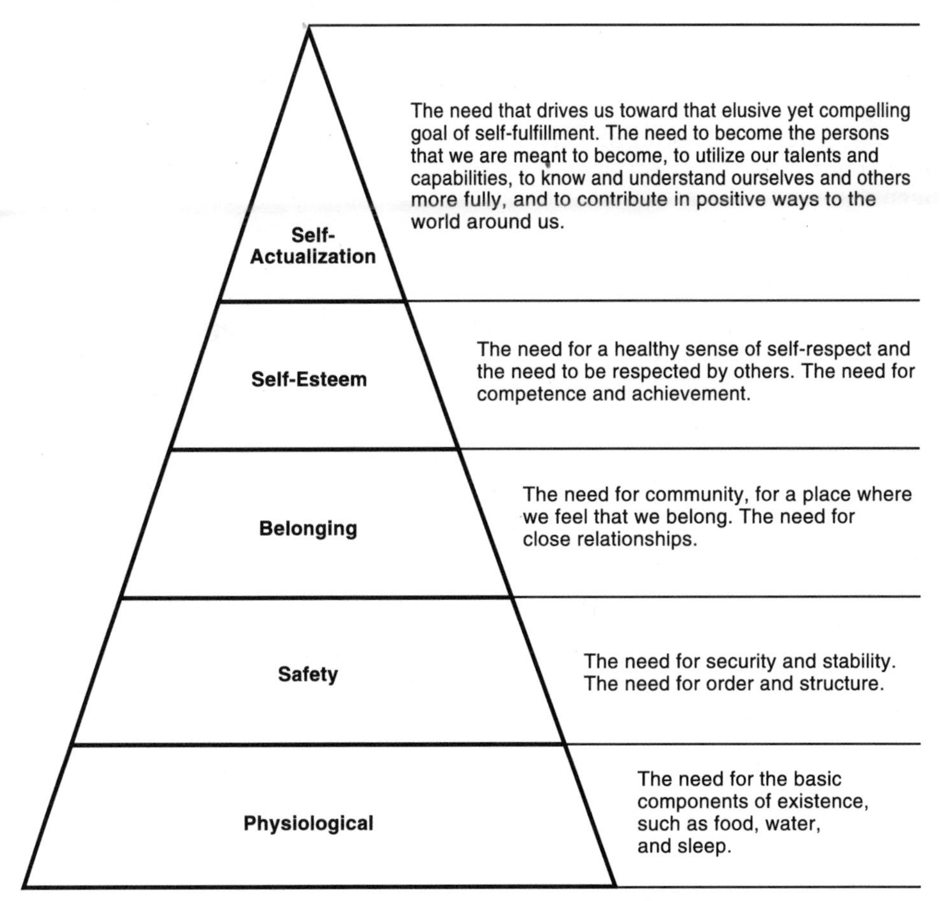

Figure 1. Abraham Maslow's Hierarchy of Needs

These needs manifest themselves each time a trainee enters a new training environment. In order to develop a productive group that is committed to achieving training objectives, you, as the trainer, must help the trainees to meet their needs:

1. *Physiological.* Do you make sure that the room is adequate for the purpose of the training, that the furniture is comfortable, that the lighting is appropriate, that the temperature is moderate, that water and/or other refreshments are continually available, that the trainees are given sufficient breaks, and that activities do not extend beyond the trainees' normal lunch time?

2. *Safety.* Do you greet and welcome each trainee as he or she enters the room? Do you create and foster a relaxed atmosphere that is conducive to learning? Do you explain the goals of the training, give an overview of the agenda, and then follow that agenda? Do you treat each trainee with respect?

3. *Belonging.* Do you take the responsibility for introducing trainees to one another and for ensuring that they become acquainted with the wide variety of resources that exist within the group? Do you provide activities that allow the trainees to work in subgroups?

4. *Self-Esteem.* Do you provide direction (clear goals, tasks, and time frames so that processes run smoothly and trainees can experience a sense of accomplishment) without exhibiting a need for power and control? Do you encourage and allow the participants to assume responsibility for their own experiential-learning opportunities?

5. *Self-Actualization.* Do you give risky assignments so that trainees can try new ideas and release their creative ingenuity? Do you provide activities in which trainees can share who they are? Do you offer activities in which trainees can work interdependently?

Few trainees express their needs to be comfortable, to be safe, to meet others, to produce something special, or to be integrated and authentic in the group. The trainees' physiological needs are fairly straightforward, but the other four needs are not; helping trainees to meet their needs for safety, belonging, self-esteem, and self-actualization can be a difficult challenge. Without the trainer's active efforts to meet these needs, many trainees become passive and deny the group the joy of knowing who they really are. Thus, as a trainer you must find and use specific techniques and tools to help satisfy trainees' needs so that the training experience is as richly rewarding as it can be for every individual.

Reference

Maslow, A.H. (1970). *Motivation and personality* (2nd ed.). New York: Harper & Row.

UP CLOSE AND PERSONAL WITH DR. MASLOW RESOURCE SHEET

When designing a training module, you start by defining the *objective*, which is based on a desired outcome. In other words, you must answer the questions "Why am I conducting this training?" and "What do I expect trainees to gain from this experience?" The objective can be likened to an organization's mission: It provides meaning or purpose.

Once you have clarified the objective, you can proceed to designing and organizing the training experience. Every training module must have three stages: (1) an opening, (2) a body, and (3) a conclusion. The opening accounts for 10 percent of the training time, the body for 80 percent, and the conclusion for 10 percent.

1. The Opening: "Tell Them What You'll Tell Them"

The opening consists of two components: (1) a "hook" (question, statistic, story, skit, role play, group sharing, or example) to capture the trainees' attention and (2) a review of the objective and the agenda for the training experience. This stage should meet trainees' needs for safety and belonging.

2. The Body: "Tell Them"

The body of the training module should have no more than three to five main ideas, and each idea should be supported with information that helps to meet the training objective. This stage should meet trainees' needs for self-esteem and self-actualization.

It is useful to vary the instructional strategies for the ideas. If you present one idea in a didactic fashion (by delivering a lecturette, for instance), then you might want to use a skit, a role play, and a group discussion to convey subsequent ideas.

3. The Conclusion: "Tell Them What You Told Them"

In the conclusion you summarize the objective and the main ideas that you presented; review action plans, if the trainees have made any, and encourage them to follow through; and answer any questions that the trainees may have. This stage should meet trainees' needs for self-actualization.

INTRODUCTION TO THE INSTRUMENTATION SECTION

The contents of the Instrumentation section are provided for training and developmental purposes. These instruments are not intended for in-depth personal growth, psychodiagnostic, or therapeutic work. Instead, they are intended for use in training groups; for demonstration purposes; to generate data for training or organization development sessions; and for other group applications in which the trainer, consultant, or facilitator helps respondents to use the data generated by an instrument for achieving some form of progress.

Most people have difficulty in describing others in nonpejorative terms, especially if others' behavior has had an adverse effect on them. One of the principal benefits of using instrumentation in human resource development (HRD) is that instruments typically provide respondents with new, relatively neutral words to use in describing others. With such a new vocabulary, one can begin to describe another person's behavior as "stemming from a strong need for inclusion" or "representing a weak economic value commitment" rather than in more subjective and emotionally laden terms that inhibit rather than enhance communication.

In addition to helping respondents to identify behavior, the comparison of scores from an instrument provides respondents with a convenient and comparatively safe way to exchange interpersonal feedback. The involvement with their own scores helps participants to understand the theory on which the instrument is based—a typical reason for using an instrument in training. Therefore, there are strong, positive reasons for using instruments in training and development work.

The trainer, consultant, or facilitator must recognize that the scores obtained by individuals on any instrument are the results of their answers to a series of verbal questions at one point in time and that those scores should not be treated with reverence. Such responses typically change over time, for a variety of reasons. The individual's interpretation of a single question the next time may affect his or her answer; a variety of experiences may change the person's self-perception; and so on. Professionals in HRD are encouraged to use instruments simply as one additional means of obtaining data about individuals, with all the risks and potential payoffs that any other data source would yield.

There are three instruments in this year's *Annual*. The first, the "Burnout Inventory," is based on the premise that burnout is alienation from work. The instrument yields four scores: three in areas related to burnout (perception of job content, perception of immediate supervisor, and perception of the organization) plus an overall burnout score derived from the three perception areas. This instrument is best used as a tool for examining burnout potential so that follow-up action planning can be done.

The second instrument, the "Locus of Control Inventory," measures internality and externality in an organizational context. The instrument is based on the notion that people with an *internal* locus of control—those who believe that outcomes are the result of their own actions—are more effective in an organization than people with an *external* locus of control—those who believe that outcomes are the result of external contingencies, such as the actions of others. The inventory helps respondents to determine how much control they believe they have in important organizational matters, how much control they believe is held by others, and to what degree they believe organizational events to be determined by luck. After completing the inventory, respondents can examine how to increase internality and reduce externality.

The final instrument, the "Total Quality Management (TQM) Inventory," offers respondents an opportunity to assess an organization's current emphasis on each of eight key criteria of TQM. This instrument can be used to diagnose an organization's readiness for involvement in TQM, to initiate discussions about the organization's level of activity in each of the eight criteria, and to provide data for action planning to foster TQM.

Readers of earlier *Annuals* will note that the theory necessary for understanding, presenting, and using each instrument now is included with the instrument itself. This eliminates the necessity of referring to several sections of the *Annual* in order to develop a program based on any of the instruments. All interpretive information, scales or inventory forms, and scoring sheets are also provided for each instrument. In addition, Pfeiffer & Company publishes all of the reliability and validity data contributed by the authors of instruments; if readers want additional information on reliability and validity, they are encouraged to contact instrument authors directly. (Authors' addresses and phone numbers are provided in the Contributors list that follows the Professional Development section.)

BURNOUT INVENTORY

Wm. Randolph Warley

BURNOUT AS ALIENATION FROM WORK

Much of the literature on burnout in the work place suggests that the source of burnout is the individual who experiences it—that burnout is primarily an outcome of physical, psychological, and emotional exhaustion. However, it seems more likely that exhaustion is symptomatic rather than causal and that burnout is actually a form of alienation from one's work (Kohn, 1976; Seeman, 1959, 1975; Warley, 1983). The Burnout Inventory is based on the view of burnout as alienation. The instrument incorporates three kinds of factors that play a critical role in the development of burnout: work-context factors, organizational factors, and alienation factors.

Work-Context Factors

The work context is a major contributor to burnout (Carroll & White, 1982). The following *work-context factors* linked to burnout were used in the construction of the Burnout Inventory and are based on those identified by Hackman and Oldham (1974, 1975), Hill (1975), Miller and Carey (1979), Vaugh (1975), and Warley (1983):

1. *Boredom:* The degree to which an employee feels that his or her work is monotonous, uninteresting, and dull;
2. *Upward Communication:* The degree to which an employee's position requires direct communication with individuals in higher positions;
3. *Decision Influence:* The degree to which an employee's position provides substantial opportunity for independent decisions and control in areas of personal responsibility;
4. *Growth Opportunities:* The degree to which an employee's position provides opportunities for personal growth and development in work-related skills and/or knowledge;
5. *Personal Control:* The degree to which an employee's position allows him or her to function autonomously;
6. *Salary:* The degree to which the salary an employee receives is appropriate compensation for the work required in the position;
7. *Task Identity:* The degree to which an employee's position requires the completion of a whole and identifiable piece of work;

8. *Task Responsibility:* The degree to which an employee's position demands personal accountability and responsibility for the tasks performed by the employee;
9. *Task Significance:* The degree to which an employee's position has a substantial impact on the lives and work of others;
10. *Skill Variety:* The degree to which an employee's position requires a variety of different activities and involves the use of many different skills and talents;
11. *Specialized Skills:* The degree to which an employee's position requires a highly complex level of skill or expertise in a specialized area;
12. *Supervisor Support:* The degree to which an employee's immediate supervisor supports the employee's work efforts; and
13. *Work Load:* The degree to which an employee perceives his or her work load to be heavy, light, or satisfactory.

Organizational Factors

In addition to the work-context factors, there are *organizational factors* or characteristics that influence employees' behaviors, attitudes, and feelings with regard to their work. The importance of four of these factors in particular—effective leadership (Miner, 1980), planning (Branch, 1983; Steiner, 1979), policies and procedures, and organizational philosophy or mission (Peters & Waterman, 1982; Stonich, 1982)—is frequently discussed in both organizational research and popular literature. According to the literature, these four factors appear to influence job satisfaction; if they are not present in an organization, their absence may contribute to employee burnout. These factors, as used in the development of the Burnout Inventory, are defined as follows:

1. *Leadership Effectiveness:* The degree to which an employee perceives the organizational leadership as effective in terms of getting work done and inspiring excellence;
2. *Planning:* The degree to which an employee perceives that planning is an integral part of organizational processes;
3. *Clarity of Policies and Procedures:* The degree to which an employee perceives that organizational policies and procedures are clearly articulated and meaningful; and
4. *Organizational Philosophy/Mission:* The degree to which an employee perceives the organization's philosophy/mission as guiding people's work throughout the organization.

Alienation Factors

The third kind of factor used in the construction of the Burnout Inventory has to do with alienation. The alienation factors developed for the inventory are based on Seeman's work on worker alienation (1959, 1975). These factors are defined as follows:

1. *Meaninglessness:* An employee's expectancy that his or her future will not be good in a current position or profession;
2. *Cultural Estrangement:* An employee's assignment of low reward value to goals that are typically highly valued by the organization;
3. *Powerlessness:* An employee's expectancy that his or her own behavior will not determine the outcomes or reinforcements that he or she seeks;
4. *Social Isolation:* An employee's sense of exclusion or rejection;
5. *Work-Activity Estrangement:* The degree to which the activities and tasks of an employee's position no longer bring the employee enjoyment or satisfaction; and
6. *Worker Alienation:* The degree to which an employee disassociates from a work identity to which he or she claims membership by virtue of practice, certification, or employment.

THE INSTRUMENT

Format

The Burnout Inventory consists of seventy-three statements that an individual evaluates on a six-point scale ranging from Strongly Disagree to Strongly Agree. The inventory statements incorporate the work-context, organizational, and alienation factors; responses to the statements reflect the individual's total response to his or her work and its environment.

Scoring and Interpretation

Completing the inventory allows an individual to examine the three kinds of factors and thereby assess the likelihood that he or she will experience burnout in the present job. The results yield four scores. The first three are based on the respondent's perceptions, and the fourth is the total burnout score. The following paragraphs describe the four areas in which scores are given:

1. *Perception of Job Content.* This scale measures how an individual experiences his or her job and its content: Do I perceive opportunities for advancement from my current position? Do I feel indifferent or excited about my work? Does my work have meaningful goals and a significant influence on others? Does my job provide me with a sense of responsibility? Does it include a reasonable work load? How do I view my opportunities for personal growth? How satisfied am I with my salary? How much autonomy and power do I have to get things done? What visible outcomes do I see in my work? How do I perceive my activities and tasks? All of these issues contribute to an individual's perception of job content.

2. *Perception of Immediate Supervisor.* This scale measures how an individual perceives his or her relationship with the immediate supervisor: Do my supervisor and I communicate openly? Do I receive appropriate feedback from my supervisor? Does my supervisor support me in my work? Do I respect my supervisor? This

relationship is one of the most important that an employee has; if it is positive, then the likelihood of burnout is low.

3. *Perception of the Organization.* This scale measures how an individual perceives the general organizational environment: How well and how clearly does the organization put forth its philosophy or mission? Are the organization's policies and procedures clearly articulated? Is the organization's leadership effective in accomplishing its goals and objectives? Does planning take place, and does it occur at all levels of the organization so that all employees are involved? This scale also measures an individual's perception of the organization's contributions to his or her work.

4. *Overall Burnout.* The fourth score combines the three perception scores into an overall evaluation of the individual's potential for burnout in his or her current job.

After the instrument has been completed, the administrator distributes copies of the scoring sheet. After scoring, the participants are given copies of the interpretation sheet and are asked to read this sheet and to plot their scores on the continua. Subsequently, the administrator leads a discussion based on the content of the interpretation sheet, emphasizing that how each individual respondent perceives his or her work environment *is reality* for that person. Within the same organization and even the same work team, one person may view the work context and the organization as the best of all possible worlds, whereas another person may have an entirely different view. All perceptions must be viewed as legitimate.

The content of the interpretation sheet is based on generalizations. An individual respondent may or may not be able to relate to all of the characteristics given in a particular description. If respondents express concerns about any of their scores in a particular category (Perception of Job Content, Perception of Immediate Supervisor, or Perception of the Organization), the administrator should suggest that they examine the individual statements that comprise that category.

Validity, Reliability, and Suggested Uses

No validity or reliability data are available on the Burnout Inventory, but it does have face validity and is best used as a tool for examining burnout potential so that follow-up action planning can be done. The inventory may be used to establish a group burnout assessment of a department or a work team. Each member of the department or team responds to the instrument; then the scores are aggregated, divided by the number of respondents, and interpreted for the group. Individual items may be examined for identification of problem areas.

REFERENCES AND BIBLIOGRAPHY

Biddle, B.J. (1979). *Role theory: Expectations, identities, and behaviors.* New York: Academic Press.

Branch, M.C. (1983). *Comprehensive planning: General theory and principles.* Pacific Palisades, CA: Palisades Publishers.

Carroll, J.F.X., & White, W.L. (1982). Theory building: Integrating individual and environmental factors within an ecological framework. In W.S. Paine (Ed.), *Job stress and burnout: Research, theory, and intervention perspectives.* Beverly Hills, CA: Sage Publications.

Hackman, J.R., & Oldham, G.R. (1974). *The job diagnostic survey: An instrument for the diagnosis of jobs and the evaluation of job redesign projects* (Technical Report No. 6). New Haven, CT: Yale University, Department of Administrative Services.

Hackman, J.R., & Oldham, G.R. (1975). Development of the job diagnostic survey. *Journal of Applied Psychology, 60*(2), 159-170.

Hill, A.B. (1975). Work variety and individual differences in occupational boredom. *Journal of Applied Psychology, 60*(1), 128-131.

Kohn, M.K. (1976). Occupational structure and alienation. *American Journal of Sociology, 82*(1), 111-130.

Miller, J.O., & Carey, S.D. (1979). *Defining roles and work dimensions as a function of selected complementary categories with complex organizations.* Unpublished manuscript, Educational Studies Division, Emory University, Atlanta, GA.

Miner, J.B. (1980). *Theories of organizational behavior.* Hinsdale, IL: The Dryden Press.

Mintzberg, H. (1973). *The nature of managerial work.* New York: Harper & Row.

Peters, T.J., & Waterman, R.H., Jr. (1982). *In search of excellence.* New York: Warner.

Seeman, M. (1959). On the meaning of alienation. *American Sociological Review, 24*(6), 783-791.

Seeman, M. (1975). Alienation studies. In A. Inkeles, J. Coleman, & N. Smelser (Eds.), *Annual review of sociology* (Vol. 1). Palo Alto, CA: Annual Reviews.

Steiner, G.A. (1979). *Strategic planning.* New York: The Free Press.

Stonich, P.J. (Ed.). (1982). *Implementing strategy: Making strategy happen.* Cambridge, MA: Ballinger.

Vaugh, C. (1975). Personal responsibility as a cure for job boredom. *Supervisory Management, 20*(3), 2-8.

Warley, W.R. (1983). *A study of need fulfillment and professional alienation among Georgia public school teachers.* Ann Arbor, MI: University Microfilms International.

Wm. Randolph Warley, Ph.D., *is an assistant professor of business and human services in the University College of Mercer University, Forsyth, Georgia. He specializes in research methodology, organizational behavior, and creative thinking for decision making. His professional activities include teaching and research, and he is the founding editor of the New Church Business Review. Dr. Warley has served as a head librarian and registrar and is responsible for implementing a university-wide on-line student information system. He has published articles on burnout, values, and leadership.*

BURNOUT INVENTORY

Wm. Randolph Warley

Instructions: For each of the seventy-three statements in this inventory, refer to the following scale and decide which option corresponds to your level of agreement with the statement. Then write the letter(s) representing your level of agreement in the blank beside the statement. For example, if you Moderately Disagree with the first statement, you would write MD in the blank beside that statement.

Strongly Disagree	Disagree	Moderately Disagree	Moderately Agree	Agree	Strongly Agree
SD	D	MD	MA	A	SA

_____ 1. I have many chances for learning new and interesting things in my work.

_____ 2. The policies and procedures of this organization are well articulated.

_____ 3. My pay is inadequate for the work I do.

_____ 4. My work has visible outcomes; I can see how it fits with the whole of the organization.

_____ 5. Planning contributes directly to the ongoing activities of this organization.

_____ 6. Communications with key people at work are difficult for me.

_____ 7. I have enough power to accomplish my objectives in my current position.

_____ 8. I feel indifferent about my work.

_____ 9. I have freedom in scheduling my work.

_____ 10. Even if I did a poor job in my work, I would receive little or no criticism about it.

_____ 11. Since there is no future in my present position, I will probably seek another position.

_____ 12. The leadership of this organization inspires excellence.

_____ 13. The activities and tasks of my work bring me little or no enjoyment or satisfaction.

_____ 14. Management involves me in the decisions that influence my work.

_____ 15. My immediate supervisor is very supportive of my work efforts.

Strongly Disagree	Disagree	Moderately Disagree	Moderately Agree	Agree	Strongly Agree
SD	D	MD	MA	A	SA

_______ 16. The planning done at this organization reflects the input of most employees.

_______ 17. I cannot make up my mind about whether the goals of my job are important to me.

_______ 18. My work has little or no influence on the lives or work of others.

_______ 19. I have more work than I can handle effectively.

_______ 20. My immediate supervisor seldom gives me information about my work performance.

_______ 21. I feel a high level of self-motivation to do my work.

_______ 22. This organization's policies and procedures are objective and workable.

_______ 23. I am leaving my job as soon as possible.

_______ 24. My work has clear beginnings and endings.

_______ 25. I feel inadequately compensated for my work.

_______ 26. The organization's philosophy/mission is clearly reflected in the way work is carried out.

_______ 27. I have no power to accomplish my objectives in my current position.

_______ 28. My work is interesting.

_______ 29. My future is limited in my current position.

_______ 30. The leadership of this organization is competent.

_______ 31. I frequently feel that my work does not make any difference to anyone.

_______ 32. The activities and tasks of my work bring me only moderate enjoyment or satisfaction.

_______ 33. I control how my work is performed.

_______ 34. The day-to-day activities of this organization are supported by timely planning.

_______ 35. The goals of my job are very important to me.

Strongly Disagree SD	Disagree D	Moderately Disagree MD	Moderately Agree MA	Agree A	Strongly Agree SA

______ 36. I do not have enough work to do.

______ 37. My immediate supervisor is antagonistic toward me.

______ 38. I no longer want to be associated with my colleagues at work.

______ 39. This organization's policies and procedures are flexible enough to allow attainment of goals.

______ 40. I have great respect for my immediate supervisor's capabilities.

______ 41. I lack the "inner drive" to do my work effectively.

______ 42. I cannot make up my mind about whether I should leave my job.

______ 43. This organization has a well-articulated philosophy/mission that guides employees in their work.

______ 44. When management is considering a change in my areas of responsibility, I am consulted.

______ 45. I have insufficient power to accomplish my objectives in my current position.

______ 46. The organization's mission is vague.

______ 47. I have opportunities for personal growth and development in my work.

______ 48. My future is good in my current position.

______ 49. In this organization, planning involves most employees.

______ 50. The activities and tasks of my work bring me enjoyment and satisfaction.

______ 51. The leadership of this organization is effective.

______ 52. The goals of my work are no longer important to me.

______ 53. My work load is about right.

______ 54. I have a clear sense of being personally accountable for the quality and quantity of work that I do.

______ 55. Even when given the opportunity, I have little association with my colleagues at work.

Strongly Disagree	Disagree	Moderately Disagree	Moderately Agree	Agree	Strongly Agree
SD	D	MD	MA	A	SA

_______ 56. The philosophy of this organization creates a positive work environment.

_______ 57. I am committed to my work.

_______ 58. Communications between me and my immediate supervisor are good.

_______ 59. My work is part of a process with no identifiable beginning and end.

_______ 60. The leadership of this organization needs much improvement.

_______ 61. In this organization, policies and procedures support individual effort.

_______ 62. My work has substantial impact on the lives or work of others.

_______ 63. There are few prospects for personal growth and development in my work.

_______ 64. I have a satisfactory level of autonomy in my work.

_______ 65. Management makes decisions about my work without seeking my advice.

_______ 66. I receive appropriate compensation for the work I do.

_______ 67. I receive sufficient feedback from my supervisor about my work performance.

_______ 68. It is difficult to get my work done because my supervisor is seldom available for consultation.

_______ 69. When given the opportunity, I actively associate with my colleagues at work.

_______ 70. I would prefer working for someone else other than my immediate supervisor.

_______ 71. The mission of this organization is clearly defined.

_______ 72. My work is boring.

_______ 73. My supervisor provides me with enough information to do my work.

BURNOUT INVENTORY
SCORING SHEET

Instructions:

1. The numbers in sections A, B, and C below correspond to the item numbers in the Burnout Inventory. In the blanks below, write the numerical values of your responses to the items. Your responses will have different values, depending on the items:
   - If the item number shown below is **boldface** and circled, your responses have the following values:

     SD = 6; D = 5; MD = 4; MA = 3; A = 2; SA = 1

     Go through sections A, B, and C below and write in the values of your responses for all the items that are boldface and circled.
   - The responses for the remaining (uncircled) items have the following values:

     SD = 1; D = 2; MD = 3; MA = 4; A = 5; SA = 6

     Go through sections A, B, and C again and write in the values of your responses for the remaining (uncircled) items.
2. For each of sections A, B, and C, add up all of your responses to obtain your *total score.*
3. For each of sections A, B, and C, divide the total score by the number indicated to obtain your *average score.*
4. To arrive at your *overall burnout score,* follow the formula presented in section D.

A. Perception of Job Content

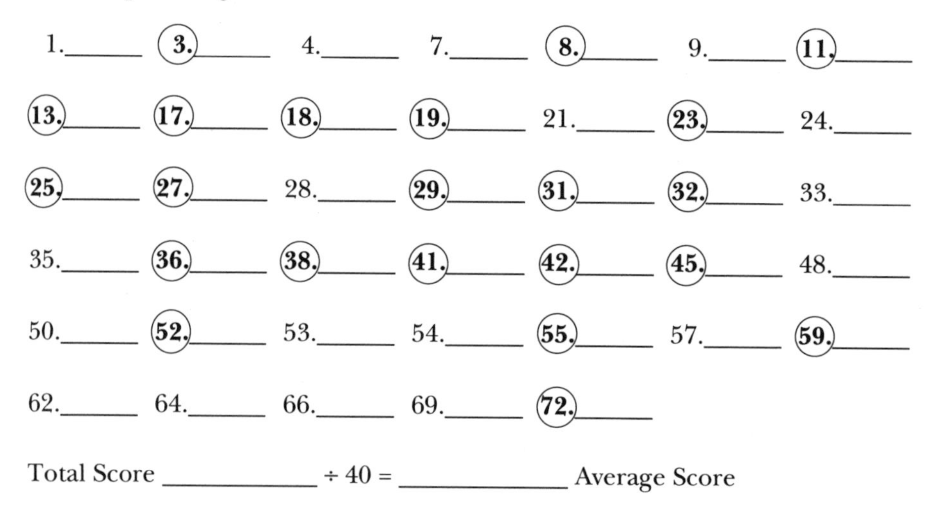

1.______ **(3.)**______ 4.______ 7.______ **(8.)**______ 9.______ **(11.)**______

(13.)______ **(17.)**______ **(18.)**______ **(19.)**______ 21.______ **(23.)**______ 24.______

(25.)______ **(27.)**______ 28.______ **(29.)**______ **(31.)**______ **(32.)**______ 33.______

35.______ **(36.)**______ **(38.)**______ **(41.)**______ **(42.)**______ **(45.)**______ 48.______

50.______ **(52.)**______ 53.______ 54.______ **(55.)**______ 57.______ **(59.)**______

62.______ 64.______ 66.______ 69.______ **(72.)**______

Total Score __________ ÷ 40 = __________ Average Score

B. Perception of Immediate Supervisor

(10.)_____ 15._____ (20.)_____ (37.)_____ 40._____ 58._____ 67._____

(68.)_____ (70.)_____ 73._____

Total Score __________ ÷ 10 = __________ Average Score

C. Perception of the Organization

2._____ 5._____ (6.)_____ 12._____ 14._____ 16._____ 22._____

26._____ 30._____ 34._____ 39._____ 43._____ 44._____ (46.)_____

47._____ 49._____ 51._____ 56._____ (60.)_____ 61._____ (63.)_____

(65.)_____ 71._____

Total Score __________ ÷ 23 = __________ Average Score

D. Overall Burnout

Use the *total scores for sections A, B, and C (before division)* to calculate your overall burnout score. Add the total score for A to three times the total score for B; then add the score for C and divide the total by 93.

(A)______ + (3 x B)______ + (C)______ = ______ ÷ 93 = ________
Overall Burnout Score

BURNOUT INVENTORY
INTERPRETATION SHEET

Your Average Scores in the Perception Categories

Scores below 3 indicate a high potential for experiencing burnout. If your average scores fall in this range, your work life is unfulfilling for you. Serious attention and action on your part are warranted if you want to experience any level of fulfillment in your work life.

Scores in the 3-to-4 range indicate a degree of satisfaction that can be very deceiving. If your average scores are in this range, you are experiencing an ambiguous state that is neither fulfillment nor burnout. Your work life is neither so great that you love it nor so bad that you feel compelled to leave it. You may perceive things as being "O.K."; therefore, you may not be motivated to change. However, you might want to consider making some changes to make your work life a more positive experience for you.

Scores approaching 5 or 6 indicate a work life that is exciting and fulfilling. If your average scores fall in this range, any "down" times that you experience are infrequent and short lived. Nevertheless, you might want to check back through the inventory to pinpoint specific items that you evaluated at a level that you consider unacceptable; then you can plan action to take to address those items.

The following paragraphs describe the perception categories in which you received scores.

Perception of Job Content

Your perception of the content of your job is based on three elements:

1. *How you see yourself in your job.* Do you see yourself as a flunky or as an important contributor to your organization's goals and objectives? Or do you have a high-paying job that is dull and uninteresting?

2. *How you feel about the work you do.* Your feelings about your work are closely tied to, but still different from, your image of yourself in your job. For example, you may see yourself as a flunky but still enjoy and feel good about your work.

3. *Whether and how much you enjoy the tasks and activities of your job.* Do you enjoy performing your day-to-day activities at work? Are your tasks the types of things you typically like to do?

4. *Whether and to what degree your job is right for you.* You may perceive your organization as fine, your supervisor as supportive, and your work as enjoyable, but the job still may not be right for you. Because of surrounding favorable conditions, you may not see a level of dissatisfaction with your job that could eventually lead to burnout. If the working environment is good and there is a mismatch between you and the job, you will experience boredom or apathy about your job. This means you have limited fulfillment from what you are doing. An average score of 3 in this

category would indicate this condition and would warrant further examination of current feelings about the job.

Your feelings about your job content may be complex. For instance, you may enjoy your work but feel that your job does not fit your self-image. Conversely, the content of your job may be unpleasant to you, but you may feel that the job makes a positive difference in people's lives; thus, your work may seem worthwhile to you. However, it is important to realize that work that you perceive as unpleasant or inappropriate in some way may eventually cause you to experience burnout.

Plotting your score with an X on the following continuum will give you a general idea of how you experience the content of your job:

Perception of Immediate Supervisor

Your relationship with your immediate supervisor is one of the most important relationships, if not the most important, that you have in the organization. Without the support of your supervisor, your work day can be very unpleasant, leading to dissatisfaction and burnout. Good communications are the key to a good relationship with your supervisor. Receiving appropriate feedback and complete information can make even the most difficult job much easier. How you view your relationship and your communication with your supervisor is closely related to the satisfaction you derive from your work.

Plot your score with an X on the following continuum to obtain an idea of how you perceive your relationship with your immediate supervisor:

Perception of the Organization

Every organization has a mission that incorporates its philosophy. The philosophy and mission of your organization create an environment that may or may not be compatible with your personal values, philosophy, and mission. If these two sets of values, philosophy, and mission are incompatible, then you will be uncomfortable in the organizational environment. Unfortunately, not every organization articulates its philosophy and mission clearly; when this is the case, ambiguity about what the organization is trying to accomplish can also lead to burnout.

The organization's philosophy and mission are reflected in its policies and procedures, both written and unwritten. Thus, clear policies and procedures are important in creating a supportive work environment. When you are certain about what the organization expects, you know what management perceives as appropriate or inappropriate. Whether you agree or not, your knowledge of what is expected creates a certain security that ambiguity cannot. Similarly, good, effective leadership gives you direction and clarity in your work and contributes to the likelihood of a clearly articulated philosophy and mission.

Plot your score with an X on the following continuum to illustrate your perception of your organization:

1 2 3 4 5 6

Nonsupportive organization — Supportive organization

Overall Burnout Score

Your overall burnout score is an indication of your potential for burning out on the job. You may already be burned out, or you may be headed for burnout sometime in the future. In either case you need to examine inventory items that indicate dissatisfaction or unfulfillment (ones indicating a negative perception that you agreed with and ones indicating a positive perception that you disagreed with). Examining specific statements in this way will tell you the sources of your potential or existing burnout.

In some cases you may be able to change the situation. In other cases you may be unable to change the situation because the source of your burnout is beyond your control. However, even in situations that appear to be out of your control, you may find that some creative thinking and negotiating will go a long way toward improving your level of satisfaction and fulfillment.

Plot your overall burnout score on the following continuum:

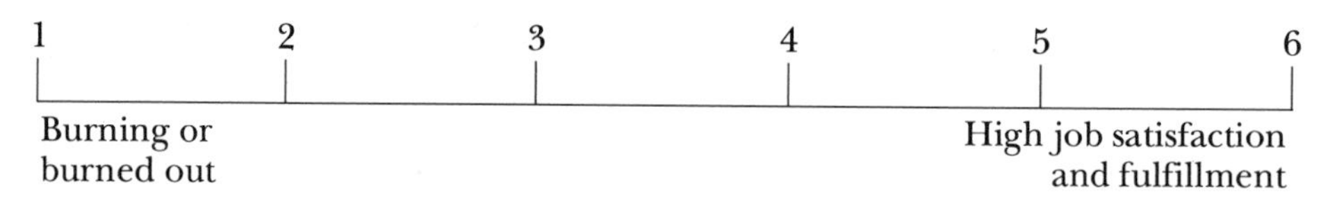

LOCUS OF CONTROL INVENTORY

Udai Pareek

There are two contrasting attitudes regarding the way rewards and outcomes are determined. Some people believe that we can neither predict nor influence significant events, whereas others believe that we can do both. Issues related to prediction and causation of social and personal matters have intrigued philosophers, politicians, behavioral scientists, and psychologists alike.

REVIEW OF RESEARCH

One of the most popular terms developed for discussing these issues is *locus of control.* This was suggested by Rotter (1954) and subsequently generated a great deal of research. The concept is based on the extent to which people perceive the contingencies that affect outcomes. Individuals who have low perceptions of such contingencies are said to have an *internal* locus of control; they believe that their own actions produce outcomes. Those who have high perceptions of contingencies are characterized by an *external* locus of control; they believe that outcomes are the result of contingencies rather than of their own actions. Internal and external loci of control are represented by the terms *internality* and *externality,* respectively. Similarly, people with high internality are called *internals;* those with high externality, *externals.*

Internality is related to effectiveness and adjustment. When compared to externals, internals have been reported to be more sensitive to new information, more observant, more likely to attend to cues that help resolve uncertainties (Lefcourt & Wine, 1969), and more prone to both intentional and incidental learning (Wolk & DuCette, 1984). The association of internality with various aspects of learning (for example, curiosity, eagerness to obtain information, awareness of and desire to understand situations and their contexts, and the ability to process the available information) seems to make good sense. For example, in order to influence or control outcomes, the person with an internal approach must acquire as much information as possible and then process that information as quickly as possible. Evidence supports the assumption that an internal locus of control leads to academic achievement (Crandall, Katkovsky, & Crandall, 1965; Harrison, 1968; Lessing, 1969).

Some studies have also shown a high and positive correlation between internality and perseverance, which is characterized by extra time spent on work (Franklin, 1963), continued involvement in difficult and complex tasks, and willingness to defer gratification (Mischel, 1966). Lefcourt (1976) summarized the research on the relationship between internality and deferred gratification. Involvement in long-term goals requires deferment of gratification; and persistence in effort requires undivided attention, which is not possible unless the temptation of immediate gratification is resisted. Because internals believe that their efforts lead to favorable outcomes, they can rely on their own understanding and predictability. In contrast, externals—perceiving a lack of personal predictability and fearing that unforeseen external factors will affect outcomes—may find it more attractive to seek immediate gratification than to try to achieve distant goals.

Internality was found to be an important characteristic of people with high achievement motivation (McClelland, 1961). It was further reported that internal locus of control generates moderate or calculated risk taking, and one study indicated that the correlation between achievement motivation and preference for moderate risk was significant and positive among internals but almost zero among externals (Wolk & DuCette, 1984).

Internality seems to be a cornerstone of the process of *valuing*, which includes awareness of one's own values, willingness to declare those values in public, and adherence to them and the behavior associated with them in spite of outside pressures. This process of developing ethical norms and using those norms even in periods of crisis has also been called *inner-direction*—the state of being directed by one's own, internalized standards rather than merely conforming to outside expectations, norms, or pressures.

Some studies have indicated a significant relationship between internality and morality, which leads to resistance of temptation (Johnson, Ackerman, Frank, & Fionda, 1968), helping others (Midlarski, 1971), and low Machiavellianism (Miller & Minton, 1969). Apparently internality is important in the development of standards for judging one's own behavior. Both personal autonomy and responsibility are involved in the process of valuing, which is necessary for the development of a healthy and proactive society.

One study (Mitchell, Smyser, & Wood, 1975) uncovered relationships between internality and certain organizational attitudes and behaviors. For example, internals experienced greater job satisfaction than externals did. Internals also preferred a participatory management style, whereas externals preferred a directive style. Further comparisons indicated that internals believed that working hard was more likely to lead to rewards and that they had more control over the ways they worked. Supervisors with an internal orientation believed that persuasive power was the most productive approach, whereas their external counterparts relied on coercive power. Furthermore, the use of rewards, respect, and expertise was seen by internally focused supervisors as the most effective way to influence subordinates; those with an external orientation saw coercion and their formal positions as most effective.

The sum of these findings indicates that internality plays an important role in human development and meaningful living. Nevertheless, the internal pays a price. Those who perceive their own abilities and actions as solely responsible for their failures are likely to experience stress and may become self-punitive. Attribution of failure or negative conditions to external factors can help people to cope with adverse experiences more effectively, to perceive social reality in the proper perspective, to fight injustice, and to rectify undesirable situations.

Rotter (1966) developed the first instrument to measure internality and externality. Although Rotter's instrument has been used extensively in research and training, his unitary concept of internality has been challenged. On the basis of factor analysis of the responses on Rotter's instrument, several studies found multidimensionality in Rotter's instrument, which seemed to contain items related to control ideology, personal control, system modifiability, and race ideology (Gurin et al., 1969; Guttentag, 1972; McDonald & Tseng, 1971; Minton, 1972; Mirels, 1970). Levenson (1972) questioned putting three external factors (chance, fate, and powerful others) together. Levenson also proposed a new scale to measure internality and externality; instead of viewing these elements along a continuum, Levenson proposed to measure both internality (I) and externality (E). Furthermore, Levenson proposed two subscales for externality: one to measure perceived influence of chance (EC) and the other to measure perceived influence of powerful others (EO). Gutkin, Robbins, and Andrews (1985) reported factor-analysis results of a health locus-of-control scale that revealed internal and external factors.

THE INSTRUMENT

Although Levenson's scale has been used in many organizational studies, the instrument was not developed specifically for organizations. Therefore, Levenson's (1972) concept of locus of control was used to develop the Locus of Control Inventory, which was designed to measure internality and externality in the organizational context. An earlier version of this instrument contained Levenson's six-point scoring system and twenty-four items (parallel to Levenson's instrument). The current five-point system appears to be a superior measure; and the thirty-item version contains ten statements each for internality (I), externality- others (EO), and externality-chance (EC).

A locus-of-control orientation is reflected in the way a person views what happens in an organization; that is, how much control the person believes that he or she has in important organizational matters, how much control the person believes is held by certain others, and to what degree the person believes events are a matter of luck. The Locus of Control Inventory links the locus of control to seven areas:

1. General
2. Success or Effectiveness
3. Influence
4. Acceptability
5. Career
6. Advancement
7. Rewards

Using the Instrument

The Locus of Control Inventory can be used for both research and training purposes in human resource development, organization development, or training packages. It was developed, however, primarily for training purposes.

Scoring

Numbers that respondents have assigned to the instrument items are transferred to the scoring sheet and a total is computed for each column. Scores will range from zero to forty for each of the three columns (Internality, Externality-Other, and Externality-Chance).

Norms

Based on data from more than three hundred managers, mean and standard-deviation (SD) values are presented in Table 1. High and low scores were calculated by adding or subtracting one-half SD value to or from the mean, respectively. Similarly, very high and very low scores were obtained by adding or subtracting one SD value to or from the mean. Such norms can be worked out for specific organizations for interpretation purposes.

Table 1. Mean and Standard-Deviation Values

	Mean	SD	Very High	High	Low	Very Low
I	25	8	33	29	21	17
EO	25	9	34	29.5	20.5	16
EC	19	9	28	23.5	14.5	10

Reliability

Levenson (1972) reported moderately high internal consistency, with Kuder-Richardson reliabilities (coefficient alpha) of .64, .77, and .78 and split-half reliabilities of .62, .66, and .64 for I, EO, and EC, respectively. Retest reliability for a one-week period for the three subscales were .64, .74, and .78, respectively. Reliabilities of the Levenson instrument were also moderately high in another study (Sen, 1982) in India.

Split-half reliability coefficients for the earlier version of the Locus of Control Inventory were .43, .45, and .55, and even-odd reliability coefficients were .41, .48, and .54 for I, EO, and EC subscales, respectively. The current version has similar reliability coefficients.

Validity

There was a high correlation (.89) between Levenson's instrument and the Locus of Control Inventory in a sample of twenty-six bankers. This finding indicates the validity of the Locus of Control Inventory. Using Levenson's scale, Surti (1982) reported a highly significant coefficient of correlation (.70) between EO and EC in a sample of 360 professional women and correlation values of .00 and .06 between I and EO and between I and EC, respectively. This finding shows the validity of Levenson's two-factor concept.

Twenty-seven managers responded to the Locus of Control Inventory, to Rotter's instrument of locus of control and an adaptation of that instrument (Rotter, 1966), and to Valecha's (1988) adaptation of Rotter's instrument. The data indicated acceptable validity of the Locus of Control Inventory, and other data have established construct validity for the instrument.

Correlates of Internality and Externality

In a study of four hundred bankers using Levenson's instrument, Sen (1982) found a high positive correlation (significant at the .001 level) between internality and role efficacy (see Pareek, 1980a and 1980b, for the concept) and a negative correlation (significant at the .01 level) between I and both EO and EC. Surti (1982) reported similar results when 320 professional women completed the instrument.

There is some evidence that externals, especially those who believe things are controlled by powerful others, experience higher role stress. When forty women entrepreneurs completed the Levenson instrument, Surti (1982) found positive correlation (significant at the .01 level) between EO and the following role stresses: inter-role distance, role overload, result inadequacy, resource inadequacy, role inadequacy, and total entrepreneurial role stress. See Pareek (1990a) for the concept of entrepreneurial role stress. There were significant positive correlations (at the .01 level) between EC and inter-role distance and between EC and role overload. Surti also reported positive and negative correlations, respectively, between EC and avoidance style and between EC and approach styles (both significant at the .05 level). See Pareek (1987) for the concept of coping styles.

Using the Motivational Analysis of Organizations—Behavior (Pareek, 1986), Sen (1982) found positive correlations between internality and operational effectiveness of five motives. The levels of significance are shown in parentheses: achievement (.001), influence (.003), extension (.05), affiliation (.01), and dependence (.001). He also reported significant negative correlations (most of them significant at the .001 level) with both EO and EC and operational effectiveness of all six motives. This indicates that internals use the motivational behavior more effectively in organizations than externals do.

Using the Locus of Control Inventory with 212 managers in engineering firms, Keshote (1989) found negative correlations (significant at the .05 level) between both EO and EC and interpersonal trust, measured by the Rotter (1967) scale. Externals seem to have low interpersonal trust.

Keshote, using the Locus of Control Inventory and the Pareek (1990b) instrument to measure perception of and the need for coercive and persuasive power, found positive correlation (significant at the .01 level) between I and perception of having persuasive power and between EO and perception of having coercive and persuasive power. The EC scores had positive correlation (significant at the .05 level) with perception of having persuasive bases of power. These correlations indicate that internal managers use more persuasive bases of power, EO managers use more coercive bases, EC managers use less persuasive bases, and externals of both types want more coercive power.

When using the Locus of Control Inventory and an instrument to measure styles of managing conflict (Pareek, 1982a, 1983), Keshote found significant positive correlation between negotiation style and internality. Externals of both types showed preference for other styles. Regarding interpersonal styles (Pareek, 1984), EO managers were found to have lower operating effectiveness on task orientation; and EC managers, lower operating effectiveness on regulating, task-innovative, and confronting styles.

In summary, internal managers tend to have higher role efficacy, to experience less role stress, to use problem-solving approaches to stress and conflict, to use their motivational behavior more effectively, and to use more persuasive bases of power in working with their employees. Externals seem to do the opposite and to have lower interpersonal trust. Externals want more coercive power; EOs use more coercive bases of power while working with their employees, and ECs use less persuasive bases.

Development of Internality

Organizational climate and environments seem to influence the development of internality. Baumgartel, Rajan, and Newman (1985), using four indices of organizational environment (freedom-growth, human relations, performance pressure, and person benefit) with a group of 3,200 student respondents (78 percent men, 22 percent women) in a center for postgraduate management education in India, found clear evidence of the influence of organizational environments on locus of control as measured by the Levenson instrument. However, this effect was more striking for female than for male postgraduates. Regression analysis (based on data from 320 professional women) that used role efficacy as a variable indicated that out of the fourteen variables that finally emerged in the stepwise regression, organizational climate alone explained about 34 percent of the variance, showing a very large effect on role efficacy (Surti, 1982).

ADMINISTERING THE INSTRUMENT

The respondents complete the instrument by evaluating each statement according to a five-point scale ranging from zero (seldom or never agree) to five (strongly agree). The responses must be transferred to the scoring sheet, which presents three scores (internality, externality-others, and externality-chance).

If possible, the scoring sheets should be completed in advance, so that the mean and standard deviation can be calculated prior to a discussion of the scores. Norms can be created as demonstrated in Table 1.

The facilitator leads a discussion based on the concepts and findings included in this article. Respondents are asked to predict their own levels (high, medium, or low) of the three dimensions. In very open groups, each member of a triad can estimate the levels of the other two triad members.

Completed scoring sheets are distributed to the respondents, as well as copies of the interpretation sheet. Triads are formed to discuss discrepancies between actual scores and both self-predicted and other-assessed levels. The discussions should be based on observed behavior.

The facilitator presents implications of internality for employee effectiveness and leads a discussion on how to increase internality and reduce externality. The discussion should include which organizational practices promote I, EO, and EC. Table 2 shows which of the thirty items in the Locus of Control Inventory are related to each of the seven areas addressed by the instrument.

Table 2. Distribution of Items in Locus of Control Inventory

	Internality	Externality (Others)	Externality (Chance)
General	1, 27	4, 30	7, 24
Success or Effectiveness	3, 10, 16	6, 19, 22	9, 13, 21
Influence	28	17	26
Acceptability	25	29	18
Career	2	5	8
Advancement	23	11	14
Rewards	20	15	12

Another important discussion would deal with how to increase internality among the employees (Pareek, 1982b). Material that would help the facilitator lead this discussion includes Baumgartel et al. (1985), Reichard (1975), Mehta (1968), and DeCharms (1976).

REFERENCES

Baumgartel, H.J., Rajan, P.S.S., & Newman, J. (1985). Educational environments and attributions of causality: Some exploratory research findings. *Quality of Work Life, 2*(5-6), 309-328.

Crandall, V.C., Katkovsky, W., & Crandall, W.J. (1965). Children's beliefs in their control of reinforcements in intellectual academic achievement behaviors. *Child Development, 36,* 91-109.

DeCharms, R. (1976). *Enhancing motivation: Change in the classroom.* New York: Irvington.

Franklin, R.D. (1963). Youth's expectancies about internal versus external control of reinforcement related to N variable. *Dissertation Abstracts, 24,* 1684. (University Microfilms No. 63-6493)

Gurin, P., Gurin, G., Lao, R., & Beattie, M. (1969). Internal-external control in the motivational dynamics of Negro youth. *Journal of Social Issues, 25*(3), 29-53.

Gutkin, J., Robbins, R., & Andrews, L. (1985). The health locus of control scales: Psychometric properties. *Educational and Psychological Measurement, 45*(2), 407-410.

Guttentag, M. (1972). *Locus of control and achievement in minority middle school children.* Paper presented at the meeting of the Eastern Psychological Association, Boston, MA.

Harrison, F.I. (1968). Relationship between home background, school success, and adolescent attitudes. *Merrill-Palmer Quarterly of Behavior and Development, 14,* 331-344.

Johnson, R.C., Ackerman, J.M., Frank, H., & Fionda, A.J. (1968). Resistance to temptation and guilt following yielding and psychotherapy. *Journal of Consulting and Clinical Psychology, 32,* 169-175.

Keshote, K.K. (1989). *Personnel and organizational correlates of conflict management styles.* Unpublished doctoral dissertation, University of Gujarat, India.

Lefcourt, H.M. (1976). *Locus of control: Current trends in theory and research.* Hillsdale, NJ: Lawrence Earlbaum.

Lefcourt, H.M., & Wine, J. (1969). Internal versus external control of reinforcement and the development of attention in experimental situations. *Canadian Journal of Behavioral Science, 1,* 167-181.

Lessing, E.E. (1969). Racial differences in indices of ego functioning relevant to academic achievement. *Journal of Genetic Psychology, 115,* 153-167.

Levenson, H. (1972). *Distinctions within the concept of internal-external control: Development of a new scale.* Paper presented at the meeting of the American Psychological Association, Hawaii.

McClelland, D.E. (1961). *The achieving society.* Princeton, NJ: Van Nostrand.

McDonald, A.P., & Tseng, M.S. (1971). *Dimension of internal vs. external control revisited: Toward expectancy.* Unpublished paper, West Virginia University.

Mehta, P. (1968). *Increasing achievement motive in high school boys.* New Delhi: National Council of Education Research and Training.

Midlarski, E. (1971). Aiding under stress: The effects of competence, dependency, visibility, and fatalism. *Journal of Personality, 39,* 132-149.

Miller, A.G., & Minton, H.L. (1969). Machiavellianism, internal-external control and the violation of experimental instructions. *Psychological Record, 19,* 369-380.

Minton, H.L. (1972). *Internal-external control and the distinction between personal control and system modifiability.* Paper presented at the meeting of the Midwestern Psychological Association, Cleveland, OH.

Mirels, H. (1970). Dimensions of internal vs. external control. *Journal of Consulting and Clinical Psychology, 34,* 226-228.

Mischel, W. (1966). Theory and research on the antecedents of self-imposed delay of reward. In B.A. Maher (Ed.), *Progress in experimental personality research* (Vol. 3). New York: Academic Press.

Mitchell, T.R., Smyser, C.M., & Wood, S.E. (1975). Locus of control: Supervision and work satisfaction. *Academy of Management Journal, 18*(3), 623-631.

Pareek, U. (1980a). Dimensions of role efficacy. In J.W. Pfeiffer & J.E. Jones (Eds.), *The 1980 annual handbook for group facilitators* (pp. 143-145). San Diego, CA: Pfeiffer & Company.

Pareek, U. (1980b). Role efficacy scale. In J.W. Pfeiffer & J.E. Jones (Eds.), *The 1980 annual handbook for group facilitators* (pp. 100-105). San Diego, CA: Pfeiffer & Company.

Pareek, U. (1982a). *Conflict and collaboration in organizations.* New Delhi: Oxford & IBH.

Pareek, U. (1982b). Internal and external control. In J.W. Pfeiffer & L.D. Goodstein (Eds.), *The 1982 annual for facilitators, trainers, and consultants* (pp. 174-181). San Diego, CA: Pfeiffer & Company.

Pareek, U. (1983). Preventing and resolving conflicts. In L.D. Goodstein & J.W. Pfeiffer (Eds.), *The 1983 annual for facilitators, trainers, and consultants* (pp. 195-203). San Diego, CA: Pfeiffer & Company.

Pareek, U. (1984). Interpersonal styles: The SPIRO instrument. In J.W. Pfeiffer & L.D. Goodstein (Eds.), *The 1984 annual: Developing human resources* (pp. 119-130). San Diego, CA: Pfeiffer & Company.

Pareek, U. (1986). Motivational analysis of organizations—behavior (MAO-B). In J.W. Pfeiffer & L.D. Goodstein (Eds.), *The 1986 annual: Developing human resources* (pp. 121-133). San Diego, CA: Pfeiffer & Company.

Pareek, U. (1987). Role pics: Measuring strategies of coping with stress. In J.W. Pfeiffer (Ed.), *The 1987 annual: Developing human resources* (pp. 91-107). San Diego, CA: Pfeiffer & Company.

Pareek, U. (1989). Motivational analysis of organizations—climate (MAO-C). In J.W. Pfeiffer (Ed.), *The 1989 annual: Developing human resources* (pp. 161-180). San Diego, CA: Pfeiffer & Company.

Pareek, U. (1990a). Entrepreneurial role stress scale. Unpublished manuscript.

Pareek, U. (1990b). Persuasive and coercive power scale. Unpublished manuscript.

Reichard, B.D. (1975). *The effect of a management training workshop altering locus of control.* Unpublished doctoral dissertation, University of Maryland.

Rotter, J.B. (1954). Social learning and clinical psychology. Englewood Cliffs, NJ: Prentice-Hall.

Rotter, J.B. (1966). Generalized expectancies for internal versus external control of reinforcement. *Psychological Monographs, 80*(1, Whole No. 609).

Rotter, J.B. (1967). A new scale for the measurement of interpersonal trust. *Journal of Personality, 35,* 651-665.

Sen, P.C. (1982). *Personal and organizational correlates of role stress and coping strategies in some public sector banks.* Unpublished doctoral dissertation, University of Gujarat, India.

Surti, K. (1982). *Some psychological correlates of role stress and coping styles in working women.* Unpublished doctoral dissertation, University of Gujarat, India.

Valecha, G. (1988). *A locus of control scale.* Unpublished manuscript.

Wolk, S., & DuCette, J. (1984). Intentional performances and incidental learning as a function of personality and task direction. *Journal of Personality and Social Psychology, 29,* 90-101.

Udai Pareek, Ph.D., *is a freelance writer, researcher, and consultant. Most recently he was an organization development advisor (US-AID) to the Ministry of Health of the Republic of Indonesia. For a number of years he was Larsen & Toubro Professor of Organizational Behavior at the Indian Institute of Management in Ahmedabad. He has been the president of the Indian Society of Applied Behavioural Science and a fellow of the National Training Laboratories. His fields of interest are organization development, human resource development, and action research.*

LOCUS OF CONTROL INVENTORY[1]

Udai Pareek

Instructions: The following thirty statements represent employees' attitudes toward their work in an organization. Read each statement carefully; then indicate the extent to which you agree with it by writing a number in the blank provided. There are no right or wrong choices; the one that is right for you is the correct answer. If the responses do not adequately indicate your own opinion, use the number *closest* to the way you feel. Use the following key:

Strongly Agree	Generally Agree	Agree Somewhat	Agree Only Slightly	Seldom or Never Agree
4	3	2	1	0

_____ 1. I determine what matters to me in the organization.

_____ 2. The course of my career depends on me.

_____ 3. My success or failure depends on the amount of effort I exert.

_____ 4. The people who are important control matters in this organization.

_____ 5. My career depends on my seniors.

_____ 6. My effectiveness in this organization is determined by senior people.

_____ 7. The organization a person joins or the job he or she takes is an accidental occurrence.

_____ 8. A person's career is a matter of chance.

_____ 9. A person's success depends on the breaks or chances he or she receives.

_____ 10. Successful completion of my assignments is due to my detailed planning and hard work.

_____ 11. Being liked by seniors or making good impressions on them influences promotion decisions.

[1] This instrument is based on ideas that appeared in *Distinctions Within the Concept of Internal-External Control: Development of a New Scale,* a paper written by Hanna Levenson and presented at the meeting of the American Psychological Association in Hawaii, 1982. The Locus of Control Inventory, written by Udai Pareek, applies these concepts to the organizational environment and is used here with the permission of Hanna Levenson.

Strongly Agree	Generally Agree	Agree Somewhat	Agree Only Slightly	Seldom or Never Agree
4	3	2	1	0

_______ 12. Receiving rewards in the organization is a matter of luck.

_______ 13. The success of my plans is a matter of luck.

_______ 14. Receiving a promotion depends on being in the right place at the right time.

_______ 15. Preferences of seniors determine who will be rewarded in this organization.

_______ 16. My success depends on my competence and hard work.

_______ 17. How much I am liked in the organization depends on my seniors.

_______ 18. Getting people in this organization to listen to me is a matter of luck.

_______ 19. If my seniors do not like me, I will not succeed in this organization.

_______ 20. The way I work determines whether or not I receive rewards.

_______ 21. My success or failure in this organization is a matter of luck.

_______ 22. My success or failure depends on those who work with me.

_______ 23. Any promotion I receive in this organization will be due to my ability and effort.

_______ 24. Most things in this organization are beyond the control of the people who work here.

_______ 25. The quality of my work influences decisions on my suggestions in this organization.

_______ 26. The reason I am acceptable to others in my organization is a matter of luck.

_______ 27. I determine what happens to me in the organization.

_______ 28. The degree to which I am acceptable to others in this organization depends on my behavior with them.

_______ 29. My ideas are accepted if I make them fit with the desires of my seniors.

_______ 30. Pressure groups in this organization are more powerful than individual employees are, and they control more things than individuals do.

LOCUS OF CONTROL INVENTORY SCORING SHEET

Instructions: The numbers below correspond to the numbers of the items in the Locus of Control Inventory. Please transfer the numbers you assigned by writing them in the appropriate blanks below. Then total the numbers you transferred to each column.

Item Number	Number You Assigned	Item Number	Number You Assigned	Item Number	Number You Assigned
1	______	4	______	7	______
2	______	5	______	8	______
3	______	6	______	9	______
10	______	11	______	12	______
16	______	15	______	13	______
20	______	17	______	14	______
23	______	19	______	18	______
25	______	22	______	21	______
27	______	29	______	24	______
28	______	30	______	26	______
Column Total	______	**Column Total**	______	**Column Total**	______
	I		**EO**		**EC**

LOCUS OF CONTROL INVENTORY
INTERPRETATION SHEET

The following information will be helpful in interpreting your scores. These scores represent the way you view what happens in your organization; therefore, no score has to be permanent. If you are not happy with the way you have marked the answers, you may create an action plan that will help to change the way you look at things.

Select the column with the highest total. Then read the section below that pertains to that column. Next read the section pertaining to your lowest total. Then read the remaining section. The paragraph on ratios may also be helpful.

I (Internal)

A person with an *internal* orientation believes that his or her future is controlled from within. A total I score of 33 or above indicates a very high internality tendency. It represents self-confidence in a person's ability to control what happens to him or her in an organization. However, this person may sometimes be unrealistic in assessing difficulties and may ascribe personal failure to situations over which he or she had no control.

A score from 29 to 32 shows high trust in one's ability and effort and is likely to lead to effective use of these. A score of 18 to 21 indicates that the individual lacks such self-trust and needs to examine his or her strengths by using feedback from others.

A low score (17 or less) in this area represents little self-confidence and could hinder a person from utilizing his or her potential.

EO (External-Others)

A person with an *external-others* orientation believes that his or her future is controlled by powerful others. Very high EO scores (30 or higher) indicate dysfunctional dependence on significant other people for achieving one's goals. A score of 21 to 29 reflects a realistic dependence on supervisors, peers, and subordinates. A score of 17 to 20 shows an independence orientation, and a score below 17 indicates counterdependence.

EC (External-Chance)

A person with an *external-chance* orientation believes that his or her future is controlled primarily by luck or chance. To an extent, the lower the EC score, the better, because a person with a low EC orientation is more likely to utilize his or her potential in trying to achieve goals. However, a score of 10 or below may reflect problems in coping with frustrations when unforeseen factors prevent achievement of goals.

Ratios of Scores

The ratio of your I and E scores can also provide information about your orientation. If your I/total-E ratio is more than one (that is, if your I score is greater than the total of your E scores), you have an internal orientation. If your I/EO ratio is more than one, you have more internality than externality-other. If your I/EC ratio is greater than one, you are more internal than external-chance. Ratios greater than one are beneficial, and action plans can be created to change ratios that are lower than desired.

TOTAL QUALITY MANAGEMENT (TQM) INVENTORY[1]

Gaylord Reagan

Often the process of total quality management (TQM) serves to differentiate successful organizations from unsuccessful ones. After inventing and then discarding the principles of TQM approximately five decades ago, American managers once again are learning *continuous improvement* for the quality of products and services they offer to internal as well as external customers. The basic criteria of TQM are simultaneously very simple and highly complex; however, they can be mastered by committed organizations. A necessary first step in learning about and implementing TQM is to assess the emphasis that an organization places on these eight basic criteria.

THE INSTRUMENT

Theoretical Framework

Total quality management is not a short-term, morale-boosting and efficiency-improvement program. In fact, TQM is not a "program" at all. It can be defined best as a strategic, integrated management philosophy based on the concept of achieving ever-higher levels of customer satisfaction. These higher levels are a result of the emphasis that an organization's senior managers place on using participative management, total employee involvement, and statistical methods to make continual improvements in their organization's processes.

The Total Quality Management (TQM) Inventory is based on the eight criteria identified by the President's Council on Management Improvement, the Office of Personnel Management, the Federal Quality Institute, and the Office of Management and Budget. In turn, specific content of the criteria is based on the following models: Deming's (1982) statistical process control, Juran's (1986) project-by-project continuous improvement, Crosby's (1986a) zero defects, and Feigenbaum's (1983) total quality control.[2]

---

[1] This instrument is based on the Federal Quality Institute's *Federal Total Quality Management Handbook 2: Criteria and Scoring Guidelines for the President's Award for Quality and Productivity Improvement*, Washington, DC: Office of Personnel Management, 1990.

[2] Through mid-1991, four publications on these topics have been published by the Federal Quality Institute; another eight are scheduled to be released at later dates. Following are the titles published through mid-1991: (1) *How To Get Started: Implementing Total Quality Management—Part 1;* (2) *How To Get Started: Appendix—Part 1A;* (3) *Criteria and Scoring Guidelines: The President's Award for Quality and Productivity Improvement;* and (4) *Introduction to Total Quality Management in the Federal Government.*

Following are the eight TQM criteria:

Criterion 1: Top-Management Leadership and Support. This criterion examines upper management's role in building and maintaining a total-quality environment. It focuses on the following factors: visible, senior-management involvement in TQM; existence of written policies and strategies supporting TQM; allocation of human and other resources to TQM activities; plans for removing barriers to TQM implementation; and creation of a value system emphasizing TQM.

Criterion 2: Strategic Planning. This criterion probes the level of emphasis placed on total quality during the organization's planning process. The focus here is on the existence of strategic TQM goals and objectives, the use of hard data in planning for TQM, the involvement of customers and employees in planning for TQM, and the injection of TQM into the organization's budget process.

Criterion 3: Focus on the Customer. This criterion examines the degree to which the organization stresses customer service. It focuses on assessing customer requirements, implementing customer-satisfaction feedback mechanisms, handling customer complaints, empowering employees to resolve customer problems, and facilitating the communication processes required to support these activities.

Criterion 4: Employee Training and Recognition. This criterion explores the extent to which the organization develops and rewards behaviors that support total quality. It centers on the existence of a training strategy designed to support TQM, the use of needs assessments to identify areas in which TQM training is needed, the allocation of funds for TQM training, the assessment of the effectiveness of TQM training, and the recognition of employee accomplishments.

Criterion 5: Employee Empowerment and Teamwork. This criterion delves into the breadth and depth of total-quality involvement that organizational members are encouraged to demonstrate. Its focus is on increasing employee involvement in TQM activities, implementing feedback systems through which organizations can become aware of employee concerns, increasing employee authority to act independently, identifying ways to increase employee satisfaction, and using data to evaluate human resource management practices within the organization.

Criterion 6: Quality Measurement and Analysis. This criterion scrutinizes the organization's use of data within a total-quality system. The focus here is on using hard data to assess TQM results and on using the results of that assessment to identify changes needed to achieve higher levels of customer satisfaction.

Criterion 7: Quality Assurance. This criterion looks at the organization's use of total-quality practices in connection with the products and services provided to customers. It focuses on implementing new methods for achieving greater customer satisfaction, using rigorous scientific methods to verify that the new methods actually achieve their intended purposes, and assessing the outcomes of the new methods.

Criterion 8: Quality- and Productivity-Improvement Results. This criterion explores the actual results produced by the organization's total-quality efforts. Its focus is on identifying specific instances in which the organization's TQM efforts over a long period of time (three to six years) actually resulted in higher levels of customer satisfaction in areas such as timeliness, efficiency, and effectiveness.

Extensive detail on the eight criteria can be found in the Federal Quality Institute's publication, *Criteria and Scoring Guidelines for the President's Award for Quality and Productivity Improvement* (Federal Quality Institute, 1990).[3] As the publication's editors point out (p. vi), "Other management systems may contain certain elements of these criteria, [but] it is the combination of all eight that distinguishes TQM."

Reliability and Validity

The Total Quality Management (TQM) Inventory is designed for use as an action-research tool rather than as a rigorous data-gathering instrument. Applied in this manner, the inventory has demonstrated a high level of face validity when used with audiences ranging from executive managers to non-management personnel.

Administration

The following suggestions will be helpful to the facilitator who administers the instrument:

1. Before respondents complete the inventory, discuss briefly the concept of TQM. It is important that respondents understand that TQM is not another faddish, short-term, productivity-improvement "program." Instead, TQM is a strategic, culture-based commitment to meeting customer requirements and to continually improving products and services. The foundations on which that commitment is built can be found in the eight criteria forming the core of the instrument. Similar criteria are included in Japan's Deming prizes and in the United States' Baldrige award (Walton, 1986).
2. Distribute copies of the Total Quality Management (TQM) Inventory Theory Sheet. Review the descriptions of the eight criteria to ensure that respondents understand the focus of each one. Explanatory remarks should be simple and to the point. The purpose of this step is to clarify the meanings of the criteria, not to encourage respondents to initiate a premature discussion of their organizations' placements on criterion-ranking scales.
3. Distribute copies of the instrument and read the instructions aloud as the respondents follow.
4. Instruct the respondents to read each of the six statements listed under each criterion. Each respondent chooses the statement that best

[3] The President's Award is the United States Federal government's version of its private sector's Malcolm Baldrige National Quality Awards and Japan's Deming prizes.

describes how he or she perceives the present situation in his or her organization. Choices range from exceptionally strong performance to total absence of performance for each criterion.

5. Request that the respondents wait to score the instrument until everyone has completed it.

Scoring

Each respondent should be given a copy of the Total Quality Management (TQM) Inventory Scoring Sheet. The left column of the scoring sheet lists the eight criteria of total quality management. The right column of the scoring sheet lists point values for each of the six possible responses to each criterion. Respondents simply transfer their answers from the Total Quality Management (TQM) Inventory to the appropriate rows and columns on the scoring sheet. After responses have been circled for all eight criteria, each respondent totals the circled point values to obtain an overall score for the inventory.

Interpretation and Processing

When respondents finish determining their overall scores on the inventory, the facilitator should distribute the Total Quality Management (TQM) Interpretation Sheet. The Interpretation Sheet consists of five score categories ranging from "world-class TQM" to "absolutely no interest in learning about TQM." Each category offers brief guidelines for preparing appropriate TQM goals.

The numbers listed in the Response Categories/Points section of the scoring sheet also represent the approximate weights attached to each individual TQM criterion by the Federal Quality Institute's President's Award. For example, note that an organization's score for "Quality- and Productivity-Improvement Results" is much more central to successful TQM implementation efforts than its score on a criterion such as "Employee Training and Recognition"—although it is difficult to see how the former could be achieved without the presence of the latter. Respondents may wish to refer back to "A" statements for each criterion as bases for discussing "world-class" TQM activities.

Some groups find it useful to prepare a copy of the scoring sheet on a newsprint flip chart. In this case, the facilitator polls the individual respondents as to the option letter they selected for each criterion. Their differing perceptions then form the basis for discussion. In order to provide respondents with group norms, it may also be useful to compute average scores for each of the eight criteria and for the overall score.

Uses of the Instrument

The Total Quality Management (TQM) Inventory is designed to accomplish the following objectives:

1. To offer the respondents the opportunity to identify and to define eight key criteria of TQM;

2. To differentiate the importance of each criterion;
3. To provide a framework for respondents to assess an organization's current emphasis on each of the eight criteria;
4. To initiate discussions about the adequacy of the organization's level of activity for each of the eight criteria; and
5. To stimulate planning designed to increase the organization's level of TQM involvement.

Therefore the TQM Inventory can be used to diagnose the organization's readiness for involvement in total quality management. The instrument can focus on perceptions of the overall organization or of individual units or departments within the organization.

SELECTED BIBLIOGRAPHY AND REFERENCES

Clements, R.R. (1988). *Statistical process control and beyond.* Malabar, FL: Robert E. Krieger.

Crosby, P.B. (1984). *Quality without tears: The art of hassle-free management.* New York: New American Library.

Crosby, P.B. (1986a). *Quality is free: The art of making quality certain.* New York: New American Library.

Crosby, P.B. (1986b). *Running things: The art of making things happen.* New York: New American Library.

Crosby, P.B. (1990). *Let's talk quality: 96 questions you always wanted to ask Phil Crosby.* New York: Plume.

Deming, W.E. (1982). *Out of the crisis.* Cambridge, MA: Massachusetts Institute of Technology Center for Advanced Engineering Study.

Federal Quality Institute. (1990). *Federal total quality management handbook 2: Criteria and scoring guidelines for the President's award for quality and productivity improvement.* Washington, DC: Office of Personnel Management.

Feigenbaum, A.V. (1983). *Total quality control.* New York: McGraw-Hill.

Gabor, A. (1990). *The man who discovered quality: How W. Edwards Deming brought the quality revolution to America—the stories of Ford, Xerox, and GM.* New York: Times Books.

Juran, J.M. (1988a). *Juran on planning for quality.* New York: The Free Press.

Juran, J.M. (Ed.). (1988b). *Juran's quality control handbook* (4th ed.). New York: McGraw-Hill.

Juran, J.M. (1989). *Juran on leadership for quality: An executive handbook.* New York: The Free Press.

The memory jogger: A pocket guide of tools for continuous improvement. (1988). Methuen, MA: GOAL/QPC.

Townsend, P.L., & Gebhardt, J.E. (1990). *Commit to quality.* New York: John Wiley.

Walton, M. (1986). *The Deming management method.* New York: Perigee Books.

***Gaylord Reagan, Ph.D.**, is the human resource manager for Weyerhaeuser Paper Company (Containerboard Packaging Division) in Omaha, Nebraska. He is also an independent management training and development consultant who has conducted programs for managers in corporations, government, health care, and publishing. In addition, he is a faculty member at Century University in Albuquerque, New Mexico. Dr. Reagan has done extensive internal and external consulting with senior managers who are implementing total quality management in their organizations.*

TOTAL QUALITY MANAGEMENT (TQM) INVENTORY THEORY SHEET

The Total Quality Management (TQM) Inventory is based on eight criteria identified by the President's Council on Management Improvement, the Office of Personnel Management, the Federal Quality Institute, and the Office of Management and Budget. Following are the eight criteria:

Criterion 1: Top-Management Leadership and Support

This criterion examines upper management's role in building and maintaining a total-quality environment. It focuses on the following factors: visible, senior-management involvement in TQM; existence of written policies and strategies supporting TQM; allocation of human and other resources to TQM activities; plans for removing barriers to TQM implementation; and creation of a value system emphasizing TQM.

Criterion 2: Strategic Planning

This criterion probes the level of emphasis placed on total quality during the organization's planning process. The focus here is on the existence of strategic TQM goals and objectives, the use of hard data in planning for TQM, the involvement of customers and employees in planning for TQM, and the injection of TQM into the organization's budget process.

Criterion 3: Focus on the Customer

This criterion examines the degree to which the organization stresses customer service. It focuses on assessing customer requirements, implementing customer-satisfaction feedback mechanisms, handling customer complaints, empowering employees to resolve customer problems, and facilitating the communication processes required to support these activities.

Criterion 4: Employee Training and Recognition

This criterion explores the extent to which the organization develops and rewards behaviors that support total quality. It centers on the existence of a training strategy designed to support TQM, the use of needs assessments to identify areas in which TQM training is needed, the allocation of funds for TQM training, the assessment of the effectiveness of TQM training, and the recognition of employee accomplishments.

Criterion 5: Employee Empowerment and Teamwork

This criterion delves into the breadth and depth of total-quality involvement that organizational members are encouraged to demonstrate. Its focus is on increasing employee involvement in TQM activities, implementing feedback systems through which organizations can become aware of employee concerns, increasing employee authority to act independently, identifying ways to increase employee satisfaction, and using data to evaluate human resource management practices within the organization.

Criterion 6: Quality Measurement and Analysis

This criterion scrutinizes the organization's use of data within a total-quality system. The focus here is on using hard data to assess TQM results and on using the results of that assessment to identify changes needed to achieve higher levels of customer satisfaction.

Criterion 7: Quality Assurance

This criterion looks at the organization's use of total-quality practices in connection with the products and services provided to customers. It focuses on implementing new methods for achieving greater customer satisfaction, using rigorous scientific methods to verify that the new methods actually achieve their intended purposes, and assessing the outcomes of the new methods.

Criterion 8: Quality- and Productivity-Improvement Results

This criterion explores the actual results of the organization's total-quality efforts. Its focus is on identifying specific instances in which the organization's TQM efforts over a long period of time (three to six years) actually resulted in higher levels of customer satisfaction in areas such as timeliness, efficiency, and effectiveness.

TOTAL QUALITY MANAGEMENT (TQM) INVENTORY

Gaylord Reagan

Instructions: For each of the eight total quality management criteria listed below, choose the statement that best describes the present situation in your organization. Write the letter of that statement in the blank to the left of each criterion.

_____ **Criterion 1: Top-Management Leadership and Support**

A. Top managers are directly and actively involved in activities that foster quality.

B. Top managers participate in quality-leadership activities.

C. Most top managers support activities that foster quality.

D. Many top managers are supportive of and interested in quality improvement.

E. Some top managers are beginning to tentatively support activities that foster quality.

F. No top-management support exists for activities involving quality.

_____ **Criterion 2: Strategic Planning**

A. Long-term goals for quality improvement have been established across the organization as part of the overall strategic-planning process.

B. Long-term goals for quality improvement have been established across most of the organization.

C. Long-term goals for quality improvement have been established in key parts of the organization.

D. Short-term goals for quality improvement have been established in parts of the organization.

E. The general goals of the organization contain elements of quality improvement.

F. No quality-improvement goals have been established anywhere in the organization.

_____ **Criterion 3: Focus on the Customer**

A. A variety of effective and innovative methods are used to obtain customer feedback on all organizational functions.

B. Effective systems are used to obtain feedback from all customers of major functions.

C. Systems are in place to solicit customer feedback on a regular basis.

D. Customer needs are determined through random processes rather than by using systematic methods.

E. Complaints are the major methods used to obtain customer feedback.

F. No customer focus is evident.

_____ **Criterion 4: Employee Training and Recognition**

A. The organization is implementing a systematic employee-training and recognition plan that is fully integrated into the overall strategic quality-planning process.

B. The organization is assessing what employee training and recognition is needed, and the results of that assessment are being evaluated periodically.

C. An employee training and recognition plan is beginning to be implemented.

D. An employee training and recognition plan is under active development.

E. The organization has plans to increase employee training and recognition.

F. There is no employee training and there are no systems for recognizing employees.

_____ **Criterion 5: Employee Empowerment and Teamwork**

A. Innovative, effective employee-empowerment and teamwork approaches are used.

B. Many natural work groups are empowered to constitute quality-improvement teams.

C. A majority of managers support employee empowerment and teamwork.

D. Many managers support employee empowerment and teamwork.

E. Some managers support employee empowerment and teamwork.

F. There is no support for employee empowerment and teamwork.

_____ **Criterion 6: Quality Measurement and Analysis**

A. Information about quality and timeliness of all products and services is collected from internal and external customers and from suppliers.

B. Information about quality and timeliness is collected from most internal and external customers and from most suppliers.

C. Information about quality and timeliness is collected from major internal and external customers and from major suppliers.

D. Information about quality and timeliness is collected from some internal and external customers.

E. Information about quality and timeliness is collected from one or two external customers.

F. There is no system for measuring and analyzing quality.

_____ **Criterion 7: Quality Assurance**

A. All products, services, and processes are designed, reviewed, verified, and controlled to meet the needs and expectations of internal and external customers.

B. A majority of products, services, and processes are designed, reviewed, verified, and controlled to meet the needs and expectations of internal and external customers.

C. Key products, services, and processes are designed, reviewed, verified, and controlled to meet the needs and expectations of internal and external customers.

D. A few products and services are designed, reviewed, and controlled to meet the needs of internal and external customers.

E. Products and services are controlled to meet internally developed specifications that may or may not include customer input.

F. There is no quality assurance in this organization.

_____ **Criterion 8: Quality- and Productivity-Improvement Results**

A. Most significant performance indicators demonstrate exceptional improvement in quality and productivity over the past five years.

B. Most significant performance indicators demonstrate excellent improvement in quality and productivity over the past five years.

C. Most significant performance indicators demonstrate good improvement in quality and productivity.

D. Most significant performance indicators demonstrate improving quality and productivity in several areas.

E. There is evidence of some quality and productivity improvement in one or more areas.

F. There is no evidence of quality and productivity improvement in any areas.

TOTAL QUALITY MANAGEMENT (TQM) INVENTORY SCORING SHEET

To determine your scores on the inventory, complete the following three steps:

1. For each of the *Total Quality Management Criteria* listed in the left column, find the letter under the heading labeled *Response Categories/Points* that corresponds to the one you chose on the questionnaire.
2. Then circle the one- or two-digit *Point* number that corresponds to the letter you chose.
3. Finally add up the points circled for all eight criteria to determine your *Overall Score.*

Note: The numbers you are about to circle correspond to the relative weights attached to individual Quality/Productivity Criteria in the President's Award.[1] Therefore, in addition to helping to score your responses, the points also identify the categories that are more significant than others. For example, scores on Criterion 8 (Quality- and Productivity-Improvement Results) are better indicators of an organization's orientation toward quality and productivity than are its scores on Criterion 4 (Employee Training and Recognition).

Total Quality Management Criteria	**Response Categories/Points**					
	A	B	C	D	E	F
1. Top-Management Leadership and Support	20	16	12	8	4	0
2. Strategic Planning	15	12	9	6	3	0
3. Focus on the Customer	40	32	24	16	8	0
4. Employee Training and Recognition	15	12	9	6	3	0
5. Employee Empowerment and Teamwork	15	12	9	6	3	0
6. Quality Measurement and Analysis	15	12	9	6	3	0
7. Quality Assurance	30	24	18	12	6	0
8. Quality- and Productivity-Improvement Results	50	40	30	20	10	0
SCORES FOR CHOICE CATEGORIES:	____	____	____	____	____	____

OVERALL SCORE: ____ (Range: 0-200)

[1] This instrument is based on the Federal Quality Institute's *Federal Total Quality Management Handbook 2: Criteria and Scoring Guidelines for the President's Award for Quality and Productivity Improvement,* Washington, DC: Office of Personnel Management, 1990.

TOTAL QUALITY MANAGEMENT (TQM) INVENTORY INTERPRETATION SHEET

160-200 points: An overall score in this range indicates a "world-class" organization with a deep, long-term, and active commitment to improving quality and productivity. At this level, goals should focus on the challenge of maintaining gains as well as seeking ways to attain even higher levels of quality and productivity.

120-159 points: An overall score in this range indicates that an organization with a sound, well-organized philosophy of quality and productivity improvement is beginning to emerge. At this level, goals should focus on fully implementing a sound TQM effort while continuing to build on current levels of excellence.

80-119 points: An overall score in this range indicates an organization that is starting to learn about and plan quality and productivity improvements. At this level, goals should focus on moving from the planning stages to actually implementing a TQM effort in order to gain the necessary hands-on experience.

40-79 points: An overall score in this range indicates an organization that is vaguely aware of quality and productivity improvement but has no plans to learn about or implement such activity. Scores at this level approach the danger point; if long-term organizational viability is sought, progress must be made quickly. Goals should focus on strongly encouraging top managers to learn more about TQM while re-examining their assumptions about possible contributions that the process can make to the health of their organization.

0-39 points: An overall score in this range indicates an organization that currently has neither an awareness of nor an involvement with quality- and productivity-improvement programs. Unless an organization has an absolute, invulnerable monopoly on extremely valuable products or services, this level represents a de facto decision to go out of business. Goals should focus on an emergency turnaround. Learning about total quality management must occur at an accelerated rate, and plans to bring quality and productivity consciousness to the organization must be implemented immediately.

INTRODUCTION TO THE PROFESSIONAL DEVELOPMENT SECTION

This is the ninth year of the *Annual's* Professional Development section, which was introduced in the 1984 *Annual* to bring together a variety of materials that would be useful to human resource development (HRD) practitioners in their personal and professional development. Included in this section are articles that HRD practitioners can use as resources for information, bring to the attention of management, or use in a training session. Such articles often are useful in documenting or supporting a position or in explaining a complex or subtle point. In addition, these articles can be used to help HRD professionals to "sell" a broader understanding of the HRD function to line managers.

This year's section consists of eleven articles, plus Pfeiffer & Company's guidelines for contributors. The first article, "Emotional Isolation and Loneliness: Executive Problems," offers a research-based perspective on the four forces in modern American culture that contribute to the problems of emotional isolation and loneliness for executives. It also discusses the impact of emotional isolation on health and the implications of this issue for HRD professionals.

Memberships in professional associations are effective means of avoiding isolation, gaining expertise, making networking contacts, and keeping one's knowledge current. The next article, entitled "A Directory of Professional Associations: Human Resource Development and Beyond," lists professional associations in areas related to human resource development.

"Group Size as a Function of Trust," the third article in this section, offers a method for making the decision about what size of group or subgroup to use in a training situation on the basis of the trust level present among the participants. The author discusses how the issue of trust is borne out with individual work, with dyads, with triads, with subgroups, and with whole groups.

Job aids are important resources for enhancing performance. Those HRD professionals who become experts at developing and using job aids will better meet the needs of their organizations. In the next article in this section, "Developing Successful Job Aids," the authors describe six formats for job aids and outline six steps to follow in developing effective job aids.

The fourth article, "Career Planning and the Fallacy of the Future," builds on the predictions made in *Megatrends* (Naisbitt, 1984). The author presents the career-plan implications of each of Naisbitt's predictions, the influences that will determine the future growth of various industries, and recommendations to organizations about the best ways to adapt to changing conditions.

"From Controlling to Facilitating: How to L.E.A.D." is the sixth article in this section. The author presents an easy-to-follow model for leading a work group in a facilitative way. She also discusses the differences between facilitating and the older, more traditional pattern of leadership, which she refers to as "controlling."

Two generations that will continue to have profound impacts in the workplace are the baby boomers and the baby busters. In "An Annotated Bibliography on the Work Force of the Twenty-First Century: Baby Boom and Bust," the author presents fascinating information and speculations on the members of these two generations, both as workers and as prospective customers. Practitioners can use the bibliography to educate themselves and managers about trends that will affect critical organizational activities such as strategic planning.

Baby boomers and baby busters are two factors that contribute to diversity in the workplace. The eighth article in the section, "Managing Diversity in the Workplace," addresses the impact of diversity, how cultural clashes develop and what their outcomes can be, and what the HRD professional can do to help an organization to manage diversity. Highlights include a brief historical perspective on diversity, four questions to ask of employees to determine whether an organizational climate supports cultural differences, and a handout called "The Cultural Component of Problem Solving" that can be used in diversity training.

Another of this year's key training topics is faster cycle time. In "Time-Based Evolution and Faster Cycle Time," the author uses the metaphor of the evolutionary process to make the case for faster cycle time. As the author explains, organizational evolution, like human and animal evolution, depends on continual adaptation to environmental influences. The article outlines the principles of faster cycle time, key steps in its implementation, and its implications for HRD practitioners.

An appreciation for the importance of individual differences and personality types enhances a person's ability to succeed in an organization. The article entitled "Using Personality Typology to Build Understanding" reviews personality typology, the role of temperament and management style, and action steps that can be taken to enhance understanding in the workplace.

The final article, "Managing Green: Defining an Organization's Environmental Role" describes the current trends in managing green and the reasons behind these trends. It outlines practical approaches to minimizing waste and maximizing resources and concludes with ways in which an HRD professional can assist an organization in defining its environmental role.

"Guidelines for Contributors to Pfeiffer & Company Publications" completes this section. These guidelines describe the specifications for the structured experiences, instruments, and professional development articles that are published in the *Annual* and are provided for the convenience of potential contributors.

As is the case with every *Annual,* several topics are covered in this volume; not every article will appeal to every reader. Nonetheless, the range of articles presented should encourage a good deal of thought-provoking, serious discussion about the present and the future of HRD.

REFERENCE

Naisbitt, J. (1984). *Megatrends: Ten new directions transforming our lives.* New York: Warner.

EMOTIONAL ISOLATION AND LONELINESS: EXECUTIVE PROBLEMS[1]

James Campbell Quick, Debra L. Nelson, Janice R. Joplin, and Jonathan D. Quick

Emotional isolation and loneliness are problems that affect many people in American culture and particularly executives, those at or near the top in the organizational hierarchy. These problems are important because of the adverse health consequences that result from them as well as the organizational problems they can create. Emotional isolation can lead to behavior that others find difficult to understand or respond to. For example, an executive whose emotional isolation leads to interacting with people in a manner that they find aloof and uncaring may experience difficulty in developing any mutual comfort or interdependence in working relationships. Often the behavior of a person experiencing emotional isolation can lead to recurrent, intense conflicts with others, sometimes creating unresolvable problems. Once the situation reaches this worst-case scenario, the individual experiencing the isolation and exhibiting the difficult behavior may resign or be asked to leave the organization.

In this article the authors identify the forces that contribute to emotional isolation and loneliness for executives, examine the adverse health consequences of these feelings, and explore the implications for human resource development (HRD) professionals.

FORCES CONTRIBUTING TO EMOTIONAL ISOLATION

There are four forces in the late Twentieth-Century American culture that contribute to the problems of emotional isolation and loneliness for executives. These forces, depicted on the left side of Figure 1, are (1) the value that the American places on independence, (2) the corporate hierarchy, (3) the behavioral strategy of counterdependence, and (4) interpersonal defensiveness in working relationships. These forces are examined in the following paragraphs.

Independence: A Cultural Value

The American culture places great value on independence (Hofstede, 1980a, 1980b). This value is reflected in the heroic figures that have emerged during the Twentieth Century, such as Superman, the Lone Ranger, and John Wayne. These

[1] Based on Chapter 7, "Loneliness: A Lethal Problem" in *Stress and Challenge at the Top: The Paradox of the Successful Executive* (pp. 147-161) by J.C. Quick, D.L. Nelson, and J.D. Quick, 1990, Chichester, England: John Wiley & Sons, Ltd.

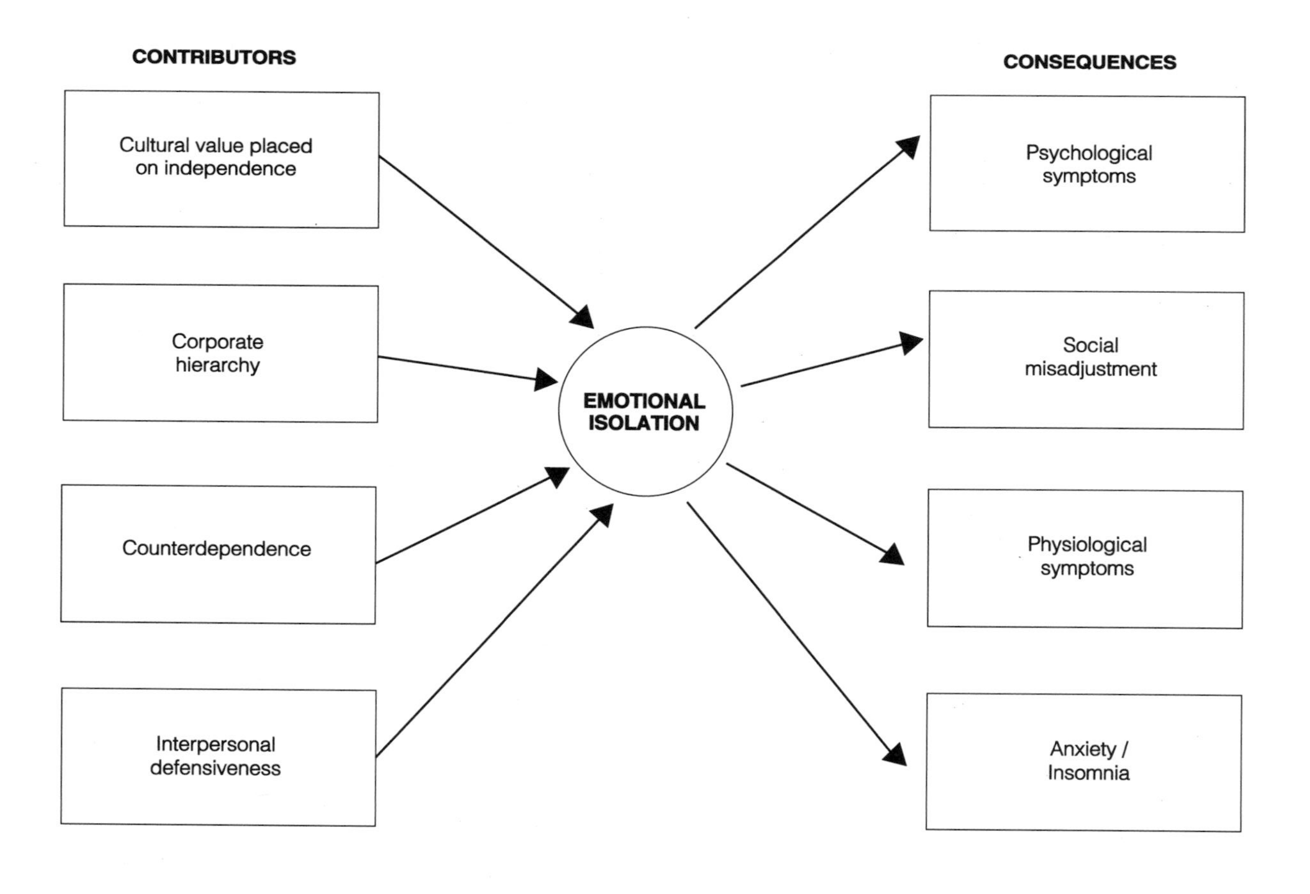

Figure 1. Forces Contributing to Emotional Isolation and Possible Consequences

figures appear solitary and self-sufficient, communicating an omnipotence that is the basis of the myth of independence. The myth suggests that a "real" man or woman can grow up, if he or she is healthy, and not need anyone else. The reality is that achieving total self-sufficiency is a physiological, psychological, and practical impossibility.

However, the truth or falsehood of the logic inherent in this myth is less important than the extent to which people accept the myth. The executive who believes in this cultural myth is more likely to engage in autonomous behavior, which in the extreme can lead to emotional isolation and loneliness. Furthermore, the American value placed on independence results in a dynamic that emphasizes the individual and leads to a process of separating the individual from the group. The consequences of this process are emotional isolation and loneliness.

Not all cultures foster this myth. In a study of 160,000 working people in sixty countries, Hofstede (1980a, 1980b) found significant differences across cultures with regard to the value placed on independence and individualism. While Americans prize this value, the Oriental cultures place much less importance on independence and individualism. Instead, the values they prize emphasize the family system and the group. This different value system leads to a social process of attachment as opposed to separation. The consequence of attachment is bonding in human relationship, not emotional isolation.[2]

Individual personality differences also operate within the larger value framework of a culture. For example, Zaleznik (1977) describes leaders and managers as fundamentally different types of personalities. In particular, he makes the point that leaders have the capacity to work in a solitary fashion for periods of time, whereas managers do not. This does not necessarily mean that leaders are lonely; there is a difference between being alone and experiencing loneliness. The ability to work alone for periods has to do with a phenomenon of human maturation: Over time people develop the ability to incorporate various perspectives into their internal conversations; they look at issues from different perspectives and carry on a kind of dialog with those perspectives. According to Zaleznik, leaders have a higher degree of this ability than managers do; managers need much greater social contact to avoid a sense of emotional isolation and loneliness. Also, in most organizational structures, managers—particularly front-line managers—must interact extensively with others to accomplish their work. Leaders, on the other hand, may tend to isolate themselves more than managers do not only because that is their inclination but also because their work is less dependent on interaction with others. Consequently, leaders may be at greater risk of emotional isolation than managers are.

The Corporate Hierarchy

Men and women have organized themselves in complex organizational hierarchies for millennia, most likely beginning with the temple corporations of ancient

[2] It is important to keep in mind that although emotional isolation may not be a problem within the Oriental cultures, there may be an inhibition of individualistic and exploratory behavior that limits freedom.

Mesopotamia (Sterba, 1976). The advent of the Industrial Revolution over the past two centuries has led to the evolution of the business corporation as the dominant organizational form in American and other Western cultures. The vertical nature of a hierarchy forces those who are higher in that hierarchy to be increasingly isolated from those who are lower in the hierarchy. The discrimination that leads to this separation is based on authority and responsibility.[3]

Schwartz (1990) explains very well the psychological problems created by vertical separation in a corporate hierarchy. He refers to the situation as "ontological differentiation" because of the self-enhancing bias created for those higher in the hierarchy and the self-diminishing bias created for those lower in the hierarchy. The implicit message is that executives who are at or near the top of the hierarchy are better or more perfect than other employees; consequently, there is a social distance in relationships that feeds the problem of emotional isolation in organizations.

Schein (1989) argues that because we typically perceive working relationships in hierarchical terms, we do not have good alternative models for relationships of a different nature. Yet, he continues, the computer and information-system revolutions have confronted us with the issue of how to reconceptualize work and our relationships at work. If he is correct and the future demands an organizational structure that is not hierarchical, the potential benefit for executives is less exclusion from human relationships.

Counterdependence

The corporate hierarchy and the value of independence are culture-based forces that move executives into positions of isolation. However, there are also personality-based forces that can contribute to emotional isolation. One of these forces is counterdependence.

Normal human development is dependent on a child's process of *attachment* (Bowlby, 1982), which consists of connecting himself or herself to reliable "attachment figures"—generally parents—during times of threat or danger. If the child knows that the attachment figure(s) will be there and will provide what is needed, that child will grow to become a self-reliant adult, accepting responsibility for his or her well-being and, at the same time, maintaining a support network of people who will be available and willing to help in times of need (Quick, Nelson, & Quick, 1991). However, if a child's attachment figures are absent, unreliable, or unresponsive during the developmental years, that child experiences separation anxiety. People who experience separation anxiety frequently and intensely during childhood may begin to employ alternative, dysfunctional strategies for achieving a sense of felt security in times of danger or threat (Bowlby, 1973; Kobak & Shaver, 1987).

One of these dysfunctional strategies is overdependence, a desperate clinging to others. The fundamental problem of the overdependent personality is the

[3] Not all organizational forms create the degree of vertical separation that becomes problematic in terms of emotional isolation. For example, Mintzberg (1979) discusses "adhocracy" as a professional form of bureaucracy that does not emphasize the vertical dimension.

lack of autonomy or the ability to stand on one's own. Although this strategy may have a negative effect on an executive's decision-making ability and job performance, the authors have found no indication that overdependence is related to any psychological or physical disorders.

However, the same cannot be said of the second dysfunctional strategy, that of counterdependence. In working with groups of managers and graduate students, the authors have found a significant, positive relationship between counterdependence and a range of health disorders (see the section entitled "The Impact of Emotional Isolation on Health" in this paper). The counterdependent strategy consists of avoiding or denying one's needs in times of threat or danger. It represents an attempt on the individual's part to achieve self-sufficiency in relation to others. The fundamental problem of the counterdependent personality is the lack of close, personal or professional relationships on which to draw in times of need.

Situations involving danger or threat naturally trigger the experience of anxiety and fear. Counterdependent people attempt to achieve a sense of security in such situations by distancing themselves from others. Hence, counterdependent people become isolated and lonely at precisely the times when it is least appropriate to be so.

Interpersonal Defensiveness

Another personality-based force that can contribute to emotional isolation is interpersonal defensiveness. Although there are times in which it may be appropriate to defend oneself from physical and/or psychological attack, Wells (1980) has demonstrated how interpersonal defensiveness in working relationships can lead to powerlessness, isolation, loneliness, and other destructive outcomes for everyone involved. Interpersonal defensiveness always establishes barriers between people, creates distance in relationships, and may result in a wide range of communication dysfunctions.

Interpersonal defensiveness may take either an active or a passive form. The active form comes from the mind-set of "I am right and you are wrong." This aggressive, controlling, dictatorial form of interpersonal interaction is illustrated in comments such as "Don't argue; just do as I say" or "Now see, that proves my point." The executive who uses an active defense likes to hold the upper hand in relationships. The passive form of interpersonal defensiveness comes from the mind-set illustrated in Willie Nelson's song "Excuse Me for Livin'." It is a submissive, withdrawn, nonaggressive and nonassertive form of interpersonal interaction. It may be best characterized by comments such as "I'm just doing what I was told" or "O.K., whatever you say." Apologies that are inappropriate to the situation and serious self-deprecation are clearly forms of passive defensiveness.

Both of these forms of interpersonal defensiveness create distance and alienation in relationships. The alternative to interpersonal defensiveness is nondefensive interpersonal interaction, which is characterized by responsibility, nonreactivity, power, control, openness, and choice. The executive who is nondefensive chooses how to relate interpersonally and is not simply reacting to the behavior of the other person. Nondefensive interactions have the potential to build and strengthen working relationships. Even though two people may not necessarily agree about the issues at hand or their positions, when they interact nondefensively they have a better understanding and appreciation for each other as individuals. Hence, mutual respect and common understanding are the least one might expect from nondefensive interactions.

THE IMPACT OF EMOTIONAL ISOLATION ON HEALTH

As depicted on the right side of Figure 1 (page 166), several health consequences of emotional isolation are suggested in the literature. For example, House, Landis, and Umberson (1988) reported that lower levels of social support resulted in higher levels of distress and death. Specifically, they concluded that there is strong empirical evidence for the causal impact of social relationships on health. In addition, they concluded from their analysis of experimental and quasi-experimental studies that isolation is a major risk factor for mortality from a wide variety of causes. Emotional isolation, loneliness, and the absence of social relationships have been tied to mortality and a range of health disorders in earlier studies as well (Lynch, 1977). The authors' research has confirmed a set of significant, positive relationships between counterdependence and a range of health disorders: psychological symptoms, social misadjustment, physiological symptoms, and anxiety/insomnia. These disorders are discussed in the following paragraphs.

Psychological Symptoms

Emotional isolation can lead to a wide range of psychological symptoms of distress, including depression and burnout. Depression may be the most common of the psychological symptoms and is akin to emotional deprivation. Although the psychological consequences of emotional isolation appear rather early in infants and children, parallel effects in the adult stages of life may take significantly longer to manifest themselves for two reasons.

First, it is rare that an individual experiences total social isolation or loneliness. Instead, adults are far more likely to become "psychologically anemic" by operating "a quart low" in the arena of social relationships. Hence, an executive may have a mild depression that continues untreated for extended periods of time because it has minimal impact on the executive's personal and work life. However, the depressed executive may experience decreased abilities in the areas of decision making, judgment, and other key cognitive processes. Depression awareness and treatment programs in industry have found that early awareness is often the best cure.

Second, it may take longer for the depression and other psychological symptoms to show up in an adult than in a child because an adult has a larger reservoir of emotional and life-history reserves to draw on. Thus, an executive may operate in a deficit position for an extended period before totally depleting his or her emotional reserves. Also, in some cases, the internal reserves may be strong enough to avert serious depression with only minimal social contact. For example, Brigadier General Bobby Reisner tells of his experience of emotional isolation in a North Vietnamese prisoner-of-war (POW) camp during the Seventies. He found that he was able to avert serious depression by (1) developing a self-talk dialog about all of the positive events of his entire life and (2) forming as much of a POW support network as possible within the confines of the camp. Few executives will face constraints as severe as General Reisner's, so the risks are not insurmountable.

Social Misadjustment

Executives and managers rely heavily on a wide range of social cues and role-related information developed within the network of relationships in the work environment. Thus, isolation leads to the loss of key information and expectations that flow through the network. Although mild social misadjustment may not lead to disaster, serious social misadjustment may result in errors from which it is difficult to recover: decision-making errors, miscalculations of planning risks, or problem-solving failures. In addition, social misadjustments can lead to distrustful and/or hostile working relationships and morale problems.

The authors' research has found a significant relationship between counterdependence and social dysfunction. The dynamic for this relationship is the denial and defensive distancing process that counterdependent personalities use in relationships with others. The attachment process, spoken of earlier, results in the formation of a support network that serves as a "guidance system" in times of need, analogous to any guidance system used by aircraft to effect safe landings. In times of need, counterdependent people disconnect parts of their "guidance systems"; hence the dysfunctions and misadjustments.

Physiological Symptoms

There are a variety of physiological symptoms that may result from emotional isolation, the most serious being premature death from any of a wide range of causes. Less-serious physiological and medical health problems, many of which fall into the realm of psychosomatic disorders, often precede premature death. Hence, health awareness is a very important issue for executives. Because of individual differences, these early-warning signs in the body may turn up in a variety of physiological systems, such as the digestive, respiratory, cardiovascular, musculoskeletal, and nervous systems.

The research on emotional isolation and the impact of relationships on physical health have not identified specific physical pathways through which the effects are developed. The point of impact of the physiological symptom is determined to a great extent by the "Achilles heel" phenomenon, also known as the "weak-organ hypothesis," which states that the physiological or medical breakdown occurs in the weakest link of the body. Studying family history is one of the best ways to identify a person's Achilles heel. For example, an executive whose family history contains cardiovascular or digestive problems is most likely at risk for the same disorders.

Anxiety/Insomnia

As mentioned earlier, the authors have found anxiety and insomnia associated with higher levels of autonomy in the work environment. They have found an even stronger, positive relationship between these symptoms and counterdependence. People who are counterdependent have distanced themselves in social relationships. The resultant anxiety is analogous to the separation anxiety experienced by the child in need who is unable to connect to attachment figures. Although averting the experience of anxiety is obviously not the sole purpose for being in a relationship, the key issue is to have people who are accessible in times of threat, danger, or need.

Self-reliant people display decisive, active behavior that is sometimes erroneously confused with counterdependence. The difference between the counterdependent person and the self-reliant person lies in the well-developed support network that the self-reliant person draws on in times of need and to achieve effectiveness. It is the support network that frees a self-reliant person to engage in autonomous behavior that may look like counterdependence. The counterdependent person, however, does not reach out in times of threat, danger, or need and instead internalizes the experience in the form of anxiety. The experiences of anxiety and insomnia are overcome through supportive attachments and relationships.

IMPLICATIONS FOR HRD PROFESSIONALS

Although executives in particular are at risk of experiencing emotional isolation and loneliness, these problems can occur at any level of an organization. The human resource development (HRD) professional can take a number of steps to help prevent or minimize the experience of emotional isolation and loneliness:

1. Promote awareness by distributing copies of this article to the top-management team and leading a discussion on its content. Educate executives and others about the risks of isolation.

2. Encourage the establishment and maintenance of personal support networks. Use activities and instruments such as the structured experience entitled “Supporting Cast: Examining Personal Support Networks” in this *Annual* and the “Self-Reliance Inventory” by Quick, Nelson, and Quick in the 1991 *Annual* (see References and Bibliography at the end of this article). Also refer to the “Burnout Inventory” in this *Annual* for a discussion of burnout as a form of alienation.

3. Conduct team building, starting with the top-management team. Promote the view that teamwork is essential not only for front-line employees but for all levels of the organization.

4. Suggest that top management reward teamwork throughout the organization. Help top managers to set up and implement an appropriate reward system. Urge all teams in the organization to congratulate themselves and to celebrate successful team efforts.

5. Encourage top managers and other employees to develop an awareness of their health: to have annual physicals; to chart their family medical histories; and to recognize digestive problems, anxiety, insomnia, and other symptoms as early-warning signs that require attention.

6. Model self-reliant functioning by developing and nurturing your own support network and monitoring your own health.
7. Conduct training to build skills in nondefensive behavior in interpersonal transactions.
8. Support and encourage membership in interorganizational networks and professional societies.
9. Develop a mentoring system, and encourage mentoring at all levels.
10. Set up support systems for people at work. Give special attention to high-risk groups: new employees; those who travel frequently; those whose work environments are physically arranged in a manner that contributes to isolation; and those near retirement, who may gradually disengage from the work environment to the detriment of their health.
11. Develop a list of resource people that employees can consult in times of special need.

Ironically, American organizations are now stressing the importance and the impact of group work—something that Americans have been taught is less valuable than individual achievement. However, the importance of teamwork in alleviating the problems of emotional isolation and loneliness has been largely overlooked. The HRD professional now has an opportunity to make this connection known and to take advantage of it to the benefit of executives and the entire organization.

REFERENCES AND BIBLIOGRAPHY

Bowlby, J. (1973). *Attachment and loss* (Vol. II: Separation anxiety and anger). New York: Basic Books.

Bowlby, J. (1982). *Attachment and loss* (Vol. I: Attachment, rev. ed.). New York: Basic Books.

Hofstede, G. (1980a). *Culture's consequences: International differences in work-related values.* Beverly Hills, CA: Sage Publications.

Hofstede, G. (1980b, Summer). Motivation, leadership, and organization: Do American theories apply abroad? *Organizational Dynamics,* pp. 42-63.

House, J.S., Landis, K.R., & Umberson, D. (1988). Social relationships and health. *Science, 241,* 540-545.

Kobak, R., & Shaver, P. (1987). *Strategies for maintaining felt security: A theoretical analysis of continuity and change in styles of social adaptation.* Prepared for the Conference in Honor of John Bowlby's 80th Birthday, Bayswater, London.

Lynch, J. (1977). *The broken heart: The medical consequences of loneliness.* New York: Basic Books.

Mintzberg, H. (1979). *The structuring of organizations.* Englewood Cliffs, NJ: Prentice-Hall.

Quick, J.C., Joplin, J.R., Nelson, D.L., & Quick, J.D. (in press). Behavioral responses to anxiety: Self-reliance, counterdependence, and overdependence. *Anxiety Research.*

Quick, J.C., Nelson, D.L., & Quick, J.D. (1990). *Stress and challenge at the top: The paradox of the successful executive.* Chichester, England: John Wiley.

Quick, J.C., Nelson, D.L., & Quick, J.D. (1991). Self-reliance inventory. In J.W. Pfeiffer (Ed.), *The 1991 annual: Developing human resources* (pp. 149-161). San Diego, CA: Pfeiffer & Company.

Schein, E.H. (1989). Reassessing the "divine rights" of managers. *Sloan Management Review, 30*(2), 63-68.

Schwartz, H.S. (1990). *Narcissistic process and corporate decay: The theory of the organization ideal.* New York: New York University Press.

Sterba, R.L.A. (1976). The organization and management of the temple corporations in ancient Mesopotamia. *Academy of Management Review, 1,* 16-26.

Wells, T. (1980). *Keeping your cool under fire.* New York: McGraw-Hill.

Zaleznik, A. (1977). Leaders and managers: Are they different? *Harvard Business Review, 55,* 67-78.

James Campbell Quick, Ph.D., *is a professor of organizational behavior in the Department of Management at the University of Texas at Arlington. He consults and conducts research in the field of stress, with a special emphasis on chief executives and top management, and is a stress expert for the American Psychological Association. He is co-editor of* Work Stress: Health Care Systems in the Workplace, *which received the 1987 Distinguished Service Award from the UTA College of Business Administration. In addition, he is co-editor of* Work and Well-Being: Assessments and Interventions for Occupational Mental Health.

Debra L. Nelson, Ph.D., *is an associate professor of management in the College of Business Administration at Oklahoma State University. She has consulted with a variety of organizations, including AT&T, Exxon Corporation, and Aerospatiale Helicopter Corporation. She is co-author of* Stress and Challenge at the Top: The Paradox of the Successful Executive, *and her research in the area of stress management has appeared in the* Academy of Management Executive, Academy of Management Journal, Personnel, Organizational Dynamics, *and* Journal of Organizational Behavior. *She has also published research on the subjects of newcomer socialization and technology management.*

Janice R. Joplin *is a doctoral student in organizational behavior at the University of Texas at Arlington. She is currently conducting research in the areas of social support and self-reliance in organizational settings. Her other areas of interest are preventive stress management and executive-information processing. She has been employed by the Department of Defense and has served as a consultant to not-for-profit organizations and small businesses in both the United States and Europe.*

Jonathan D. Quick, M.D., *is a program director for the Management Sciences for Health (MSH) and is presently serving as a health care planner/evaluator on the Kenya Health Financing Project, funded by the United States Agency for International Development. He is also an adjunct associate professor in the School of Public Health, Boston University, Massachusetts. He consults and conducts research internationally in the fields of public health, pharmaceutical drug logistics, and stress. He is co-editor of* Work Stress: Health Care Systems in the Workplace.

A DIRECTORY OF PROFESSIONAL ASSOCIATIONS: HUMAN RESOURCE DEVELOPMENT AND BEYOND

Professionals in many fields gain expertise, networking contacts, and the latest information and news through membership in various professional associations. The same is true for human resource development (HRD) professionals, and there are many associations whose emphases are related to HRD.

The readers of Pfeiffer & Company's *Annuals* are a professionally diverse group. Our readership includes organization-development consultants, strategic planners, university professors, educators, personnel specialists, trainers, counselors, managers, military personnel, career-development specialists, and many others. With these various areas in mind, the *Annual* staff has prepared the following directory of professional associations.

The associations in the directory are categorized as follows:

- Training and Development;
- Organization Development;
- Counseling/Personnel/Career Development;
- Total Quality Management/Quality Circles;
- Management/Planning;
- Education/Adult Development; and
- International Associations.

Each listing contains the address and phone number of the national office of the association; the contact name (if applicable); the number of members; and whether or not the association has local/regional chapters or affiliates. Several associations are organized with local chapters; therefore a new member will join not only the national association but the closest local chapter or region as well. Other associations do not govern local *chapters* per se but are *affiliated* with other (often smaller) associations. Still others have no local chapters or affiliations at all.

Professional associations afford their members varying kinds of benefits, events, publications, meetings, and conferences. For information about membership dues, benefits, conferences and other events, and local chapter membership, contact the association's national headquarters.

TRAINING AND DEVELOPMENT

American Society for Training and Development (ASTD)
P.O. Box 1443
1640 King Street
Alexandria, Virginia 22313-9833
(703) 683-8100 (Main Office)
(703) 683-8187 (Conference Director)
Members: 70,000
Local Chapters: Yes

Association for Sales Training (AST)
P.O. Box 2902
Palos Verdes, California 90274
(213) 378-2666
Members: 600-700
Local Chapters: No

Council of Hotel and Restaurant Trainers (CHART)
Natalie Milholland, Secretary
Richards Restaurants, Inc.
R.R. 1, Box 180-B
Bryant, Indiana 47326
(219) 997-6823 ext. 218
OR
(permanent mailing address)
3712 North Broadway, Suite 306
Chicago, Illinois 60613
Members: 225
Local Chapters: No

Instructional Systems Association (ISA)
P.O. Box 1196
Sunset Beach, California 90742
(714) 846-6012
Members: 103
Local Chapters: No

National Association of State Training and Development Directors (NASTADD)
Governmental Services Center
Kentucky State University
Fourth Floor, Academic Services Building
Frankfort, Kentucky 40601
(502) 564-8170
Members: 75-100
Local Chapters: No

National Society for Performance and Instruction (NSPI)
1300 L Street, N.W., Suite 1250
Washington, DC 20005
(202) 408-7969
Members: 5,000
Local Chapters: Yes

National Society of Sales Training Executives (NSSTE)
203 East Third Street
Sanford, Florida 32771
(407) 322-3364
Members: 173
Local Chapters: No

National Training Labs (NTL) Institute
1240 North Pitt Street Centre, Suite 100
Alexandria, Virginia 22314-1403
(703) 548-1500
Members: 461
Local Chapters: No

National Training Systems Associations
2425 Wilson Boulevard, Suite 457
Arlington, Virginia 22201
(703) 243-1655
Members: 40 (corporate)
Local Chapters: No

Society for Applied Learning Technology (SALT)
50 Culpeper Street
Warrenton, Virginia 22186
(703) 347-0055
Members: 900
Local Chapters: No

Training Directors Forum
50 South Ninth Street
Minneapolis, Minnesota 55402
(612) 333-0471, ext. 508
Members: 2,500 (subscribers)
Local Chapters: No

ORGANIZATION DEVELOPMENT

OD Network
Ruth Emory and Rene Pino,
Administrators
P.O. Box 69329
Portland, Oregon 97201
(503) 246-0148
Members: 2,500+
Local Chapters: 22 regional OD networks

Professional Organizational Development Network (PODN)
c/o David Graf
Instructional Development Office
Exhibit Hall South
Iowa State University
Ames, Iowa 50011
(515) 294-2316
Members: 700
Local Chapters: No

COUNSELING/PERSONNEL/CAREER DEVELOPMENT

American Association for Counseling and Development (AACD)
Dr. Theodore P. Remley, Jr., JD, NCC
Executive Director
5999 Stevenson Avenue
Alexandria, Virginia 22304-9990
(703) 823-9800
Members: 58,362
Local Chapters: No

American College Personnel Association (ACPA)
Dr. Leila V. Moore, President
Division of Student Programs
210 Eisenhower Chapel
Pennsylvania State University
University Park, Pennsylvania 16802
(814) 863-4926
(814) 863-2463 (FAX)
Members: 8,637
Local Chapters: No

American Mental Health Counselors Association (AMHCA)
Dr. William Krieger, President
401 Louisiana, S.E., #D
Albuquerque, New Mexico 87108
(505) 255-1551
(505) 265-6988 (FAX)
Members: 11,917
Local Chapters: No

American Psychological Association (APA)
1200 Seventeenth Street, N.W.
Washington, DC 20036
(202) 955-7600
Members: 108,000 (including affiliates)
Local Chapters: Yes (affiliated state associations)

American Rehabilitation Counseling Association (ARCA)
Dr. Martha L. Walker, President
Professor, Rehabilitation Counseling
Room 310, White Hall
Kent State University
Kent, Ohio 44242
(216) 672-2662
(216) 672-3407 (FAX)
Members: 2,693
Local Chapters: No

American School Counselor Association (ASCA)
c/o American Association for Counseling and Development
5999 Stevenson Avenue
Alexandria, Virginia 22304
(703) 823-9800
Members: 12,502
Local Chapters: Yes

Association for Adult Development and Aging (AADA)
Marilyn S. Edwards, President
Director of Admissions and Social Services
Bloomington Convalescent Center
714 South Rogers Street
Bloomington, Indiana 47403
(812) 336-6893
(812) 336-4833 (FAX)
Members: 2,037
Local Chapters: No

Association for Counselor Education & Supervision (ACES)
Dr. Harold L. Hackney, President
Professor and Director, Community and School Counseling Program
Graduate School of Education and Allied Professions
Fairfield University
Fairfield, Connecticut 06430
(203) 254-4000, ext. 2396
Members: 2,983
Local Chapters: No

Association for Humanistic Education and Development (AHEAD)
Dr. JoAnna F. White, President
Assistant Professor, Department of Counseling and Psychological Services
Georgia State University
Atlanta, Georgia 30303
(404) 651-2550
Members: 2,781
Local Chapters: No

Association for Measurement and Evaluation in Counseling and Development (AMECD)
Dr. Patricia B. Elmore, President
Professor, Department of Educational Psychology
Southern Illinois University at Carbondale
Carbondale, Illinois 62901-4618
(618) 453-6915
(618) 453-1646 (FAX)
Members: 1,549
Local Chapters: No

Association for Multicultural Counseling and Development (AMCD)
Mr. Clemmie Solomon, Jr., President
Acting Dean of Students
Bowie State University
Bowie, Maryland 20715
(301) 464-6526
Members: 3,254
Local Chapters: No

Association for Religious and Value Issues in Counseling (ARVIC)
Dr. Ann Marie Wallace, President
Director, Center for Spiritual Development
96 Milton Road
Rye, New York 10580
(914) 967-7328
Members: 4,086
Local Chapters: No

Association for Specialists in Group Work (ASGW)
Dr. Rosemarie S. Morganett, President
Coordinator of Counselor Education
Indiana University Southeast
4201 Grant Line Road
New Albany, Indiana 47150
(812) 941-2385
Members: 5,759
Local Chapters: No

Association of Human Resource Systems Professionals (HRSP, Inc.)
James D. Stroop, Executive Director
P.O. Box 801646
Dallas, Texas 75380-1646
(214) 661-3727
Members: 3,500
Local Chapters: Yes

Association of Outplacement Consulting Firms, Inc. (AOCF)
364 Parsippany Road
Parsippany, New Jersey 07054
(201) 887-6667
Members: 52 member firms
Local Chapters: Yes (250 branch offices)

California Association for Counseling and Development
2555 East Chapman Avenue, Suite 201
Fullerton, California 92631
(714) 871-6460
Members: 2,000
Local Chapters: No

California Career Development Association
2555 East Chapman Avenue, Suite 201
Fullerton, California 92631
(714) 871-6460
Members: 600
Local Chapters: Yes (area councils)

Employment Management Association (EMA)
4101 Lake Boone Trail
Raleigh, North Carolina 27607
(919) 787-6010
Members: 1,600-1,900
Local Chapters: No

Human Resource Planning Society (HRPS)
P.O. Box 2553, Grand Central Station
New York, New York 10163
(212) 490-6387
Members: 2,000+
Local Chapters: Yes

Industrial Relations Research Association (IRRA)
7226 Social Science Building
University of Wisconsin
1180 Observatory Drive
Madison, Wisconsin 53706-1393
(608) 262-2762
Members: 4,800
Local Chapters: Yes

International Association of Addictions and Offender Counselors (IAAOC)
Kevin P. Warwick, President
Director, Day Reporting and
Substance Abuse Program
590 West Columbus Avenue
Springfield, Massachusetts 01105
(413) 787-1780
(413) 781-6688 (FAX)
Members: 1,541
Local Chapters: No

International Association of Marriage & Family Counselors (IAMFC)
Dr. Pat Love, President
Counselor/Consultant
Austin Family Institute
2404 Rio Grande
Austin, Texas 78705
(512) 478-1175
Members: 4,661
Local Chapters: No

International Personnel Management Association (IPMA)
1617 Duke Street
Alexandria, Virginia 22314
(703) 549-7100
(703) 684-0948 (FAX)
Members: 6,000
Local Chapters: Yes

International Society of Preretirement Planners (ISPP)
11312 Old Club Road
Rockville, Maryland 20852
(301) 881-4113 or (800) 327-ISPP
Members: under 600
Local Chapters: Yes

Military Educators and Counselors Association (MECA)
Theresa Ann Locke, President
Army Education Guidance Counselor
Army Education Center
Building 5009
Andrews Avenue
Fort Rucker, Alabama 36362-5122
(205) 255-3651
Members: 609
Local Chapters: No

National Association of Personnel Consultants (NAPC)
1432 Duke Street
Alexandria, Virginia 22314
(703) 684-0180
Members: 2,100
Local Chapters: Yes

National Career Development Association (NCDA)
Dr. Deborah P. Bloch, President
Associate Professor
Box 299
Baruch College
17 Lexington Avenue
New York, New York 10010
(212) 387-1720
(212) 387-1748 (FAX)
Members: 5,587
Local Chapters: No

National Employment Counselors Association (NECA)
Roberta A. Floyd, President
Career Assessment Coordinator
Southfield Employment and Training
26000 Evergreen Road
P.O. Box 2055
Southfield, Michigan 48037-2055
(313) 354-9167
Members: 1,803
Local Chapters: No

Society for Human Resource Management (SHRM) [formerly American Society for Personnel Administration (ASPA)]
Kay Wills, Membership
606 North Washington Street
Alexandria, Virginia 22314
(703) 548-3440
Members: 44,000-45,000
Local Chapters: Yes (also has overseas chapters)

Society for Intercultural Education, Training and Research (SIETAR)
733 Fifteenth Street, N.W., Suite 900
Washington, DC 20005
(202) 737-5000
Members: 2,000
Local Chapters: Yes (also has overseas chapters)

TOTAL QUALITY MANAGEMENT/ QUALITY CIRCLES

American Society for Quality Control (ASQC)
310 West Wisconsin Avenue
Milwaukee, Wisconsin 53203
(414) 272-8575
Members: 83,000
Local Chapters: Yes

Association for Quality and Participation (AQP) [formerly International Association of Quality Circles (IAQC)]
801-B West Eighth Street, Suite 501
Cincinnati, Ohio 45203
(513) 381-1959
Members: 8,200
Local Chapters: Yes

MANAGEMENT/PLANNING

Academy of Management
Lucretia Coleman
Director of Membership
Georgia College, CPO 11
Milledgeville, Georgia 31061
Members: 9,000
Local Chapters: Yes (regional divisions)

American Management Association (AMA)
AMACOM Division
135 West Fiftieth Street
New York, New York 10020
(212) 586-8100
Members: 65,000
Local Chapters: No

National Association for Management (NAM)
1617 Murray Street
Wichita, Kansas 67212
(316) 721-4684
Members: N/A
Local Chapters: No

National Management Association (NMA)
2210 Arbor Boulevard
Dayton, Ohio 45439
(513) 294-0421
Members: 55,000
Local Chapters: Yes

The Planning Forum (The International Society for Strategic Management and Planning)
5500 College Corner Pike
P.O. Box 70
Oxford, Ohio 45056
(513) 523-4185
(513) 523-7539 (FAX)
Members: N/A
Local Chapters: N/A

EDUCATION/ADULT DEVELOPMENT

American Association for Adult and Continuing Education (AAACE)
1112 Sixteenth Street, N.W., Suite 420
Washington, DC 20036
(202) 463-6333
Members: 3,000
Local Chapters: Yes (affiliated associations)

American Association for Higher Education (AAHE)
One Dupont Circle, N.W., Suite 600
Washington, DC 20036
(202) 293-6440
Members: 8,000
Local Chapters: No

American Association of School Administrators (AASA)
Gail M. Stephens
Deputy Executive Director
1801 North Moore Street
Arlington, Virginia 22209
(703) 528-0700 or (703) 875-0771
(703) 841-1543 (FAX)
Members: 18,235
Local Chapters: Yes

American Educational Research Association (AERA)
1230 Seventeenth Street, N.W.
Washington, DC 20036
(202) 223-9485
Members: 17,000
Local Chapters: No

Association for Community Based Education (ACBE)
1805 Florida Avenue, N.W.
Washington, DC 20009
(202) 462-6333
Members: 200
Local Chapters: Yes

Association for Continuing Higher Education (ACHE)
Dr. Scott Evenbeck
Executive Vice President
Indiana University-Purdue University at Indianapolis
620 Union Drive
Room 143, North Wing
Indianapolis, Indiana 46202-5171
(317) 274-2637
Members: 1,700
Local Chapters: Yes

Association for Educational Communications and Technology (AECT)
1025 Vermont Avenue, N.W. Suite 820
Washington, DC 20005
(202) 347-7834
Members: 4,500
Local Chapters: Yes

Association for Supervision and Curriculum Development (ASCD)
1250 North Pitt Street
Alexandria, Virginia 22314-1403
(703) 549-9110
Members: 165,000
Local Chapters: Yes (affiliates)

International Association for Continuing Education and Training (IACET)
1101 Connecticut Avenue, N.W., Suite 700
Washington, DC 20036
(202) 857-1122
Members: 600
Local Chapters: No

National Academy for School Executives (NASE)
1801 North Moore Street
Arlington, Virginia 22209
(703) 528-0700
Members: 18,235
Local Chapters: No

National Community Education Association (NCEA)
119 North Payne Street
Alexandria, Virginia 22314
(703) 683-6232
Members: 1,400
Local Chapters: Yes

National Home Study Council (NHSC)
1601 Eighteenth Street, N.W.
Washington, DC 20009
(202) 234-5100
Members: 60
Local Chapters: No

National University Continuing Education Association (NUCEA)
One Dupont Circle, N.W., Suite 615
Washington, DC 20036-1168
(202) 659-3130
Members: 2,200
Local Chapters: Yes (regions)

INTERNATIONAL ASSOCIATIONS

Asian Regional Training and Development Organization (ARTDO)
Suite 2039, V.V. Solivan Building
EDSA Greenhills
San Juan 1500, Metro Manila
PHILLIPINES

Austrian Center for Productivity and Efficiency (ACPE)
Rockgasse 6
P.O. Box 131
A-1014 Vienna
AUSTRIA
222-533-8636-17

Engineering Industry Training Board (EITB)
54 Clarendon Road
Watford, Herts WD1 1LB
ENGLAND
(0923) 38441

European College of Marketing and Marketing Research (ECMMR)
(Professional Associations)
18 St. Peters Steps
Brixham, Devon TQ5 9TE
ENGLAND
(0926) 831271

European Foundation for Management Development (EFMD)
54 Postfach 1546
6200 Wiesbaden 1
GERMANY

Hotel and Catering Training Board (HCTB)
International House
High Street
Ealing W5 5DB
ENGLAND
081 579 2400, ext. 222

Industrial Relations Research Association (IRRA)
British Columbia, Canada
Mark Thompson, Secretary-Treasurer
Faculty of Commerce
University of British Columbia
2053 Main Mall
Vancouver, British Columbia V6T 1Y8
CANADA
(604) 224-8375

Industrial Relations Research Association (IRRA)
Ontario, Canada
Harish Jain
Faculty of Business
McMaster University
Building KTH-226
Hamilton, Ontario L8S 4M4
CANADA
(416) 525-9140, ext. 3952

Industrial Relations Research Association (IRRA)
Jacques Rojot, President
20 Lacepede
Paris 75005
FRANCE

The Institute of Export (IE)
64 Clifton Street
London EC2A 4HB
ENGLAND
071 247 9812

Institute of Personnel Management Australia (IPMA)
GPO Box 853
Brisbane, Queensland 4001
AUSTRALIA

Institute of Quality Assurance
10 Grosvenor Gardens
London SW1W 0DQ
ENGLAND
071 730 7154

The Institute of Training and Development (ITD)
Marlow House, Institute Road
Marlow, Bucks SL7 1BN
ENGLAND
(0628) 890123
(0628) 890208 (FAX)

International Association of Applied Psychology (Association Internationale de Psychologie Appliqué)
M.C. Knowles
IAAP Secretary-General
Graduate School of Management
Monash University
Clayton, Victoria 3168
AUSTRALIA

International Federation of Training and Development Associations (IFTDO)
Institute of Management Education
7 Westbourne Road
Southport PR8 2HZ
ENGLAND

International Society for Intercultural Education, Training and Research (SIETAR)
733 Fifteenth Street, N.W., Suite 900
Washington, DC 20005
(202) 737-5000

Petroleum Training Federation (PTF)
Room 326
162-168 Regent Street
London W1R 5TB
ENGLAND
071 439 2632

The Production Engineering Research Association (PERA)
Melton Mowbray
Leicestershire LE13 0PB
ENGLAND
(0664) 501501

Road Transport Industry Training Board (RTITB)
Capitol House, Empire Way
Wembley, Middlesex HA9 0NG
ENGLAND
081 902 8880

The Strategic Planning Society
17 Portland Place
London W1N 3AF
ENGLAND
071 636 7737

GROUP SIZE AS A FUNCTION OF TRUST

Patrick Leone

In designing workshops or training activities, human resource development (HRD) professionals are often faced with determining the size of the group. Typically, the decision is based on the content of the program. For example, if the facilitator has information to present, he or she bases the size of the group on logistics such as the size of the room and the capacity of the public-address system. However, if skill development is the goal, the facilitator plans for smaller groups. In any case, the factor of trust is generally ignored in determining group size.

This article offers a method for making the group-size decision on the basis of the trust level present among the participants. This method takes into account people's fear of speaking in front of groups and of being seen as incompetent or inadequate. The principle behind the method is that all other things being equal, the amount of trust an individual feels in a group is inversely related to the size of the group; as trust increases, the size of the group can increase with no resulting decrease in open communication.

An example of this principle is seen in staff meetings called by senior executives to share information and lead discussions with large numbers of middle managers. A senior executive may gather forty or fifty middle managers from as many as three levels below his or her own status and present some ideas. Then the executive is surprised when people are slow to respond. This type of gathering is the most intimidating format for receiving responses from middle managers. Those who offer comments risk embarrassing themselves in front of the executive, their managers, their peers, and perhaps even their subordinates. A preferable alternative is for the executive to meet separately with groups of four to six people so that the threat of making a contribution is not so great. Another alternative is to break the larger group into subgroups of four to six and assign facilitators to record people's ideas and then report to the total group. Either of these alternatives shows sensitivity to people's fears, acknowledges that the issue of trust affects participation, and yields better information than the total-group approach.

Every size of group is useful for certain purposes and is legitimate as long as the facilitator is sensitive to the needs of the participants. The following paragraphs discuss how the issue of trust is borne out with different sizes of groups:

Individual Work. When the facilitator's objective is to have the participants generate information, it is useful to ask them to focus privately on a topic and pinpoint their ideas and feelings—and perhaps even write down their thoughts. This approach is appropriate as long as the participants know in advance that they are not required to share their ideas and that they can be the judges of how much or how little they share in the total group. After the participants have been given a few moments to think, it is important for the facilitator to use language that *invites* rather than *pressures.* Then only those who are comfortable with the level of risk involved will talk in front of the group. Informing people in advance and using inviting terminology can increase the participants' feelings of safety in this situation.

Dyads or One-on-One Interaction. Dyads are ideal for opening up communication and building trust. They are also one of the safest methods for sharing information. Two individuals can share their ideas with each other without fear of negative responses from numerous people. Each person is concerned with the reactions of his or her partner only, and the partner is more likely to feel responsible for listening and giving positive feedback in this situation. As a result, this is a powerful way to short-circuit people's fear of speaking in front of a group. Dyads are particularly useful when the participants are strangers to one another and do not know the facilitator.

Triads. Although adding one individual to the dyad does not noticeably increase the number of individuals in the situation, it adds a radically new element. At any given moment, a triad is a dyad with an observer. The observer can take an anonymous or impersonal stance, as in the case of a participant who is monitoring people's communication patterns during a skill-building activity. This stance immediately elicits the fear response from the speakers—which, in turn, leads the speakers to watch their words and guard their thinking lest they embarrass themselves. One way to manage this dynamic in skill-building sessions is to ask one participant (a) to identify a situation, (b) to observe the other two participants as they model how to implement a skill in that situation, and (c) then to practice the skill. This alternative puts the observer in the position of learner rather than evaluator.

Subgroups. The ideal size for a subgroup is four to six people. Often it is useful to combine two dyads or two triads into groups of four or six. The information gathered and the trust built in the dyad or triad situation can then be transferred to the subgroup. Subgroups are ideal for generating ideas in brainstorming sessions. Also, when brainstorming is conducted appropriately—with the subgroup members generating ideas quickly and not commenting on their viability until later—the participants have a chance to build some confidence before they must assess one another's ideas. This method is useful for generating a large amount of information in a short time and for encouraging rapid learning.

Whole Groups. Sharing information or building skills in a large-group setting is generally difficult. Although the typical reporter method of bringing small-group information back to the whole group can be helpful, some alternatives are possible. The facilitator can build up group trust by being careful never to punish or penalize individuals who make risky statements or ask questions that show a lack of knowledge. The facilitator can develop a climate and group rules that allow participants to experience success in taking risks and to feel confident in their contributions to the total group.

Generally, leaders of large groups have acquired a great deal of experience, which is—after all—part of the reason they are the leaders. However, experienced leaders sometimes forget that not everyone shares their confidence about contributing in a large-group situation. Leaders and facilitators of large groups need to remind themselves periodically that public speaking is a common fear. They must function as the architects of trust, openness, and learning—not merely as conveyors of information.

Good tactics in the large-group situation include the following:

1. Complimenting the questions and praising the input of others.
2. Paraphrasing questions to prove that they have merit.
3. Presenting a point of view and then asking for feedback. For example, the leader might say, "This is my current opinion, and I would very much like the members of this group to respond to this, so we can see if I have missed something." Although this tactic requires a great deal of security on the part of the leader, great leaders have the confidence to make themselves vulnerable.
4. Adding new meaning to a question, tactfully but openly. For example, a question may grasp only half of a situation; the leader can answer the question directly and then go on to provide additional information that conveys to the group how important the question was.

In planning group activities, the facilitator or the program designer should consider the level of trust among the participants as well as the level of trust between the facilitator and the participants. If the total group size cannot be altered to fit the situation, then smaller groupings (dyads, subgroups, and so on) should be woven into the training design.

Patrick Leone, Ph.D., *is the manager of management development for Field Human Resources of IDS Financial Services, Minneapolis, Minnesota. He develops individual programs for high-potential sales managers. Out of these programs, which focus on communication, training, management, and sales issues, have come powerful methods that have improved the IDS sales organization. Dr. Leone works primarily on ways to make the workplace highly productive as well as responsive to worker needs.*

DEVELOPING SUCCESSFUL JOB AIDS

Allison Rossett and Jeannette Gautier-Downes

WHAT IS A JOB AID?

The human memory is not infallible, and everyone relies on "memory joggers" such as lists, calendars, directories, and instruction sheets in their professional and personal lives. The primary function of such memory joggers is to supply information that is essential for accomplishing a task but that does not need to be memorized in order to complete the task successfully.

In organizations, "memory joggers" are known as *job aids* and have evolved into much more sophisticated forms with a wide range of uses. As defined by human resource development (HRD) professionals, a job aid is a *repository for information, processes, or perspectives that is external to the individual and that supports work and activity by directing, guiding, and enlightening performance.* Job aids enable people to plan, to execute, and to evaluate work; they give specific, ordered instructions to workers in situations in which an error would be catastrophic; and they enhance enthusiasm and confidence as resources for necessary information and guidance.

As guides, job aids provide steps, illustrations, and examples that keep performance on track. For example, creating a new voice message for a telephone answering machine is an occasional activity for many people; the steps are familiar but are not committed to memory. In this case, an illustrated document guides the user through the steps. Job aids are found on shelves above employees' desks, on walls beside equipment and chemicals, in drawers beneath computer keyboards, and underneath telephones. Because job aids are separate and can be relied on when the need arises, the individual is not forced to rely on memory.

Job aids also support the more informal parts of people's lives. Cookbooks, shopping lists, to-do lists, personal calendars, planners, and address books all enable people to meet mundane and personal needs without committing information and details to memory.

Not everything connected with a job is a job aid. For example, tools are not job aids and instruction is not a job aid. Tools, like screwdrivers and office chairs, often are confused with job aids because they support people in their work. However, there is an important distinction between tools and job aids: Tools are used by people in performing jobs; job aids are repositories for information.

For a comprehensive guide to job aids, see *A Handbook of Job Aids,* by Allison Rossett and Jeannette Gautier-Downes, 1991, San Diego, CA: Pfeiffer & Company. Copyright © 1991 by Pfeiffer & Company.

Bookmarks, pencils, tractors, hard hats, and file cabinets are tools; user documentation, safety signs, and procedure lists are job aids.

JOB AIDS AND HRD TRAINING

Job aids contribute to the HRD function in the following ways:

Promoting Clarity. Before employing job aids, key questions should be asked: What do employees need to know? In detail, what skills, knowledge, and perspectives are essential? What goals and objectives must be achieved? What information or action makes a difference? What policies, procedures, or approaches are essential? Effective job aids cannot be written for undefined content, intangible goals, or murky procedures.

Reducing the Length of Training. Job aids reduce the time needed for training—in a way. If the content and objectives are held stable—that is, if no more skills, knowledge, or perspectives are added—then training time can be reduced through job aids. However, as the nature of work expands, training is expected to have more impact on the individual in the same period of time. This is where job aids can help. Research findings support the contention that training can be reduced when job aids supplant or supplement instructor-led training.

Improving the Quality of Training. Time within a training session that is devoted to introducing and coaching people on the use of job aids is likely to be perceived as relevant to actual work, both by the employees and by their supervisors. During a classroom practice exercise, for instance, if salespeople are asked to use reference manuals to check product and peripheral compatibilities, they are likely to perceive the training to be very much like the kind of challenges they confront when selling.

Helping with the Transfer of Training. Job aids help employees to transfer their skills from the classroom to the work site. For example, in a fast-food restaurant, employee familiarity with and reliance on job aids are included as part of a manager's presentation on the use of a new machine that prepares French fries. Then the same job aids accompany the employees back to the kitchen and to the demands of French-fry cutting and cooking. Increasing the common elements between the classroom and the job increases the likelihood of skill transfer and improves work performance.

Easing the Transfer of Personnel. Based on his research, Duncan (1985) reports that maintenance personnel who have been trained with job aids transfer more effectively from one type of operation to another.

Simplifying the Revision of Training. Although it is not easy to retrieve and revise existing job aids, this approach is much easier than altering the skills and knowledge that reside in the mind of each employee. In addition, revisions are made easier by the increasing reliance on computers in organizations. With a few keystrokes, people can bring job aids up-to-date and then disseminate the information electronically.

Expanding the Roles for Training and Development Practitioners. Many people believe that the job of an HRD practitioner is to provide whatever an organization requests. Too often this belief has resulted in an attempt to use training for challenges that training cannot solve. The planning, development, and use of job aids has the potential to contribute to an expanded perception of the following aspects of HRD:

1. That HRD is based on needs assessment, a systematic inquiry process that analyzes learners, jobs, and subject matter prior to recommending or implementing appropriate solutions.
2. That different kinds of problems and challenges should be addressed by different solutions. Figure 1 makes this point by pairing problems and interventions.

KINDS OF PROBLEMS	KINDS OF INTERVENTIONS
Lack of skills/knowledge	Training Job aids Coaching and mentoring
Flawed incentives	New policies New contracts Training for supervisors
Flawed environment	Work redesign New and better tools Better matches between jobs and people
Lack of motivation	Information about benefits Testimonials regarding value Training to build confidence

Figure 1. Matching Problems with Interventions

3. That solutions usually are multifaceted; involve whole systems; and include potential changes in job descriptions, tools, job aids, training, and incentives.

STEPS FOR DEVELOPING JOB AIDS

The job-aid development process includes the following six steps:

1. Clarify the problem to be solved by the job aid.
2. Choose the format and medium.
3. Prepare a draft of the job aid.

4. Pilot the job aid.
5. Make revisions to the job aid.
6. Manage the job aid.

As stated previously, training—and job aids—are not panaceas for every organizational ill. These steps assume that a job aid has already been determined to be the appropriate solution to the problem. Descriptions and illustrations of the preceding six steps follow.

Step One: Clarify the Problem to be Solved by the Job Aid

As is the case with any training, the first step in developing a job aid is to identify and focus on the problem to be solved. Data collection for job-aid development should follow the natural and usually chronological progression of the job or task. Typically, the job-aid developer tries to determine the best way of approaching the job, the common errors or misjudgments made by users, and the kind and level of help needed by the user.

Information can be collected in three ways: through observations, through interviews, and through performance of the job or task by the developer of the job aid. When possible, all three methods of collecting information should be used. The emphasis and time spent on each type of data-collection technique will depend on the job, task, or mental process involved. Observations should be emphasized when the job or task is observable; interviews should be emphasized when the job or task relies on mental processes such as decision making. Another useful technique is for the developer to actually do the job.

After the plan for gathering information has been developed, the observer or interviewer contacts the manager or supervisor of the people who will be observed or interviewed. This is important to ensure access to the job performers.

Observations. Job observations usually include two phases. First, the job-aid developer reviews the information that supports the job or task. This information might include documentation, policy and procedure manuals, training manuals, and information about errors or customer complaints. This observation often is completed during the initial needs-assessment stage. The information found in these documents focuses observations at the job site.

The second phase of observation takes place at the job site. There the developer can see how the job is performed in the work environment by expert, typical, and novice performers. At this stage, the developer takes explicit notes and records deviations from the model's or expert's approach to the job.

Interviews. The interview provides an opportunity for the developer to build from observations and to delve more deeply into differences or similarities in performance and outcome. The interview is the developer's primary tool for collecting information about the process, for finding out what the performer is thinking and feeling, and for shedding light on decision making. Interviews, unlike observations, provide flexibility because there are opportunities for the interviewer to ask for clarification. Interviews also create a personal connection between the developer and the performer that might encourage use of the job aid once it is completed.

Interviews answer the following questions:

- What is the performer thinking about while performing the job or task?
- What kinds of information and details do performers need?
- Why did the performer do it that way? Why are others approaching the job differently?
- Might special circumstances arise to change the way that the job or task is performed or approached?
- Are there steps or stages that are particularly difficult or often forgotten?
- How would the performer feel about using a job aid?

When a job or task cannot be observed directly, a two-phase interview is useful. In the first phase, the developer asks general and open-ended questions to get an overview of the process and to determine differences between experts and novices; the performer responds spontaneously. Some organizations assemble panels of experts for this stage of the process. These panels "quickly gather information, dispense information, and build affiliation" (Rossett, 1987, p. 176).

The second stage seeks more specific information and employs more directed questions. For example, during the first phase of interviews with people who write for non-English speakers, the interviewer might have learned that "When finished writing a document for non-English speakers, I always review the document to make sure that I have used simple sentences." The developer might follow up in the second interview with questions such as "What do you consider to be a simple sentence? How many words does it have? How long are the words? Are there any exceptions?" The answers to both phases of questions have obvious implications for the job aid.

Performance of the Job. When the job-aid developer actually performs the job, he or she gains a deeper understanding of the data gathered in the interviews and observations. The developer can use personal trials to identify tricky or confusing steps or processes. This step is especially useful when developing job aids for novice users because, in many ways, the developer is a novice. Personal performance reveals some of the same problems that novices will encounter. Of course, in certain cases, personal trials are impossible because the job is dangerous or because it requires special skills. In these cases, the developer must rely more heavily on observations and interviews.

After collecting data from observations, interviews, and from performing the job, the developer uses the characteristics of the job to create the job aid. Because the job aid needs to follow the logical order of the job, the developer watches the process or procedure from start to finish as the job is performed in the work environment, always asking the performer about what he or she does or is thinking about in order to perform the job. This process transforms debates over philosophies and theories into data about what to do, what to consider, and how to accomplish the task.

Before: What Does the Performer Need to Know, Do, or Have In Order to Do the Job or Task? At this point, the developer identifies the prerequisites for doing the job. Because job aids are about performance, it is best to start by watching a worker prepare to do the job. The developer must consider the following: Is everything established prior to the performance? Is location important? For example, does the user need to do the job on a flat surface or in a cool or quiet place? The developer looks for similarities and differences in the ways that novices and experts prepare. He or she lists or describes the preparation process and notes the names of any tools used and perhaps jots brief descriptions or sketches of these tools. Should the preparation stage be included as part of the job aid or should it be supported by an additional job aid, by training, or by a presentation from a supervisor?

During: What Is the Typical Method? Are There Special Circumstances or Safety Considerations? The developer determines how the person actually performs the job or task. He or she considers the following: What are the major steps or skills needed to perform the job? How is the job usually accomplished? The developer asks the performer to do what he or she would usually do if no one were observing and notes every observable action in detail. During the observation or just after it, the developer asks the performer about what he or she is thinking. How does the performer approach the problem? How does he or she proceed to solve the problem? What do they do or think about and in what order? Does every performer follow the same order? Does it matter? Do certain circumstances dictate that the performer must follow different steps? Might a condition arise to warrant developing a supporting job aid, such as a job aid for "saving information to a disk"? What if the inserted disk is full? How is that handled? How is another disk inserted? What if the user lacks another formatted disk?

After: What Must the User Do After Completing the Job or Task? What does the performer do once the widget is assembled or the program is debugged or the performance appraisal is completed? Are there any special precautions or reminders? These endnotes or final steps are especially useful for novice users who may not understand the entire process or who may be more likely to fumble a particular step and therefore need to recheck their work more carefully.

For more detailed information on needs assessment, the reader is referred to *Training Needs Assessment* (Rossett, 1987).

Step Two: Choose the Format and Medium

The job or task is the key to choosing a format. The following seven formats for job aids are possible:

1. *Steps.* The step format presents information, directions, and activities in sequence. This format is appropriate when the job-aid developer wants to ensure a flow of actions, in a particular order, for a narrowly defined purpose.

2. *Work Sheets.* The work-sheet format is also characterized by steps that must be performed in sequence. In addition, work sheets require the user to participate

in substantive written responses, usually in the form of calculations. The main purpose of the work sheet is to generate the result of the calculations.

3. *Arrays.* Arrays present bodies of information with meaningful organization and structure. This format allows the user to access large bodies of data, generally to support the completion of a larger job or task. The user of an array-type job aid is attempting to answer one of three questions: who, what, or where.

4. *Decision Tables.* Decision tables represent "if-then" situations. This format allows the user to identify solutions for given problems based on the conditions of the situation. The decision table is used when the problem includes several conditions that influence the selection of the correct answer or action.

5. *Flow Charts.* The flow-chart format is a sequence of questions that can be answered with "yes" or "no." When the user answers "yes" or "no," an appropriate path to the next decision is indicated. The performer follows the question path until enough information is gathered to reach a conclusive end.

6. *Checklists.* Like most job aids, the checklist format enables the user not to rely on memory. This format is distinct, however, in that its main purpose is to prompt the user to think about a job or task in a certain way. Checklist job aids are often used to list critical information that the user must consider or verify before, during, or after performing a job or task.

7. *Combinations.* The formats mentioned previously may be combined. For example, an operating-room attendant needs to follow a strict series of steps for preparing the operating room for a particular procedure that is performed infrequently. One of the steps on the list might be "Check that all surgical instruments are on the surgeon's tray." If many instruments are required, the job aid might include a separate checklist for ensuring that each instrument has been accounted for.

Other important considerations include the following: Who will be using the job aid? What is the working environment? What resources are available?

Who Will Be Using the Job Aid?

How Experienced Are the Users? Job aids developed for novice performers or frequently changing users often require more detail.

How Well Can the Users Read or Understand English? Statistics show that nearly 25 percent of all English-speaking adults are functionally illiterate. Therefore, it may be beneficial to augment the job aid with graphics, audiotapes, or videotapes.

With What Kind of Documentation Is the User Familiar? When documentation is commonplace for a job, use a familiar format. For example, computer programmers often use flow charts to depict the development of a program. Therefore, given the choice of a decision-table or a flow-chart job aid, the developer would choose a flow chart. A job aid should blend into the work environment; the user should not be forced to struggle with an unfamiliar format.

Does the User Want to Perform? A job aid is not an appropriate tool for erasing employee resistance, because the employee probably will not use it.

What Is the Working Environment?

Where Will the Job Aid Be Used? Whether the user will be fixing a sink, working in the dark, or at a computer terminal will influence the developer's choice of job aid. Information about the environment in which the job aid will be used helps to determine the best medium.

What Job-Aid Development Resources Are Available?

Who Will Help to Create the Job Aid? When planning a job aid, the developer needs to recruit people with appropriate expertise for the effort. Job-aid development might require a team consisting of the following:

- Instructional designers, training specialists, or human resource development professionals;
- Graphic artists;
- Subject-matter experts; and
- Computer programmers for on-line job aids.

How Much Time Is Available? Sometimes a job aid is needed to solve an immediate problem; in this case, a "quick-and-dirty" job aid may be appropriate. This kind of job aid solves the problem at hand and often is redeveloped when time allows.

How Much Money Has Been Allocated to the Development Process? Job aids are less expensive than training. Harless (1988) suggests that job aids are three to four times less expensive than training. He notes that the real savings happen because workers remain at the site and are productive, as opposed to training sessions, during which workers are absent and nonproductive. When the costs of sending people to training sessions—travel, fees, meals, and so on—are combined, the impact of job aids on the bottom line is striking.

Choose the Format

The work completed thus far should provide a clear picture of the job or task. The following steps are used to determine the format:

1. Decide what part of the task or job is being supported by the job aid.
2. Consider the data about the user's background, level of experience, and previous experience with documentation.
3. Use Figure 2 (on the next page) to determine which format or combination of formats is best.

Choose the Medium

Cost is a factor when choosing a medium. For example, an on-line job aid is much more expensive than a printed one. The medium is determined after the format,

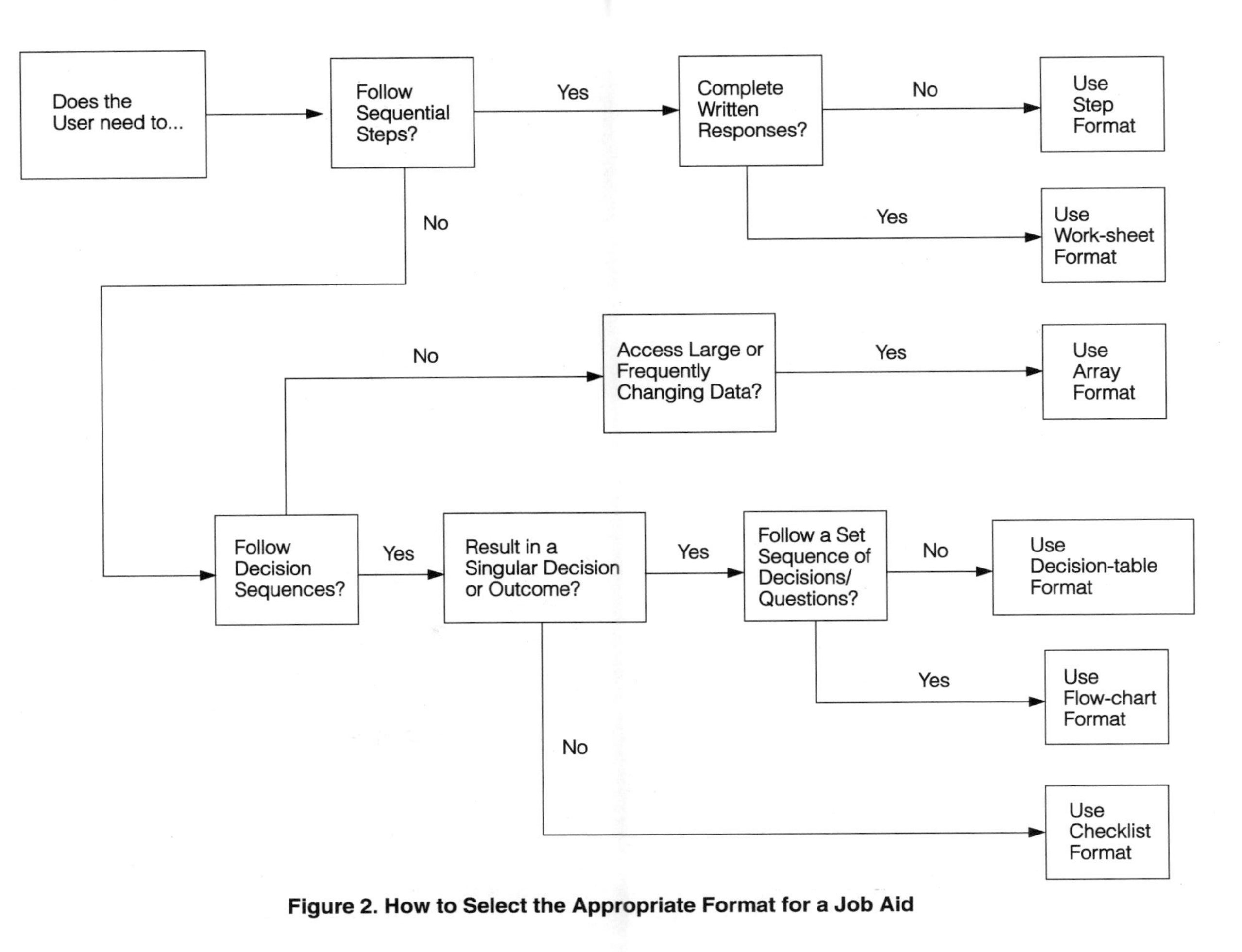

Figure 2. How to Select the Appropriate Format for a Job Aid

the working environment, and any budgetary constraints have been considered. Figure 3 serves as a guide for choosing a medium.

	Print-Poster	Extended Print	On-Line	Audio	Video
Step Format	Yes	Yes	Yes	Yes	Yes
Work-Sheet Format	No	Yes	Yes	No	No
Array Format	Yes	Yes	Yes	Yes	No
Decision-Table Format	Yes	Yes	Yes	Yes	No
Flow-Chart Format	Yes	Yes	Yes	Yes	No
Checklist Format	Yes	Yes	Yes	Yes	No

Figure 3. The Match Between Job-Aid Formats and Media

Step Three: Prepare a Draft of the Job Aid

The development team needs to be called together. When the team consists only of a designer and a subject-matter expert, this time is used to organize information. If the team is larger, the initial session is used to explain the process of drafting a job aid, including explanations of how the format and medium were chosen and the role that each person will play. It may also be useful to mention budget and time constraints.

The information collected in step one is used to break each major task into smaller subordinate steps or skills. As an example, one step in completing an automobile tune-up is to replace the spark plugs. By observing a mechanic performing a tune-up, the developer witnessed the procedure for removing spark plugs. Through interviews, the developer learned that one of the subordinate steps for replacing spark plugs is to choose the appropriate replacement spark plug. The interviewer also learned that the novice performer might be unsure about which spark plug to use because the code numbers differ from brand to brand. Therefore, for the step "Replace spark plugs," the developer must include a decision-table job aid to ensure that the novice chooses the correct spark plug every time. This also might require meeting with a subject-matter expert to determine considerations for the decision table. By breaking the job into small steps and substeps, the developer provides prompts when the user needs them.

The developer of a job aid usually begins by listing the steps or information the user needs in order to complete the task. If order is important, the developer puts the steps in the correct order. Then, if the process is a decision sequence, the developer lists all possible conditions and the appropriate responses. After listing all of the routine steps, the developer identifies circumstances in which special circumstances might arise, making an effort to account for every possible situation that the user might encounter while doing the job or task.

Zagorski (1987) suggests that the developer should include with the job aid a list of steps or information that the user will need immediately after having completed the job or task. For example, a final note on a job aid for preparing bulk-mail packages might read, "You are now ready to bring your mail to the 'Bulk Mail' Department of the Central Post Office." This step is not actually a part of the preparation of bulk-mail packages, but it is a crucial part of the overall process. Other needed "post-information" may be drawn from common errors. For example, every step of the U.S. Federal Income Tax work sheet is supported by a thorough explanation; however, a final job aid is printed on the return envelope that reads, "Sign the return? Organize your schedules and forms in proper order? Use your pre-printed label? Keep a copy for your records?" These crucial last steps are often overlooked. Sometimes a single statement will suffice. At other times, a developer may choose a supplemental job aid, based on what he or she knows about the users.

In the last part of the process, the developer creates a rough draft of the primary job aid, using the chosen format. Statements should be drafted and redrafted to eliminate extra words, to combine ideas that belong together, and to eliminate ideas that are ambiguous. This draft is crucial because it provides the infrastructure for the job aid. The statements must be as clean and pithy as possible. Before giving the job aid to a graphic artist, the developer should ask a subject-matter expert to review it for accuracy.

Specific Rules for Job-Aid Development

Step Job Aids. The step format is used for jobs that require the user to follow steps in sequence; that sequence must be clear. The steps are numbered or lettered, with each step representing only one process or procedure.

Work-Sheet Job Aids. The work-sheet format also requires the user to follow steps in sequence. Again, that sequence must be clear, with each step of the calculation numbered or lettered. The user should be able to separate the work sheet easily from the documentation that supports it. It is cumbersome to require the user to turn back and forth between instructions and the work sheet.

Array Job Aids. The array format is used for jobs that require the user to refer to bodies of information. The data need to be organized in a logical format with obvious meaning, either based on their nature or on the structure of demands that users will place on the data. Because the array format is often used for data that change frequently, the user needs to know the specific version of data that the job aid fits. For example, computer software manufacturers distribute mats that fit over computer keyboards and correspond to function keys. In order for the job aid to be effective, the user needs to know which version of software the mat accompanies.

Decision-Table Job Aids. Decision tables are developed by working backward. After deciding where the user will finish, the job-aid developer identifies the factors that lead the user to that point. First, this process involves listing all possible solutions or responses to *if* statements; the responses are *then* statements. Second, the conditions or chain of factors that lead to solutions or responses need to be determined. Third, the number of columns needed can be determined by adding the categories of possible conditions and responses or by adding the *if, and,* and *then* statements.

For example, in Figure 4, the conditions from which the personnel clerk will determine which benefits brochure to provide are the following:

1. If the Department is...
2. And the Employee is hourly,
3. Then provide brochure number....

In this case, the table must contain three columns.

Department	Hourly Employee	Benefits Brochure No.
Maintenance	Yes	123
	No	50
Housekeeping	Yes	136
	No	52
Food Service	Yes	148
	No	53
Sales	Yes	152
	No	54

Figure 4. Decision-Table Job Aid for Choosing a Benefits Brochure

Fourth, the conditions are listed in the order that they probably will occur on the job. In the preceding example, the personnel clerk gets clues about the employee's department from his or her uniform. Because the personnel clerk sees the employee's uniform first, this condition is first. The personnel clerk then must ask the employee whether he or she is hourly or salaried. Therefore, this condition is presented second.

Fifth, the job-aid developer must ensure that each decision sequence leads to only one possible answer. If a decision sequence has more than one possible answer, a checklist format should be used. Finally, it is important to keep in mind that column headers are best written as open-ended statements or questions.

Flow Charts. The process for drafting a flow chart is similar to the process for drafting a decision table. The job-aid developer lists all possible solutions or responses; these statements define the end of the sequence. For example, Figure 5 (page 201) leads the user to one of two possible solutions: "Rent a House or Apartment" or "Buy a House."

A series of binary (true/false or yes/no) questions are devised that lead to each of the possible solutions or responses. In Figure 5, the following questions were used: Do you want to own a house? Are there affordable houses in the area in which you wish to live? Do you have the "up-front" money (down payment, closing costs, and so on)? Do you plan to stay in the area for at least one year?

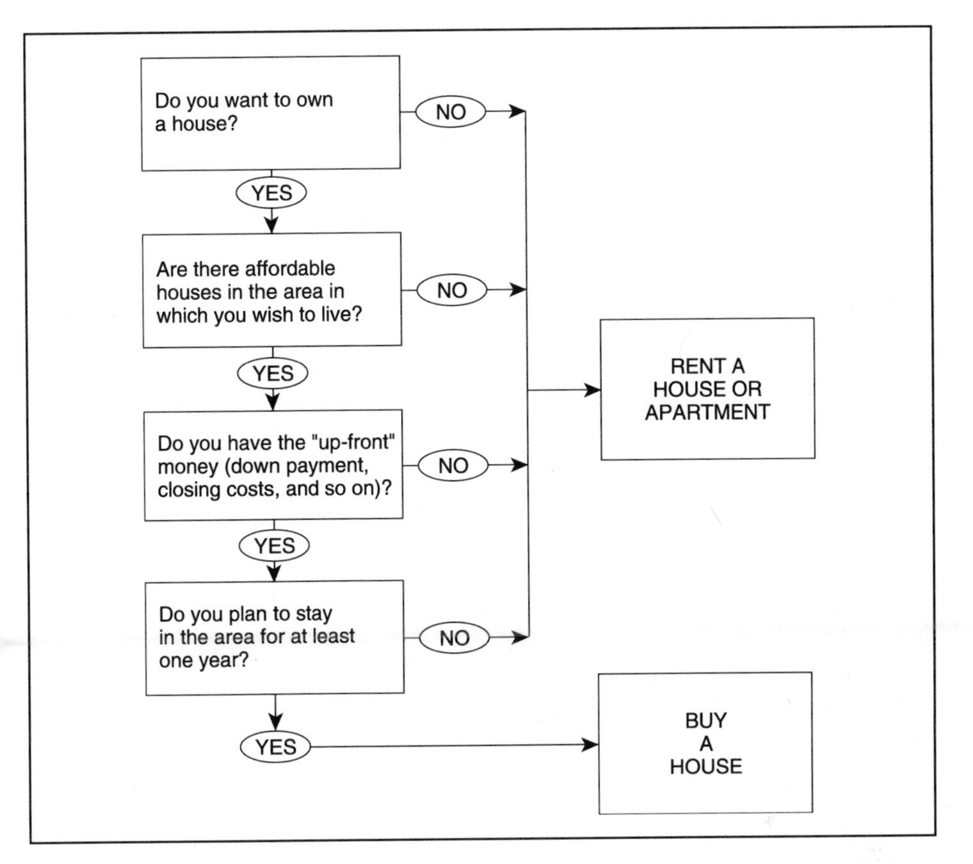

Figure 5. Flow-Chart Job Aid for Choosing to Buy or Rent a House or Apartment

Next, a diagram is drawn that represents the progression of statements leading to the end response. The flow chart will look more ordered when the lines are horizontal and vertical, not diagonal (Harless, 1988).

Checklists. The job-aid developer lists the conditions or structures the questions in the order in which the user should consider them; if there is some clear progression of information, it is used to structure the job aid. The checklist must provide enough information to guide the user to the appropriate solution. When appropriate, the range of possible answers or responses is described. Checklists do not always lead to a single response but may lead to a range of responses. If this range is defined, it should be included. For example, a book on proper nutrition during pregnancy provides categories of foods that must be represented in a woman's diet. These categories include proteins, calcium-rich foods, and so on. If a dietician were using this book, this list would suffice. The average user, however, would need examples of the foods within these categories.

Step Four: Pilot the Job Aid

Pilot testing is the process whereby the developer tries out the job aid with "real-world" end users. The developer must keep in mind that if the job aid is confusing, unclear, or inaccessible, it will not be used.

First, the developer must choose a test group that is representative of end users. The group should represent the full range of performers. In the pilot test, the developer implements the job aid as if it were being released in final form. If the job aid will be taped to an instrument panel or chained to the side of a conveyor belt, the job aid should be pilot tested there. The developer should ask employees to use the job aid to perform the task, observe their performance, and interview them about the performance and outcomes.

The checklist shown in Figure 6 can help the developer to identify any problems with the job aid.

Step Five: Make Revisions to the Job Aid

The developer should use the information collected in step four to develop the final version of the job aid. After all revisions have been implemented, a final sign-off from subject-matter experts and management should be obtained, and the master copy of the job aid should be developed. The job aid then can be reproduced and packaged for the kind of distribution that has been selected to support it.

Step Six: Manage the Job Aid

To be successful, a job aid must be managed and carefully integrated into the work environment. The first task in managing a job aid is to develop strategies to increase the chances that the job aid will be used, both initially and over time.

The fast-changing environments that make job aids desirable also threaten their usefulness over time. Job aids swiftly lose credibility if they fail to keep up with the challenges and tools that they must support. Job-aid management must institutionalize ways for a job aid to change as people and their work environments change.

People. As the work force changes, does the job aid continue to meet the new work-force needs? Are orientation, training, and coaching systems in place to help new employees to use the job aid successfully?

Work Environment. Who is responsible for introducing the initial job aid? When a new product or procedure is adopted, are revisions to job aids automatic and mandatory? How will the organization keep track of all the job aids already in existence? Is there a budget for revisions? These issues suggest the need for a systematic approach to the management of job aids and their revisions.

The Job Aid. Job aids should clearly indicate the date of the latest revision. Snow and Newby (1989) stress the importance of making the job aid accessible to all employees when they need it. Supply more than enough job aids for everyemployee or work station. If a user must rely on many job aids, each job aid must be discernible from the others.

Ask the user:

1. Do you have any questions?
2. Were you unsure at any time?
3. Were there steps that were harder to follow than others?
4. Was the job aid difficult to use at your work station?
5. Were the instructions clear?
6. Were the steps ordered correctly?
7. Were there times when you needed more information?
8. Were there times when there was too much information?
9. Was the wording of the job aid clear?
10. Were the diagrams or graphs helpful?
11. Were there typographical errors?
12. Did a circumstance arise that was not covered in the job aid?
13. Should any special circumstances be covered in the job aid?
14. Will you use it again?
15. Do you wish that you and your colleagues had a copy of this job aid?

Figure 6. Pilot Testing Job Aids

Revision System. A systematic approach to managing revision should address the following issues:

- Initiation. Who is responsible for initiating revisions? Are revisions initiated through periodic reviews or linked to changes in procedure and/or technology? Can managers request revisions easily?
- Implementation. Who implements revisions? Who collects outdated versions and introduces new versions?
- Administration. Who keeps track of existing job aids? Can the organization list the units and positions that use a particular job aid? Does everyone understand the authority and responsibility structure surrounding job aids? Is there a budget for job-aid revision?
- Incentives. Who receives recognition when job aids are successful? Who is acknowledged for their proper introduction, maintenance, and revision?

JOB AIDS AND ORGANIZATIONAL TRENDS

A variety of forces are influencing present and future job aids, including organizational shifts, demographic shifts, cost pressures, integrated work and performance systems, emphasis on performance and accomplishment, and computer technologies.

Organizational Shifts. As organizations become more customer and market responsive, service and promptness become critical to their success. Job aids, especially automated informational and coaching aids, will enable organizations to meet customer demands. Likewise, organizations are emphasizing quality, which requires a wider dissemination of information throughout the organization. Job aids will be major players in this expanding access to information. Finally, organizations are becoming flatter, with fewer middle managers to ensure productivity. As surrogates for supervisors' experience and expertise, job aids can be used to prompt and guide employees and to enlighten their performance.

Demographic Shifts. The work force is becoming increasingly female, minority, limited in English proficiency, and elderly. Futurists express concern about weak skills—especially in science and math—and inadequate English proficiency. Organizations increasingly are pressured to solve the problems that public schools and government agencies have failed to address; unfortunately, they probably will not do so. Instead, organizations probably will rely more and more heavily on job aids, which can provide information, specify detailed procedures, and coach performance within the work context and at prices perceived as affordable.

Cost Pressures. Most organizations see "cost," not "return on investment," when they examine training and development. Job aids, with their ability to diminish costs and to provide ongoing support for people on the job, will be assigned expanded roles.

Integrated Work and Performance Systems. The traditional role of training often is perceived as distinct from the world of work. However, in the future, the distinctions among systems, training, and documentation and the distinctions between work and training will blur. Training and development concepts, along with job aids, are expected to insinuate themselves earlier, continually, and seamlessly into the flow of work and the systems that support it.

Emphasis on Performance and Accomplishment. The orientation of human resources inevitably must shift to focus on the organizational goal and on helping employees to contribute to that goal. This new perspective will lead to an increased reliance on job aids.

Computer Technologies. Computer technology is now readily accessible to the instructional designer and to the human resources manager. It is impossible to overestimate the impact that decreased prices, increased speed, enhanced memory, and friendlier and more accessible systems will have on the future of job aids.

Clearly, job aids will become more and more important to organizations over the coming years. HRD professionals who become job-aid development and usage experts will better meet the needs of organizations and of the people who rely on job aids to do their work.

REFERENCES

Duncan, C.S. (1985). Job aids really can work: A study of the military applications of job aid technology. *Performance and Instruction, 24*(4), 1-4.

Harless, J.H. (1988). *Job aids workshop.* Paper presented at Job Aids Workshop by Harless Guild and Associates, Atlanta, GA.

Rossett, A. (1987). *Training needs assessment.* Englewood Cliffs, NJ: Educational Technology Publications.

Snow, N., & Newby, T. (1989). Ergonomically designed job aids. *Performance and Instruction, 28*(3), 26-30.

Zagorski, S. (1987). How I created the award-winning job aid. *Performance and Instruction, 26*(4), 29-32.

***Allison Rossett, Ed.D.**, is a professor of educational technology at San Diego State University in San Diego, California. She also serves as a consultant to corporations, agencies, and school systems in needs analysis and program design, professional development, and instructional technologies. Dr. Rossett is co-author of* A Handbook of Job Aids, *published by Pfeiffer & Company in 1991.*

***Jeannette Gautier-Downes** is a performance technologist based in Santa Barbara, California. She consults with a wide variety of organizations on performance problems, training systems, and standards. Her special interests include the evaluation of training and non-training solutions in corporate settings. Ms. Gautier-Downes is co-author of* A Handbook of Job Aids, *published by Pfeiffer & Company in 1991.*

CAREER PLANNING AND THE FALLACY OF THE FUTURE

Patrick Doyle and Jerry Zabel

When people talk about the future, they frequently fail to realize that what they are discussing is already upon them. As they consider the future, they may find that career planning is one of the most important elements in their lives. Nevertheless, they frequently postpone the planning until it is too late to create their own futures (see Ford & Lippitt, 1988). Toffler (1970) cautioned that the information age had begun its exponential growth cycle. Those who choose—through ignorance or disbelief—to disregard the warning in relation to their careers are at a serious disadvantage. About a decade later *Megatrends* (Naisbitt, 1982) provided a number of predictions that have important implications for career planning.

This paper considers the implications that the organization of the future has on today's plans for a career, and it relates them to the human resource development (HRD) professional's own career planning and to career counseling.

PREDICTIONS AND IMPLICATIONS

The following predictions are based on Naisbitt's *Megatrends*, and their career-planning implications for the HRD professional are presented.

Prediction 1: Industrial society is transforming itself into a society whose most valuable commodity would be information.

Career-Plan Implications

The job search in the industries to which we have historically turned may not be as beneficial as job searches in the new industries. In 1988 more was being produced by the same number of workers as in 1968 (Toffler, 1990), and the manufacturing sector of the economy is quickly declining in terms of the percent of total employment it provides.

Already there are organizations devoted entirely to supplying and interpreting information. For example, organizations such as Dialog and Compuserve are serving as sources of employment. Although many government agencies may decline in size, services that provide information (such as U.S. Bureau of the Census or Statistics Canada) can be expected to continue to grow. One organization in the private sector earns its income from tracking information on members of both houses of the U.S. Congress. This information relates strictly to how the members voted on specific issues and to public statements they made about various issues. The organization's customers are the Fortune 500 companies. We can expect the same trend in countries throughout the world.

The mission of some organizations is to track the advertising of their clients' competitors. They supply the information on trends in advertising but do not design advertising nor deal with it in any other way. These wave-of-the-future organizations do not require a great many *high-tech* people. The technology is centralized in the organization, and most of the jobs require only low or medium technological knowledge.

As the move continues toward providing information, career planning would be unrealistic if it did not consider this trend.

Prediction 2: Forced technology (for example, assembly-line regimentation) is giving way to high technology (robot production and computers) combined with high touch (because high technology would be rejected without active human interaction).

Career-Plan Implications

One of the great myths of the computer age is that technology will eliminate human interaction. Nothing could be further from the truth. The amount of human interaction may increase as technology allows us to interact over greater distances with more people. For example, the technology of the citizens-band radio enhanced communication between travelers instead of reducing it. Today's modems and computers should be seen as having the same potential to open up communications. Some HRD professionals will find that even though they are communicating less frequently face-to-face, opportunities to communicate with greater numbers and more diverse groups of people are continuing to increase.

The message here is clear: If human interaction is important to people, they should not dismiss high-technology organizations as being an unsuitable career choice.

Another myth is that high-tech organizations demand a significant degree of new skills not widely distributed in the general population. If there is any truth in that statement, the reason is that people have failed to develop the skills—not that the skills are difficult to acquire. Many people who think they are not capable of using computers do not realize that they in fact use computers every day—when they drive automobiles or use an automated teller.

Not everybody, of course, wants to be a programmer. That is the reason computers are being produced that require less and less expertise on the part of the operator. Software companies that are dedicated to making their packages more user friendly are flourishing. Therefore, the requirement to use a computer should not discourage a person from seeking a career that he or she really wants.

Prediction 3: National economies will have to adapt and compete in the world economy. The question is not *if* there will be free trade globally, but *when*.

Career-Plan Implications

In the Western Hemisphere, Canada and the United States already have an agreement, and very soon they will be joined by Mexico. South America will not be left out for very long. In 1992, Europe will have a true common market.

Consider companies that are competitive in the North American market for long-term careers. Having a competitive advantage in this case could be brought about by having a product that is protected by patent laws, innovative marketing techniques, or production advantages.

As the barriers between countries melt away, no one should disregard a career solely because it would take the employee outside his or her own homeland. However, training in foreign languages and diverse cultures must be considered for these types of careers.

Prediction 4: In comparing the short-term strategies of North America with the long-term strategies of Japan, it may appear that the long-term strategies have won.

Career-Plan Implications

Although long-term strategies are directed at the success of the organization, they are not necessarily related to the concept of "lifetime" employment (Ouchi, 1982). This topic can be misleading for the person planning a career. Although companies consider long-term strategies, in the future the average term of employment will decrease. The college graduate in the United States can expect to stay with one company for about six years. The two major reasons for change are (1) there are no opportunities for promotion, so the employee decides to leave, and (2) the companies focus on fast movers.

The day a person finds a new job or receives a new appointment is the day he or she updates his or her career-path plan and initiates the next series of activities to ensure its success.

Prediction 5: We are moving from a *centralized* concept of work, whereby employees report to a main location each day, to a *decentralized* concept in which employees may be working from their homes or remote offices and reporting to headquarters infrequently.

Career-Plan Implications

Major manufacturers not only cannot afford to design large office buildings so that each salesperson has an office, but they have also found that such offices entice salespeople to spend too much time in the offices and not enough with their customers. Given today's technology, there is little justification for the salesperson's office. With a computer and a modem, the salesperson can work from his or her own home.

Given this trend, people should emphasize areas in their career-path plans where they have demonstrated self-starting and self-discipline capabilities. Being able to work successfully in an independent environment is going to become more and more important, and training will be necessary to teach employees *how* to do their work at home.

Prediction 6: We are turning from institutional help to self-help programs.

Career-Plan Implications

This prediction is already being fulfilled inasmuch as major tax burdens are being shifted down to the municipal level. The concept is that if local communities want services (such as hospitals), let them raise the taxes to pay for them. Further extension of that philosophy will work its way down until it reaches the level of the individual. This has major implications for HRD programs.

Prediction 7: Representative democracies are beginning to shift to participatory democracies.

Career-Plan Implications

At all levels people are demanding a voice in the decisions that they perceive as affecting them. Technology through various means is enabling these voices to be heard. Unfortunately, while the technology enables people to participate more fully in the democracy, the "technocrats" that facilitate the running of the democracy are still trying to cope with obsolete approaches to the new demands (Toffler, 1984). Nevertheless, the future-oriented person—whether manager or subordinate—will expect participative management to be a part of his or her job.

Prediction 8: We are shifting from hierarchies to networking. Pyramid structures are being slowly dismantled for flatter, broader organizations.

Career-Plan Implications

Fewer intermediate levels of organizational structure will exist. In marketing we must announce the death of the position of sales manager. Sales personnel will be classified into sales technical support or account executives. The account executives (formerly sales representatives) will have a much broader range of responsibilities and will be part of the strategy to distribute the responsibilities of the sales manager and thus eliminate that position.

In creating career plans, focusing solely on the hierarchy of the organization may result in disappointment and frustration. The strategies of job enrichment or job expansion should be considered.

Prediction 9: Populations are shifting in the United States, and the great north-east control of the economy is giving way to the southwest.

Career-Plan Implications

The old advice to go west, young man (or young woman) is appropriate today. Or even go south or, better yet, try southwest.

Prediction 10: The either/or (yes/no, win/lose) society is becoming a multiple-option society.

Career-Plan Implications

The new society reflects momentary truth and situational ethics. Careers in this society demand broad looks at every decision. Trainers will find an increasing demand for problem-solving skills.

FUTURE GROWTH OF INDUSTRIES

Studies quoted in the *Globe and Mail* ("Business Trends," 1990) support the general information available on the influences that will determine the future growth of various industries. Some of these influences are discussed below, because they are important considerations in planning a career path.

1. *Aging.* The graying of North America is a fact of life. Young entrants into business are not able to keep up with the combination of expansion of business and the rate of retirements. Although available positions are being eliminated, the gap still indicates that we need to increase our population of the young through immigration just to fill the available positions. This may seem like a ridiculous statement in times of recession, when the heavy burden of layoffs and reductions are being imposed on the younger members of the work force. However, recessions do not last forever, and the adjustments are primarily in the areas already predicted.

2. *Two-Income Families.* The growth of the two-income family is well-established. The two-income family requires a different economy from that of the classical family of the 1940s and 1950s. Many organizations are making employment more attractive for parents, and mothers can be expected to include a lifetime of employment in their career plans.

3. *Specialization.* Markets and social demands are becoming more specialized than they were in the 1950s and 1960s. Now we question the wisdom of advertising lawn mowers to apartment dwellers. *Niche* markets or *micromarkets* will also be directed toward the service industry.

As Naisbitt predicted that democracy would become more participative, more specialized groups are demanding attention to their individualized causes.

4. *Home Operations.* More businesses are operating from the home. Various businesses—from desktop publishing to specialized furniture making—can easily operate in homes.

5. *Global Competition.* Global competition is now a fact of life. Franchisers from around the world are welcome in one another's economic environments.

RECOMMENDATIONS TO ORGANIZATIONS

Futurist Frank Odgen stated that accounting firms that have "learned to walk on quicksand and dance on electrons will survive in the next decade" (Hamilton, 1990, p. 26). This section relates some of his recommendations for the accounting industry to organizations in general.

Smaller organizations will be able to react to changing conditions better than larger organizations will. An associated concept is that organizations that have a large number of clients—each supplying a small portion of business—is in a better position than a large organization that has fewer clients, each bringing in a significant amount of the business.

As the baby boomers push through the system, the competition for higher-level jobs will increase while there will not be enough applicants for the positions at the entrance level. Organizations need to look ahead and plan for this situation.

Many people are working in jobs today that will not exist in the near future; this situation has been referred to as *discontinuous futures* (Pfeiffer, Goodstein, & Nolan, 1989). In organizations with discontinuous futures, the HRD professional will be in great demand to help employees either to fit into new careers in the organization or to make plans for careers outside.

As the eventual demise of bureaucratic organizations takes place, entrepreneurial organizations will rise. The "paperless" society is still expected, and organizations must realize that global boundaries are transparent to the electronic world.

REFERENCES

Business trends give service sector hottest growth potential. (1990, March 13). *Globe and Mail* (Toronto Metro Ed.), pp. C-1, C-3.

Ford, G.A., & Lippitt, G.L. (1988). *Creating your future: A guide to personal goal setting.* San Diego, CA: Pfeiffer & Company.

Hamilton, M. (1990, June). Into the future. *CGA Magazine,* pp. 26-31.

Naisbitt, J. (1982). *Megatrends: Ten new directions transforming our lives.* New York: Warner.

Ouchi, W.G. (1982). *Theory Z: How American business can meet the Japanese challenge.* New York: Avon.

Pfeiffer, J.W., Goodstein, L.D., & Nolan, T.M. (1989). *Shaping strategic planning: Frogs, dragons, bees, and turkey tails.* San Diego, CA: Pfeiffer & Company.

Toffler, A. (1970). *Future shock.* New York: Random House.

Toffler, A. (1984). *The third wave.* New York: Bantam.

Toffler, A. (1990). *Power shift.* New York: Bantam.

***Patrick Doyle** is the principal of High Impact Training Services and a teaching master at St. Lawrence College in Kingston, Ontario, Canada. He is active in the field of human resource development in retail, public administration, and public-health organizations. Mr. Doyle's specialty is management techniques during periods of technological change.*

***Jerry Zabel** is an associate of High Impact Training Services and a professor in Information Processing at St. Lawrence College in Kingston, Ontario, Canada. Mr. Zabel's specialty is design, selection, and management of information systems for organizations.*

FROM CONTROLLING TO FACILITATING: HOW TO L.E.A.D.[1]

Fran Rees

Styles of leadership can be placed on a continuum, with a *controlling* style at one end and a *facilitating* style at the other. A team leader's position along this continuum is determined by how much he or she shares the responsibility for decision making with subordinates.

Traditionally, the role of a leader was to control his or her subordinates' tasks and actions. Leaders made decisions and communicated them to subordinates, who carried them out. In many organizations, however, the trend is away from controlling leadership and toward facilitative leadership, in which leaders and subordinates share the responsibilities of making decisions, planning to implement decisions, and carrying out these plans. The reason for the trend is that today's organizations, with their emphases on teamwork, challenge, and motivation, have found that employees are more motivated and productive if they are allowed to share in the plans and decisions that affect them and their work.

As depicted in Figure 1, the functions and behaviors of the controlling leader differ greatly from those of the facilitative leader. The leader whose style is more controlling retains full responsibility for all work accomplished and decisions made. This leader tries to control the tasks and output of the team. In contrast, the leader whose style is more facilitative shares these responsibilities with team members.

A controlling, authoritarian style of leadership can have adverse effects on a work team's communication effectiveness and morale. Because subordinates of a controlling leader are motivated by fear, they often are reluctant to reveal problems to or share opposing opinions with their leader. The frequency of upward communication is reduced, and the information conveyed is less accurate; in fact, team members selectively send the messages that they think will bring rewards and forestall punishment. Gordon (1977) found that power struggles (gossiping, backbiting, and so on), excessive submission and conformity, squelched creativity, withdrawal (both physical and psychological), and—in those who refuse to submit—rebellion and defiance also are linked to an overly controlling leadership style.

[1] Adapted from *How to Lead Work Teams: Facilitation Skills* by F. Rees, 1991, San Diego, CA: Pfeiffer & Company. This book offers complete guidelines on the facilitative style of leading a work team.

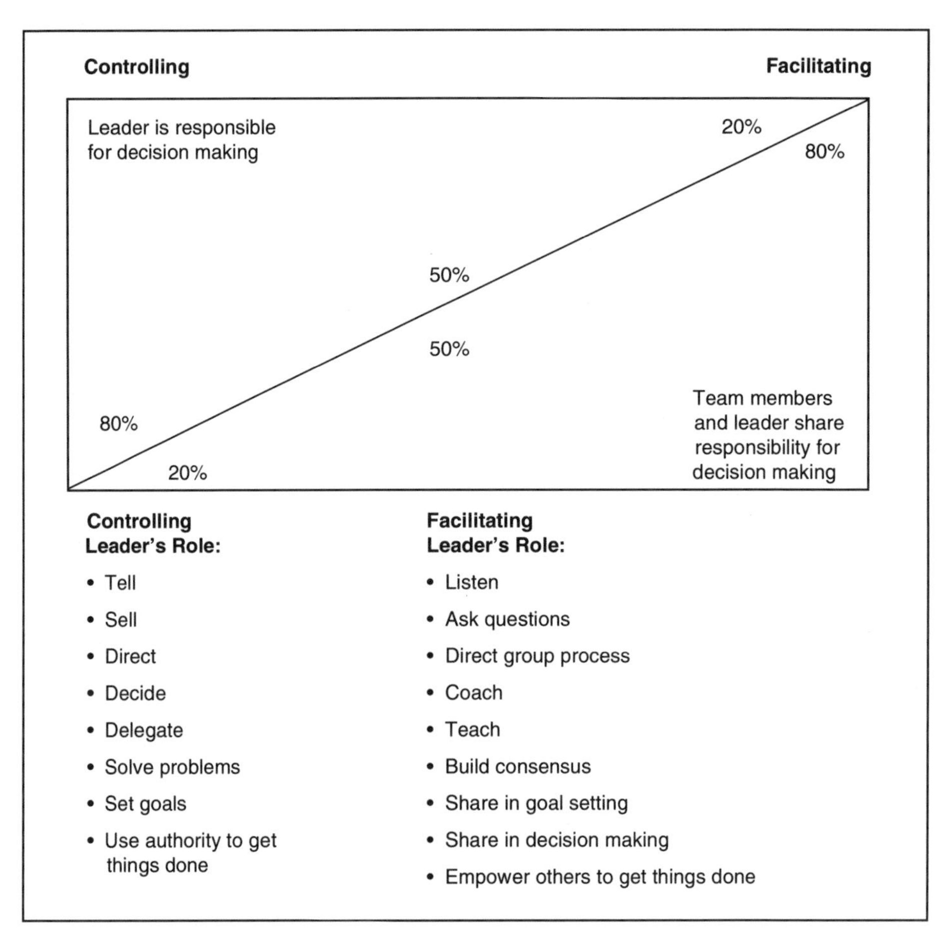

Figure 1. Controlling Versus Facilitating Styles of Leadership

POWER, THE LEADER, AND THE WORK TEAM

Controlling and facilitating leaders view power in different ways. Controlling leaders regard power as something to be hoarded and to be shared only cautiously. The results produced by work teams led by such leaders often are based on the leader's own abilities. Facilitative leaders, on the other hand, regard power as something to be shared, something that even can grow when spread among team members. Both types of leaders produce results. The difference is that facilitating leaders often produce *better* results because their subordinates are empowered and do not simply follow orders.

Under facilitative leaders, team members are more likely to support decisions because they have had input in the decision-making process. Because responsibility for implementing the decision is shared, team members' talents, experience, and knowledge are fully utilized. Teams led by facilitative leaders operate in win-win situations: They complete tasks by working together. In contrast, teams led by controlling leaders operate in what ultimately are win-lose situations: As perceived by the leaders, to give power to their teams means that they themselves must lose power. Thus, controlling leaders actually are at odds with their teams.

BECOMING A FACILITATIVE LEADER: BASIC PRINCIPLES FOR INITIATING CHANGE

Leaders who wish to move from a controlling to a facilitative style must alter their leadership styles, their patterns of interaction with subordinates, their performance standards, their work habits, and their norms of relating to team members. It is important for leaders to realize from the outset that these changes will not necessarily be easy or smooth.

Leaders who are making the transition to a more facilitative approach will do well to remember three principles of change:

- Change takes *time.*
- Change is a *process,* not a decision.
- *Experience and practice* are essential in order to become comfortable with new behaviors.

Leaders seeking to change must acknowledge the vast effort that change requires and must not give up when more time and practice than anticipated are necessary. Change is a *process*—sometimes a very long and tedious one. Leaders who effectively implement change ensure that they and their teams have plenty of opportunities to practice new behaviors.

Following are some additional principles that will help leaders to make the transition to facilitation:

- Make one or two changes at a time. Do not attempt to revamp an entire system at once.
- Allow time for changes to solidify. Change is never easy, and people need time to learn new ways of working together.
- Reward people's efforts to change; otherwise, they will not change.
- Keep the goal in mind: to increase productivity and employee satisfaction.
- Strive to reach planned, periodic milestones toward the goal. Do not let time go by without moving in the desired direction.
- Use action plans and regular evaluations as tools to move toward the goal.
- Have patience with people. Change is difficult and even threatening for some.
- Do not overestimate your power and influence. Be realistic but positive about what can be accomplished, considering the organizational culture

and any existing constraints. Acknowledge that one person alone cannot change the organization, and plan accordingly.

A PROCESS FOR TRANSITION

Some leaders faced with the prospect of change may feel overwhelmed by the enormity of the situation and may feel that they do not know where to begin. The changes to be made may seem enormous and impossible, or the particular situation may not seem applicable to the process described in this article.

By breaking up the change process into smaller chunks, however, the leader can make the task manageable. The following outline of steps will help the leader to translate the conceptual change process into a series of concrete, verifiable tasks and goals:

1. *List all desired changes in the team's functioning or in the style of leadership used.* Think in terms of long-term improvements—many months to several years.

2. *Determine the strengths, support systems, and other resources that already exist and that can help in the change process.* Plan to use these strengths to advantage when beginning to make changes.

3. *Break each large change down into small steps.* For example, if the leader's goal were to become a better listener, he or she might create the following list of action steps toward the goal:

- Ask at least three questions of subordinates this week. Make an effort to listen without interrupting.
- Take a course in listening.
- Ask a friend or significant other to tell me both when I interrupt and when I appear to demonstrate good listening skills.

What to Expect

It is human nature to resist change, even when the change is for the better. Change disrupts people's lives, challenges their beliefs about themselves and their world, and creates confusion and disorientation. Therefore, it is unrealistic for a leader to expect others to welcome his or her new persona without reservations or to be supportive immediately, even when the change is beneficial to them. In fact, subordinates may act almost antagonistic at first.

This phenomenon may be quite frustrating to the leader who is making an honest effort to change. It may be helpful in such situations for the leader to remember how subordinates interact with controlling leaders. They are somewhat fearful and distrustful; they have learned not to be the bearers of bad news or to disagree. When a formerly controlling leader begins to draw people out and to listen, his or her motives initially will be suspect. Subordinates may avoid saying anything controversial. Furthermore, unless the leader has been a good listener in the past, subordinates may not be accustomed to expressing their feelings and ideas to him or her.

Other people may welcome the solicitation of their feelings and opinions and may vent many of their frustrations all at once. This deluge of negativity may be difficult to deal with. The leader should try to remain open to what often are valuable criticisms; should listen actively, asking for clarification or examples when necessary; and should take notes. *Active listening* is listening without becoming defensive and without sermonizing or judging. The leader should avoid making promises during the listening session. He or she should explain that the purpose of the listening session is to look for opportunities to involve the team members in plans and decisions and that, together, they will discuss these issues at a later date.

HOW TO L.E.A.D.

Leaders can use a simple four-step model to ensure employee participation and to increase productivity:

Lead with a clear purpose.

Empower to participate.

Aim for consensus.

Direct the process.

The L.E.A.D. model includes key leadership functions: setting clear goals and objectives, getting people involved, reaching consensus on important items, and paying attention to both tasks (the work) and relationships (the team).

If the leader uses this model, the following ten essentials of teamwork will be met:

1. Paying attention to all four parts of the model provides the *leadership* that any team needs.
2. Leading with a clear, stated purpose meets the need for *common goals.*
3. Empowering members to participate facilitates the high levels of *interaction and involvement* that team members need.
4. Participation and consensus help to maintain the *individual team members' self-esteem.*
5. Participation and consensus also encourage *open communication.*
6. Participation and consensus also help to build *mutual trust.*
7. Good teamwork includes a healthy *respect for differences among team members.*
8. Effective communication in teamwork includes an avenue for *constructive conflict resolution.*
9. Using all four parts of the L.E.A.D. model will ensure that there is *power within the team to make decisions.*
10. Leading with a clear purpose and directing the process ensure that the leader will pay *attention to both process and content.*

The following paragraphs offer a more detailed analysis of the L.E.A.D. model.

Lead with a Clear Purpose

When a person leads with a clear purpose, he or she uses goals to motivate the team. To be motivating, goals must be challenging, positive, and realistic. A leader can bring power and focus to a team's goals in several ways.

First, the leader should set realistic, team-oriented goals that support organizational goals. Team-oriented goals apply specifically to an individual team; they are necessary because organizational goals are not "close to home" enough to motivate a team.

Next, the leader must publish the goals and display them for all team members to see. People will not remember the goals if they are not discussed and referred to often. The goals could be posted in a meeting room on flip charts or posters; the important thing is to display visual reminders to keep the goals in front of everyone. The leader should refer to the goals often in memos, presentations, and meetings. Whenever possible, the goals should be used to guide decisions. For example, if a subordinate came to the leader with a problem or suggestion, the leader might say, "In light of our goal of 95-percent on-time deliveries, what do you think is the best solution?"

The leader should work with the team to identify milestones that will indicate progress toward the team's goals. The milestones should be prominently displayed and should have deadlines whenever possible. For example, the team that wishes to achieve 95-percent on-time delivery could post the following milestones:

- 85 percent by the end of the third quarter;
- 90 percent by the end of the fourth quarter;
- 93 percent by the end of the first quarter of next year; and
- 95 percent by the end of the second quarter of next year.

The team's progress should be tracked and recorded. Milestones achieved should be acknowledged and celebrated. Over time, the leader should allow his or her team to set its own goals, to monitor its own progress, and to plan its own celebrations.

Empower to Participate

After goals have been established and published, the leader must empower the people in his or her team to work toward achieving the goals. To *empower* means to give power or authority, to authorize, to enable, or to permit. Therefore, the leader must begin to act as facilitator by delegating the responsibility for determining how goals will be met. Although the goals themselves may be motivators, team members will not be truly empowered if they are not allowed to participate in important decisions that will affect them and their work.

Leaders can involve their teams in the decision-making process in two ways. The leader can opt for a *consultative* decision: He or she can solicit team members' opinions and then make an independent decision. Alternatively, the leader can choose to make a *consensus* decision, in which the team members must reach consensus on the decision. In a consensus decision, the leader can choose to remain neutral and facilitate the decision-making process or to participate actively in the decision. The leader's choice of decision style will depend on several factors, including his or her comfort with delegating the decision, his or her ability to avoid overinfluencing the group, the leader's need for involvement in the implementation of the decision, and the team members' wishes.

Of course, not every team member must be involved with every decision. Before making a decision, the leader should ask, "Who will we depend on to carry out this decision?" The people named should at least be consulted before a decision is made.

There are many other ways of empowering people to participate. For instance, the leader may decide to redesign jobs and procedures so that team members will have to interact in order to complete their work. The leader also can identify which types of decisions he or she will make and which types of decisions the team or team members will make.

Facilitative leaders encourage participation by listening more than talking and by asking more than telling. Two skills are therefore critical for good facilitators: listening and asking questions. Effective or *active listening* is required in order to make sure that one has accurately heard what the other person has said. To listen actively, the listener must observe the speaker as well as hear the words being said. Body language, tone of voice, eye contact, and other signals provide the listener with additional information about the speaker's message. The active listener must indicate his or her receptiveness and attentiveness to the speaker's message with body language: maintaining an open posture, nodding the head, remaining quiet without restless movements, and maintaining eye contact. Active listening also requires that the listener not be distracted by others, by the surrounding environment, or by difficulties that the speaker may have in getting his or her message across. It means not thinking about what one is going to say while the speaker is talking. The listener also must postpone judgment of the message until he or she has heard it in its entirety.

In addition to knowing how to listen, an active listener needs to know when to ask questions to clarify the speaker's message. The listener can repeat a brief version of what he or she thought was said (paraphrase) in order to check the accuracy of the interpretation. The listener also can ask the speaker to provide more information in order to clear up confusion. In general, it is best to give the speaker a chance to talk and to finish what he or she wants to say before jumping in with questions.

Another important step toward the empowerment of team members is for the leader to solicit their ideas, opinions, and reactions regularly without judging or punishing them. Leaders usually are busy, and some do not have much opportunity to interact with their subordinates. A good leader-facilitator, however, will make time for others' opinions and ideas, even if only for a few minutes at the coffee machine. Stopping by a person's office for the sole purpose of getting his or her opinion is particularly empowering for that person.

After one has solicited someone else's opinion, one must follow through with a facilitative response as outlined in the following steps:

1. Listen actively.
2. Ask questions or paraphrase to clarify what was said.
3. Thank the person, and *resist having the last word.*

At times, the leader will be tempted to offer an opinion—especially if others ask for it. However, one of the best ways of empowering others to participate is to listen without having the final say. Remaining neutral frees others to express their honest opinions. In addition, the leader's opinion has clout and can change others' perspectives. True honesty from subordinates can be achieved only without the leader's becoming influential or defensive.

Another empowering technique is to avoid letting others rely on the leader for answers. Instead, when someone comes to the leader for an answer or decision, the leader should ask what he or she thinks. Use of this technique does not mean that the leader has no opinion or that he or she is abdicating the leadership role. Instead, it encourages others to solve their own problems. By doing so, the leader gives others permission (empowers them) to take on some of the leadership role.

A leader who empowers his or her team to make decisions must then support the team's decisions, even if he or she was not involved in the decision-making process. The leader can demonstrate support for a decision by expressing positive feelings about the decision, by offering assistance, by "running interference," by explaining the team's actions and goals to upper management, and by giving encouragement.

Another way that leaders can encourage participation is to give teams regular opportunities (probably at team meetings) to assess themselves. Leaders can teach team members to measure their performance. In an assessment, a team should discuss both its progress toward goal achievement and its success at functioning as a team. Are good relationships being built among team members? Is there a spirit of cooperation? Are members working out differences in acceptable ways? What team norms (ground rules) are working? What norms need to be changed or added?

Last, leaders must become proficient at giving genuinely positive reinforcement to their team members. Positive reinforcement includes watching for things that people are doing well and letting them know that their efforts are appreciated. Following are some guidelines for giving praise:

- Be specific about what is being praised.
- Praise in a timely fashion; do not wait too long after the event or behavior has occurred.
- Separate praise from problems or concerns; the message of praise may get lost if it is sandwiched between problems.
- Praise regularly, but not so often that it becomes expected or meaningless.

Aim for Consensus

In this, the third step in the L.E.A.D. model, the leader helps the members of his or her team to move toward general agreement. The goal should be to strive for consensus in all interactions, not just as a final step. Conflicts are bound to occur, of course, but the leader should regard them as natural and should help the team to work through them. The role of the leader in building consensus is to bring as many ideas, opinions, and conflicts to the surface as possible and then to get people to find the approach that best meets the needs both of the organization and of the team members.

After the team has reached consensus, it is the leader's responsibility to act on the decision or to empower the team to act on it. The leader can choose either to use the team's input to make a decision or to let the team's decision stand.

Direct the Process

The last step in the L.E.A.D. model requires experience in working with groups and knowledge about the group process. An effective leader will use various techniques, such as giving clear directions, intervening to keep the team on track, and suggesting alternative processes, to help the team to accomplish its goals and objectives.

Table 1 presents the important group needs met during each step of the L.E.A.D. model and lists key tasks that must be performed by the leader and by team members.

CONCLUSION

Use of the L.E.A.D. model can help leaders to become less controlling and more facilitative, which has been found to promote better work-team results and more empowered and motivated employees. In today's volatile marketplace, organizations must strive continually to find ways to be more productive, more competitive, and more adaptable to change and progress. Empowered work teams, led by facilitative, challenging, and enabling leaders, are helping organizations to achieve these goals. Such work teams can achieve and succeed because of their leaders, whose skills of facilitation help them to blend different views into consensus so that their teams can achieve their goals. The L.E.A.D. model presented in this article can be viewed as an outline for progress toward an empowered, facilitative organization: It provides ample opportunity for employees to take part in the management of their organizations and gives leaders a critical role to play in making this happen.

REFERENCE

Gordon, T. (1977). *Leader effectiveness training (L.E.T.): The no-lose way to release the productive potential of people.* Ridgefield, CT: Wyden.

Table 1. Using the L.E.A.D. Model

Leader Functions	Group Needs Met	Leader Tasks	Team-Member Tasks
Lead with a clear purpose	• Common goals • Attention to content • Leadership	• Set boundaries • Interpret organizational goals • Facilitate team's setting of its own goals • Evaluate and track progress toward goals	• Ask questions to test own understanding • Participate in setting goals for team • Help leader track and evaluate progress toward goals
Empower to participate	• High level of involvement of all members • Maintenance of self-esteem • Leadership • Respect for differences • Trust	• Ask questions • Listen • Show understanding • Summarize • Seek divergent viewpoints • Record ideas	• Contribute ideas from own experience and knowledge • Listen to others • Build on others' ideas • Consider others' questions • Ask questions • Think creatively
Aim for consensus	• Constructive conflict resolution • Power within team to make decisions • Leadership • Trust	• Use group-process techniques (brainstorming, problem solving, prioritization, etc.) • Ask questions • Listen • Seek common interests • Summarize • Confront in constructive way	• Focus on common interests and goals • Listen to and consider others' ideas • Make own needs known • Disagree in constructive way
Direct the process	• Attention to process • Leadership • Trust	• Give clear directions • Intervene to keep team on track • Read team and adjust • Remain neutral • Suggest alternative processes to help team achieve goal	• Listen • Keep purpose in mind • Stay focused on objective • Use own energy and enthusiasm to help process along

***Fran Rees** is the owner of Rees and Associates, a Phoenix-based training and consulting firm. She is an experienced manager and seminar leader and has consulted extensively to companies such as Digital Equipment Corporation and Motorola, Inc. Ms. Rees has successfully designed and implemented a number of training programs, workshops, and organizational interventions. She has conducted training on a wide variety of topics, including meeting-facilitation skills, multicultural awareness, consulting skills, and supervision and management. In her work with companies, she has designed and facilitated strategic-planning sessions, has led focus-group and team-building sessions, and has trained trainers.*

AN ANNOTATED BIBLIOGRAPHY ON THE WORK FORCE OF THE TWENTY-FIRST CENTURY: BABY BOOM AND BUST

Mary Ellen Collins

INTRODUCTION

Part of every human resource development (HRD) practitioner's responsibility is to keep up to date with what is happening in the field of HRD. Keeping up with new developments is a challenge. We are continually confronted with trends such as total quality management (TQM), self-directed work teams, managing diversity, empowerment, coaching, managing green, and so on. Fortunately, there are many excellent books, journals, magazines, and video packages that we HRD practitioners can use to familiarize ourselves with these subjects.

However, learning about developments in the field is only part of our responsibility in educating ourselves. It is equally important to keep up with trends among workers and in the markets that our organizations serve. We need information of all three types—about HRD, about workers, and about the marketplace—if we are to assist managers and nonmanagerial personnel in meeting the challenges they face in organizations.

This annotated bibliography has been written to fill the need for information about workers and about potential customers. It offers insights about two groups: (1) the enormous baby-boom generation, whose members were born after World War II and who now dominate the American work force and marketplace, and (2) the smaller baby-bust generation, whose members are just now entering the work force and will be the consumers of the future. Because the baby-boom generation has been a powerful force for the past two decades, there are many more books and articles about this generation than there are about the baby-bust generation; this bibliography reflects those numbers, including many more entries about the baby boomers than about the baby busters.

Many sources summarized in this bibliography not only discuss current trends but also make fascinating predictions. Here the HRD practitioner can find answers—or at least educated speculations—for many questions:

1. What will employees want and expect from organizations in terms of health care and insurance benefits, lifestyle options, flexible schedules, working conditions, retirement, managerial support, telecommuting, and environmental sensitivity? What kinds of training will they want and need? What effect will they have on inflation, unemployment, and union

strength? How will they feel about participatory decision making, autonomy, organizational loyalty, open communication, hierarchies, and chains of command?

2. What will consumers want and expect? What kinds of products and services will interest them? Will they emphasize saving or buying? How will they invest their money? What will be their attitudes toward family, stability, security, and the environment? What kind of advertising will pique their interest? How much disposable income will they have? Will they favor trendy products or products that offer substance and durability? How much leisure time will they have, and what will they choose to do with it?
3. What social, political, economic, and cultural changes can be anticipated? What are the implications of such changes for teamwork and other critical organizational processes? Which developments will act in an organization's favor? Which will hold an organization back?

Some of the data covered in the bibliography will be of interest to an organization as it completes the strategic planning process. For example, certain information might be useful in environmental monitoring, identifying proposed lines of business, selecting critical success indicators, analyzing internal resources, and contingency planning.[1] The HRD practitioner may want to distribute copies of the bibliography to managers so that they can identify which trends are of interest to their organization and which materials they would like to read or add to the organization's library.

BABY-BOOM POPULATION

Books

Barry, D. (1990). *David Barry turns 40.* New York: Crown.

Highlights trends that have developed as members of the baby-boom population retain their youthful images. Barry delivers a humorous perspective of normal aging events and the impact that these events will have on the aging youth culture of the 1960s.

Coates, J., Jarrett, J., & Mahaffie, J.B. (1990). *Future work: Seven critical forces reshaping work and the workforce in North America.* San Francisco: Jossey-Bass.

Focuses on how changes are shaping the future and provides immediate interpretation of these changes for the human-resource professional. Seven major themes are discussed: (1) Increasing diversity in the work force: Making heterogeneity and flexible management work; (2) Reintegrating home life and work life: Reversing a 100-year-old trend; (3) Globalization: Facing the realities of competing in a world

[1] For detailed instructions on the strategic planning process, refer to *Applied Strategic Planning: A How to Do It Guide* by J.W. Pfeiffer, L.D. Goodstein, and T.M. Nolan, 1986, San Diego, CA: Pfeiffer & Company.

economy; (4) Expanding human-resource planning: Restructuring roles and practices to improve business-unit planning; (5) The changing nature of work: Training and re-educating; (6) Rising employee expectations: Striking a balance between demands and costs; and (7) A renewed social agenda: Expanding corporate social responsibility.

Dychtwald, K. (1989). *Age wave: The challenges and opportunities of an aging America.* Los Angeles: Jeremy P. Tarcher.

Provides insight on the trends and shifts of an aging America. The author predicts that an older America will reshape every aspect of the present culture, leaving no one untouched. Dychtwald's intent is to prepare readers for the challenges of the future.

Gerber, J., Wolff, J., Lores, W.K., & Brown, G. (1989). *Life trends: The future of baby boomers and other aging Americans.* New York: Macmillan.

Hypothesizes that as baby boomers age, they recreate the definition of old age. The authors state that the size of the baby-boom population and the following baby-bust generation will have major implications for the Twenty-First Century. They forecast the following: an emergence of a matriarchal society; a decline of early retirement; a return to the notion of "community"; the development of intergenerational coalitions; a rescued and reshaped Social Security system; a move toward more self-treatment by patients; the election of a woman president; the rewriting of developmental psychology; and a reflection of the 1960s youth culture in the elder generation.

Gottlieb, A. (1987). *Do you believe in magic? The second coming of the sixties generation.* New York: Macmillan.

Provides an in-depth analysis of events that shaped the 1960s, through detailed discussions on the people of the era, the politics, and the world situation, with a particular emphasis on the Vietnam War. The author maintains that understanding the 1960s will facilitate how this generation responds to aging and to being the major work force in the United States.

Greiller, M.M., & Nee, D.M. (1989). *From baby boom to baby bust: How business can meet the demographic challenge.* Reading, MA: Addison-Wesley.

Focuses primarily on developing human resource strategies to deal with perceived threats created by the baby-boom and baby-bust populations. The proposed long-term solutions concern acquiring, training, and retraining employees. Adaptation to the new labor pool will position organizations to thrive in the changing labor market.

Johnston, W.B., & Packer, A.E. (1987). *Workforce 2000: Work & workers for the twenty-first century.* Washington, DC: Hudson Institute.

Hypothesizes that current changes in American culture will result in a radically different America by the year 2000. These changes will reshape the economy, the work force, and the workers.

Kiplinger, A., & Knight, A. (1989). *America in the global 90's: The shape of the future and how you can benefit from it.* Washington, DC: Kiplinger Books.

Raises controversial ideas about the 1990s as a period of growth and optimism. The authors claim that the move of foreign governments toward the modeling of American democracy and free-market systems will keep America on the economic incline.

Light, P.C. (1988). *Baby boomers.* New York: W.W. Norton.

Builds on the research of social scientists, directing special attention to surveys and polls. The data indicate that the key forces that shaped the culture of the baby-boom population were social affluence and parental uncertainty. These forces resulted in an undermining of the traditional authority held by the family, the church, and the economic system. Light argues that the 1980s bear the imprint of the 1960s, evidenced by lack of personal commitment and cynical attitudes about political behaviors. The members of this postwar generation represent new kinds of Americans, making America a new kind of nation.

Miser, C. (1987). *Grown-ups: A generation in search of adulthood.* New York: Penguin Books.

Examines the best-selling book, *Passages,* by Gail Sheehy, which discusses the meaning of adulthood. Miser maintains that the book pertains to the generation of her parents but that it is not relevant to the generation of baby boomers, who have experienced many social changes. Each new generation experiences upheaval and turmoil specific to its time, necessitating a redesigning of the passages to adulthood. It is fruitless to think about adulthood without taking into account the social, political, and economic conditions that shape the adult's world; as these conditions change, so will the definition of adulthood.

Naisbitt, J., & Aburdene, P. (1990). *Megatrends 2000: Ten new directions for the 90's.* New York: William Morrow.

Discusses new directions that social, political, and cultural changes will produce. As the year 2000 approaches, these changes will shape and create a new cultural context for the Twenty-First Century. The author predicts the following trends: (1) booming global economy, (2) renaissance in the arts, (3) emergence of free-market socialism, (4) global lifestyles and cultural nationalism, (5) privatization of the welfare state, (6) rise of the Pacific Rim, (7) women in leadership, (8) age of biology, (9) religious revival, and (10) triumph of the individual.

Wallechinsky, D. (1986). *Midterm report: The class of '65; Chronicles of an American generation.* New York: Viking.

Based on personal chronicles of baby boomers as they reach the midpoints of their journeys. The author has created an intimate and broad portrait of a segment of the American population on the verge of power. The class of 1965 is given an actual midterm report that reads: Peace and Security, "B"; Standard of Living, "C"; Technology, "A"; Culture, "C"; Environment, "A"; Education, "B"; and Freedom, "B."

Articles

Aging

Beck, M. (1989-1990, Winter/Spring). The geezer boom [Special issue]. *Newsweek,* pp. 62-63.

Discusses the impact of the aging baby-boom population on American society. In 2010, the baby boomers will be in their early sixties. By 2030, the seventy-seven million members of the baby-boom population will be senior citizens. The impact of this increase of senior citizens, who may lack retirement support, will be devastating to the small numbers in the baby-bust population. There may be no place to house the generation over age eighty-five, who will quadruple in the next forty years. The housing burden will be compounded by the increased need for hospital care for those who cannot care for themselves.

Brosseau, J. (1989, September 15). The new allure of 40. *USA Weekend,* pp. 4-5.

Describes the new image that has emerged of the years beyond the age of forty. As four million baby boomers turn forty each year, this milestone is now seen as a passage into the prime of life and as a time to savor. The baby boomers are entering this milestone year quite differently from the generation before them. Members of the baby-boom population are healthier and wiser and are making choices that redefine the former myths about turning forty.

Christian, R. (1989, October 15). The aging of America: The impact of the baby boomers on personal savings and the financial market. *Vital Speeches of the Day,* pp. 29-32.

Describes the financial status of the baby boomers, with an emphasis on their personal-savings patterns. The baby boomers are the biggest consumer market in history. As they age, they are taking rising prices in stride. Although two-paycheck households have increased incomes, their rate of personal savings has not increased. An appetite for the good life and for materialistic pleasures has contributed to this. The savings rate for people twenty-five to thirty-four years old is 8 percent; for the forty-five- to fifty-four-year-old age group, the rate is 20 percent. As the baby boomers age, the personal-savings potential could be $300-500 billion per year.

Farrell, C. (1989, October 6). The age wave and how to ride it. *Business Week,* p. 112.

Analyzes the financial status of the baby boomers as they age. Farrell claims that they will save more money in their later years. These higher savings will translate into greater investments on the part of individual baby boomers. Stocks to watch include various pharmaceuticals, General Mills, Kellogg's, Tyson's, Kindercare, La Pettite, Southwestern Bell, Club Med, and others. Demographic changes will influence the provision of services such as health care and entertainment, along with day care, telecommunications, and temporary-employment agencies.

The gray 90's. (1988, December). *Psychology Today,* pp. 8-9.

Describes trends that will take shape as the baby-boom population ages. The author compares the gay 1890s with a prediction of the gray 1990s. As the baby boomers mature and abandon their dreams, a new realism and an emphasis on healthy lifestyles will emerge.

Hamilton, P. (1990). Green, gray and tired of glitz. *Dun & Bradstreet Reports, 38*(4), 24.

Focuses on trends that will impact marketing styles in the 1990s as well as into the next century. The American public is placing higher value on families, stability, security, and environmental activism. Marketing professionals should note a decrease in the effectiveness of promoting products as trendy or glitzy. Instead campaigns should focus on substance, durability, and products that are easy to use. The author notes the trend toward a broad-based coalition of consumers who are increasingly concerned about products that they perceive to be harmful to the environment.

Linden, F. (1990). The changing face of affluence. *Across the Board, 27,* 9.

Discusses the results of a national survey about income and the standards of living of members of the baby-boom population. Data from five thousand households were used to compare the standards of living of members of the baby-boom population with those of their parents. The number of households with annual incomes of $50,000 or more has nearly doubled to fifteen million in little more than fifteen years. This represents 17 percent of the total population in 1990. Linden conjectures that the primary reason for the growth is the increase in the number of women who work outside the home. Of the respondents, members of the baby-boom generation aged forty-five years or younger believe that they have a better standard of living than their parents had at their age. According to the survey, 75 percent of the men and 80 percent of the women believe that they have had greater opportunities than their parents had.

Russell, C. (1987). What's going to happen when the baby boom gets older. *American Demographics* (Instant Replay Seminar Series).

Baby boomers are turning into a cautious middle-aged culture. The four traditional themes of home, marriage, family, and work have changed. The new themes as defined by baby boomers are globalism, individualism, instant gratification, and a move away from gender-stereotyped roles. Above all, a successful approach to this population is to make opportunities fun, because fun is the key to instant gratification.

Seniority under siege. (1987, June 8). *Fortune,* p. 10.

Explores attitudes of the baby boomers in the workplace. Many of them are questioning the notion of "seniority rules." Unions are being criticized for their part in upholding seniority domination.

Wilson, L. (1988). The aging of Aquarius. *American Demographics, 10,* 64.

Discusses baby boomers and the New Age movement. Statistics show that the majority of New Age consumers are affluent members of the baby-boom generation. The *New Age Journal* reports that 91 percent of its subscribers are college educated; among these subscribers, the average household income is almost $42,000. A joint survey conducted by Louis Harris and the U.S. Department of Health and Human Services reveals that college graduates are more likely than other, less-educated citizens to have engaged the services of New Age practitioners such as spiritual healers, herbalists, and nutritionists. One estimate of the size of the New Age consumer presence is that it represents 11.5 million people, or 7 percent of the total U.S. population.

Financial Issues

Clements, K. (1990, June 4). Social issues flexing their financial muscle. *Cincinnati Business Record,* p. 28.

Provides information about baby boomers and their discovery that they can use their investment dollars to enact social change. Environmental concerns, occupational health and safety issues, and general concern for the greater good have served to influence the movement.

Demographic forecasts: Moneyed mid-life. (1986). *American Demographics, 8,* 58.

Reports on statistics about the aging baby-boom generation and their incomes. Statistics indicate that the number of households headed by individuals between the ages of thirty-five and forty-four will increase by 31 percent during the period from 1985 to 1995. In addition, median household incomes for this age group should increase 9 percent during the same time period, making the median household income $33,400 for baby boomers in 1995. The highest income groups within this group are also the fastest growing in size (because two-income families are approaching their peak earning years). The number of households headed by individuals thirty-five to forty-four years old that earn $30,000 to $39,999 will increase by 26 percent, those with incomes in the range of $40,000 to $50,000 will experience a 42-percent growth, and those above $50,000 will increase by 63 percent.

Exeter, T. (1987). Baby boom income. *American Demographics, 9,* 62.

Reveals data that show an increase in the number of households with occupants in their prime earning years as the baby-boom population ages. The median income should rise to $38,410 by the year 2000.

Gallagher, P. (1990, February 4). Budgeting in the 90's. *Cincinnati Enquirer,* p. 11.

Discusses the "double-squeeze" position that baby boomers will face as they struggle with the financial burdens of school-age children and aging parents. Many are planning ahead for these financial burdens. As the development of long-term insurance becomes a major issue in the 1990s, many corporations (for example, Procter & Gamble) are offering this benefit to employees.

Hanley, K. (1986). Making boomers buyers. *Target Marketing, 9,* 8.

Reveals the findings of a national marketing survey of six hundred Americans aged twenty-five to forty-four. The results place the members of the baby-boom population into four groups: the *satisfied selves,* who have money and confidence and are innovative; the *contented traditionalists,* who are self-assured but conservative and inactive; *the worried traditionalists,* who are trend followers, lack confidence, and buy brand names; and the *Sixties in the Eighties,* who are dissatisfied and as active as possible. Each of these groups offers different marketing and political opportunities.

In their prime. (1986). *American Demographics, 8,* 58.

Provides useful statistics on the financial status of members of the baby-boom generation. By 1995 the number of households in the United States headed by individuals between the ages of forty-five and fifty-four will be 40 percent larger than in 1985. In 1985 there were 12.5 million households headed by people in this age group; by 1995 there will be 17.5 million. The median income for households with parents aged forty-five to fifty-four is currently $31,000. This will rise to a median income of $33,900 by 1995. Many of these households have two income earners, which accounts for their 0.7-percent earnings growth. While members of households in this age bracket who earn less than $30,000 will increase in number, the fastest-growing segment of this population will be those households that earn higher incomes.

Koretz, G. (1987, October 27). Those big spending middle-aged baby boomers. *Business Week,* p. 20.

Estimates that the number of households headed by people thirty-five to forty-nine years old will increase by 47 percent by the year 2000. This means that 71 percent of households in the year 2000 will be headed by baby boomers. Also, the number of households in the thirty-five- to forty-year-old group with incomes over $50,000 will triple by the year 2000.

Koretz, G. (1989, February 6). Age vs. wage: How baby boomers may cool inflation. *Business Week,* p. 26.

Deals with factors that suggest the trade-off between low unemployment and inflation is no longer sharp. Factors include: the reduced strength of unions, a drop in percentage of jobless covered by unemployment insurance, pressures of international competition, and the changing age distribution of the population.

Linden, F. (1987). Middle-aged muscle. *American Demographics, 9,* 4.

Projects that as the baby boomers enter their peak middle years, an alignment of consumer-spending power will emerge within the United States. The author notes that marketing professionals should prepare to target middle-aged and affluent consumers as the primary buyers.

Otten, A. (1990, July 5). Baby boomers make less, but make do. *The Wall Street Journal,* p. B-1.

Reports on the earnings of members of the baby-boom population. Although some analysts argue that baby-boomer earnings have decreased, others maintain that the baby-boom generation has made lifestyle adjustments to compensate for this decrease. These economic compromises have given baby boomers a higher standard of living than their earnings figures imply.

Royer, M.P. (1988). Please give generously. *American Demographics, 10,* 35-60.

Provides information on an organization headed by Jack Sims called B.O.O.M.E.R.S. Consulting. Its aim is to help nonprofit organizations to understand a perplexing population. Traditionally most donors to not-for-profit organizations have been aged fifty-five and over. Now it is predicted that in the next two decades baby boomers can fuel a significant growth to charitable giving if they are approached in the right way. They prefer causes related to the needs of the individual, especially those individuals who have fallen between the cracks of the American system. The members of the baby-boom population appear to respond to advertisements containing emotional appeal, straight talk, and visual excitement. Not-for-profit organizations are advised to be specific about what they intend to do with donated money.

Schwartz, J. (1988). Who will borrow tomorrow? *American Demographics, 10,* 10-11.

Reports on the shrinking market of borrowers. Research from the University of Michigan's Survey Research Center indicates that consumers between the ages of twenty-five and fifty-four account for 80 percent of all consumer debt paid. The pool of prime borrowers is larger now than ever, but it will be shrinking fast in about twelve years as the members of the baby-boom population move out of their prime borrowing years.

Shangrila for starters. (1989). *American Demographics, 11,* 15.

Suggests that developers focus on building and marketing the vacation home for baby boomers instead of starter homes for young couples. The disposable income of people forty-five to fifty-four years old grows faster than their mortgage and other payments grow.

Trends

Baby boomers push for power. (1984, July 2). *Business Week,* pp. 52-56.

Describes the impact of the baby-boom generation on politics and the work force. Politically the baby boomers are a blend of liberal and conservative ideas; as they reach middle age they are pushing for more political power. In the corporate sector, the large number of well-educated baby boomers is igniting a fiery competition. This competition is most intense among baby boomers vying for positions as corporate officers. New values are reshaping corporate cultures; participatory decision making, teamwork, flexibility, autonomy, and Japanese-style management are a direct outgrowth of the 1960s generation. In spite of these trends, baby boomers do not exhibit strong loyalties to their organizations.

Baby! What a market. (1990, February). *Marketing News,* pp. 41-50.

Provides various demographic statistics, including who is having babies, historical trends, factors affecting birth rates, projections through the year 2000, and their marketing significance.

Blakely, M.K. (1986, November). Happy birthday to a generation. *Ladies' Home Journal,* p. 123.

Reports on five women of the baby-boom population who meet to celebrate their fortieth birthdays. The diversity and complexity of their lives are seen as typical of the women of their generation.

Boomers at 40-something. (1989, September 25). *Business Week,* pp. 142-143.

Focuses on the views of baby boomers as they enter their forties. The personal concerns of this group will translate into major social themes. Many baby boomers will change their careers as they seek work with social purpose.

Business Week/Harris poll: Yes, they are different. (1984, July 2). *Business Week,* p. 64.

Discusses generational differences within the U.S. political environment. Both political parties have experienced a dramatic decline in support because of an inability to balance conservative and liberal positions on issues that appeal to baby boomers.

Career Resources. (1990, Winter). People and productivity: The issue of the 90's. *The Human Edge Newsletter,* pp.1-2.

Supplies an overview of trends that will affect life in the Twenty-First Century. The article notes changes in management style from controlling to leading. There have been expanding roles for human resource managers and an increase in opportunity for consulting services to provide help for organizations with fewer middle managers.

Cutler, B. (1989). Babies boom. *American Demographics, 11,* 20.

Reports that almost fifty million children have been born to members of the baby-boom generation. This development will create a surge in products targeted to meet the needs of these new parents.

Demographic forecasts: The boom is over. (1986). *American Demographics, 8,* 70.

Predicts that the number of people between the ages of twenty-five and thirty-four who head households will peak in 1990 at 20.6 million. This number will decrease to approximately 19.8 million in 1995, corresponding with the aging of the baby-boom generation. Household incomes for members of this age group are projected to remain stable, increasing only 2 percent during the 1990s.

Dentzne, S. (1989, December 25). How we will live. *U.S. News & World Report,* pp. 62-63.

Predicts a retirement crisis as fifty-eight million people leave the workplace by the year 2025. The American Academy of Actuaries suggests that one-half of the baby boomers do not have the financial resources to retire. Decisions on issues such as Social Security benefits and the availability of long-term care will greatly affect the standard of living for the baby-boom generation. Economists propose that the only solution to this pending problem is to raise taxes or to scale back entitlement.

Edmondson, B. (1986). In the boom-boom room. *American Demographics, 8,* 20.

Describes a marketing-research and mailing-list company, known as Baby Boomers & Company, which operates in the New York and New Jersey area. With a mailing list of 30,000 baby boomers, it invites them to social/marketing events where they are introduced to new products. The company plans to expand into Philadelphia, Boston, and the Hamptons and Nantucket markets. Among the clients sponsoring Baby Boomers & Company events are Nestlé Company, Sony Corporation, and Guess? Jeans. Most events cost sponsors between $2,000 and $10,000 and are attended by four to six thousand baby boomers.

Exter, T. (1989). Baby boom voters. *American Demographics, 10,* 62.

Discusses the baby-boom generation as a growing political force. The percentage of representation among voters in this age group has increased from 33 percent in 1980 to 43 percent in 1989. However, this influence is expected to level off by 1992 unless members of the baby-boom population increase their participation in the voting process. U.S. Census Bureau projections indicate that seventy-seven million potential voters in the baby-boom population are moving into age brackets that have had consistently a higher percentage of actual voters.

Kimball, C. (1990, August 24-25). Return of the real man. *USA Weekend,* pp. 4-5.

Focuses on the signs that indicate a new era for males is emerging. A resurgence of beer instead of wine at dinner and golf instead of cocktail parties after work are some of the examples cited. The impact of feminism is seen as a major force behind the change in male roles. The author suggests that because women have been liberated, men no longer need to impress them and are free to trade their macho images for more natural behavior.

Loth, R. (1991, August 4). And now: A voice for baby boomers. *The San Diego Union,* p. C-3.

Reports on the recently formed American Association of Boomers (AAB) made up of 11,000 members all born between the years of 1947 and 1964. The author describes the increased tension between the baby-boom population and the generation that preceded it. The organization's political agenda advocates a balanced Federal budget, limited terms for Congressional members, and a reduction in benefits for wealthy retirees. Ultimately the organization's goal is to lobby for changes that will spare following generations from having to support, in the face of a massive Federal deficit, the seventy-six million people born during the boom years.

Pearce, S. (1989, December 7). Déjà-view: For baby boomers, familiarity breeds content. *Cincinnati Enquirer,* p. I-1.

Discusses the discovery by marketing professionals that familiarity breeds content among members of the baby-boom generation. In spite of radical changes in lifestyles, baby boomers have one thing in common—the past. One of the best ways to exploit a generation commercially is to validate its youth.

Pedigo, S. (1990). Riding the tide of change. *Wyatt Communicator,* pp. 4-13.

Reports on the major concerns of 247 chief executive officers (CEOs). Health care, government relations, and productivity were cited as the most important issues for the 1990s. Training was seen as the greatest need for the 1990s, with recruitment and retention gaining more emphasis than in the past. Very few of the CEOs were concerned with changing work-force demographics in light of an abundance of labor. The author describes four trends: (1) an older work force that is growing more slowly, (2) an increase in the number of women in the work force, (3) an increase in the number of minority and immigrant workers, and (4) a shift in the economy from a manufacturing to a service base.

Riche, M. (1988). Back to the 50's? *American Demographics, 10,* 2.

Analyzes the differences between today's economy and that of the 1950s. In the 1950s, a man with less than an average education was able to afford what now takes two incomes to afford. The enrollment of females in college has now reached a point that parallels the enrollment of men. The author notes that the most profound change is the fragmentation in human life cycles and lifestyles.

Rosellini, L., & Wells, S. (1986, March 10). When a generation turns forty. *U.S. News & World Report,* p. 60.

Focuses on facts and statistics pertaining to demographics. The authors include interviews with individual baby boomers concerning their attitudes on politics, health, and turning forty. Baby boomers express what is on their minds in regard to the media, trivia, music, and the future.

Samuelson, R. (1987, July 27). Middle aged America. *Newsweek,* p. 45.

Concludes that older baby boomers will not be content with stereotypical middle-age perceptions. This population will change society's concepts of the usually stable, serious, and careful period of mid-life. The author forecasts increased spending on schools, decreased leisure time, and the death of the youth culture.

A sneak preview of its baby boomer study. (Panel discussion.) (1986). *Madison Avenue, 28,* 58.

Presents a study of a sample of 1,500 consumers from the baby-boom generation. This study indicates that they can be classified into three large and distinct groups. *Self-stylers* are affluent professionals interested in understated quality; they are internally driven, independent, and the best educated of all groups. *Materialists* have a strong need to impress and are mostly interested in attractive homes, possessions, and social approval; they are the youngest of all groups. Finally, *nesters* are usually blue-collar workers mostly interested in their families and traditional middle-class values.

Work

Carey, J. (1989, September 25). The Pepsi generation heads for the corner office. *Business Week,* p. 170.

Discusses the kinds of CEOs that will emerge as members of the baby-boom population become eligible for these positions. Generally, chief executive officers take power of large companies at age fifty-one. This means that by the year 2000, most companies will be selecting candidates from the baby-boom generation. Many argue that baby boomers will have limited loyalties to companies and be more appreciative of leisure time and family. Others say they will be outspoken, confident, and thick-skinned.

Edelhart, M. (1988). Small wins for the baby boomer. *P.C. Week, 5,* C.17.

Describes the small-wins theory created by an organizational psychologist to describe the behavior of many managers of the baby-boom generation. Baby boomers have been taught that they can attain their hearts' desires if they work hard enough, want things badly enough, and scheme long enough. Attitudes such as these can lead to major disappointments for those who constantly strive for big wins. Confusion, depression, and feelings of hopelessness can seriously affect a manager's psyche. The author states that management style has a direct effect on strategic-information systems and on the design of the systems themselves in corporations. The small-wins theory focuses on small-scale, attainable goals that allow managers to feel like winners, if only occasionally. The tenets of the small-wins theory are also applied to information-system design.

Kiechel, W. (1989, April 10). The workaholic generation. *Fortune,* pp. 50-54.

Reports on baby boomers' values in the workplace. Although they have not yet taken their places in the highest echelons of organizations, they espouse values that are readily endorsed by corporate America. These values include open communications, autonomy, and loyalty to a team or project (rather than a company). For members of the baby-boom generation, work represents an arena to perform in, a place to be stroked, and a place to be creative. Boomers are most concerned with the issues of maintaining credibility, creating the environments they want, and sustaining individualism.

MacDonald, S. (1990, May 13). Part-time working moms. *Cincinnati Enquirer,* p. D-1.

Describes women of the baby-boom generation who want children and the personal satisfaction of careers. Work options have been created, including job sharing, part-time positions, home-based businesses, and computer work at home.

Moskae, J. (1990, January 28). Stay at home jobs are gaining favor. *Cincinnati Enquirer,* p. G-12.

Reports that the number of home-based jobs is increasing and predicts that the number will continue to grow because of advancing technology. Many states are finding that home-based businesses are an important part of the economy. For example, 49 percent of the forty thousand registered businesses in Montana are home based. The Small Business Administration estimates that more than 60 percent of home-based businesses are owned by women.

Motivating the baby boomers. (1986, November). *Managers Magazine,* p. 27.

Identifies those who belong to the baby-boom generation and what motivates them. Not easily motivated by financial factors, baby boomers appear to be influenced by psychological elements including the following: respect for fellow workers; interesting job duties and responsibilities; recognition for a job well done; opportunities for self-improvement and creativity; participation in problem-solving processes; observance of the result of their work efforts (for example, the final product's usefulness); and mentorship in a business relationship. Ten suggestions for encouraging employee motivation are identified: (1) Develop a mentorship training program; (2) change employee duties on a rotational basis; (3) cross-train employees to perform jobs outside their normal areas; (4) assign difficult goals and objectives to every employee; (5) promote teamwork; (6) implement special projects and assign employees to project teams; (7) introduce a suggestion system and ask employees for their ideas on operational improvements; (8) offer employees more frequent training classes; (9) reward good service with "plum" assignments; and (10) take employees to lunch to discuss employee self-improvement plans.

Solomon, C.M. (1990, April). Careers under glass. *Personnel Journal,* 2031.

Describes glass ceilings and other barriers encountered by women and minorities in the corporate environment. The author believes that if these obstacles did not exist there would be more women and minorities in executive positions. A 1985 Korn/Ferry International Survey showed that out of a sample of 1,708 senior executives there were four blacks, six Asians, three Hispanics, and twenty-nine women. Reasons for the existence of glass ceilings may include lack of strategic visibility, lack of mentoring, lack of acceptance at the senior level, and stereotyping. Some corporations have begun to recognize diversity in the work force and the different needs of individuals. For example, by 1991, Corning Industry intends to have a work force that mirrors the national demographics by increasing the number of women and minority executives in the organization.

Valenzano, J., Jr. (1990, March-April). New leadership for a changing work force. *Journal of Business Strategy,* p. 82.

Focuses on the need for corporate leaders to understand the effects that a maturing baby-boom generation has on the work force of the 1990s. Many social changes have worked to frustrate baby boomers, including crowded schools and a crowded entry-level job market. The scarcity of middle-management positions within organizations makes it difficult for individuals to achieve promotions beyond certain levels. Successful CEOs will understand this frustration and will work to develop ways to promote creativity and entrepreneurship in their corporate cultures. The author also notes that this generation, along with its children's generation, will be the segment of the population whose tastes and beliefs will dictate public policy, marketing styles, and the nature of the work environment.

Wall, S. (1989). North Americans, Europeans and 1992. *Issues and Observations, 9*(4), 1-3.

Compares American and European managers' styles and attitudes. A single European market in 1992 will promote the need for international managerial cooperation. Researchers from the Center for Creative Leadership have found that American and European managers are more similar than they are different. Both tend to focus on short-term decision making and struggle with putting their strategies into action. Both have learned to delegate and to work with other members on a management team. Europeans make fewer decisions and tend to show less respect for authority, while cross-functional cooperation is more important to Americans.

Ward, B. (1990, July). At home at the office. *Sky,* pp. 21-26.

Describes the return of combined living and working spaces, which was a common turn-of-the-century lifestyle. The new term for this space is *hoffice.* Communities are being designed to accommodate this trend. One such prototype is Creekside Commons in Stuart, Florida.

Wilkinson, L. (1989, September 5). Workplace schools help firms recruit, keep young workers. *Cincinnati Enquirer,* p. C-7.

Reports on corporations' needs for recruiting and retaining quality employees and parents' needs for quality and involvement in the education of their children. These factors have inspired organizations to include workplace kindergartens and day-care programs as recruitment tools.

Workplace of the future. (1990, June 4). *The Wall Street Journal,* p. R-1.

Highlights new trends in the workplace. Some examples include an increase in the use of sophisticated technology, flexible work formulas, work centers closer to employees, flattened organizational pyramids, and working in the home.

BABY-BUST POPULATION

Angier, N. (1989, August). 25 and taking over: The high expectation, low-sweat generation. *Mademoiselle,* pp. 214-215.

Explains the differences between members of the baby-bust generation and the baby boomers who came before them. Members of the baby-bust population have entirely different attitudes toward work. They want to be successful and well-balanced social beings. Because of their fewer numbers and the self-confidence they exude, this generation will have a special kind of strength in the workplace. They will be able to pick and choose from a broad variety of positions. They will want more input in corporate decisions and will be impatient with corporate hierarchies, job titles, and chains of command. Baby busters are well educated and technically savvy and exhibit a renewed concern in social issues. Employers will attract this group with lifestyle options, such as allowing them to work at home, to schedule their own work hours, and to have more vacation time.

Brody, E.W. (1988). Credibility and productivity: New rules of organizational survival. *Public Relations Quarterly, 23,* 15.

Focuses on the problems organizations will encounter when the majority of the work force comprises the baby-bust population. The baby-bust generation will cause a reduction in the size of the future work force; this will threaten business organizations by creating a reduction in the number of entry-level personnel. These workers of the future were reared in an era of uncertainty and volatility, making them mobile, hard to retain, and skeptical. They expect to be listened to and kept informed. Brody suggests that companies ensure senior management's commitment to an equitable, success-based distribution of rewards. These rewards should be directed at work groups instead of individuals. Communications systems developed to keep employees in touch with planning and strategy will accommodate the needs of the baby-bust population in the work force.

DeMott, J.S. (1987, February 23). Welcome America to the baby bust. *Time,* pp. 28-29.

Analyzes American society as it adjusts to an era of smaller, leaner times. When the baby-bust generation enters adulthood, it may discover the benefits of doing without as job competition, unemployment, and demand for housing increase. These elements will result in confusion for businesses. The author discusses crime and its correlation with the number of men aged fifteen to eighteen. He also describes how the composition of social classes is changing.

Krier, B.A. (1990, June 28). Busters: A generation overshadowed. *Cincinnati Enquirer,* p. E-9.

Discusses the resentment baby busters feel about being in the shadow of the baby boomers. The U.S. Census Bureau admits that it has done few studies on the busters as a group. An aging America has paid little attention to its youth.

Liberatore, P. (1990, March 4). Teens in the global village. *Cincinnati Enquirer,* p. E-4.

Suggests that in spite of a trend toward globalization, teenagers remain loyal to their own cultures and countries. The *Whole Earth Review* initiated the first large-scale survey of teenagers' values and opinions worldwide.

MacDonald, S. (1990, June 4). Drugs, sex: Pressure points for teens in facing grown-up years. *Cincinnati Enquirer,* p. B-1.

Identifies the effects of peer pressure on teenagers. The author states that the intense pressure on today's teens to try drugs and sex can be positive or negative. This pressure comes not only from peers, but from all aspects of society. Because teenagers today are mostly unsupervised and have few adult role models, they look to their peers for values and advice.

Nix, S. (1990, August 30). Post boomer generation not rushing to the altar. *San Francisco Chronicle,* p. D-5.

Describes the twenty-something generation's reluctance to settle down and commit to marriage. As latch-key kids and children of divorce, they are skeptical about the permanence of love. Baby busters maintain a high desire for autonomy and experience disillusionment in the values of the yuppie generation that preceded them.

Quinn, J.B. (1987, November 23). Investing in the baby bust. *Newsweek,* p. 57.

Reveals the implications of North America's declining population growth on the economy. Statistics show that the present economy is built for a more rapid increase in demand than will exist. Fewer young workers may result in a decrease of consumer demands, but the decline may also mean higher wage levels and more disposable incomes.

Ramsey, K. (1990, June 5). Job vs. school: Education, social life suffer when teens work. *Cincinnati Enquirer,* p. B-1.

Suggests that many teenagers are having to balance the pressures of everyday life with an increasing need to work. Time for school work, social life, and even sleep often becomes a luxury for teenagers who work. Research by social scientists suggests that as the number of hours of employment increase, the harmful effects of employment outweigh the benefits.

Smith, L. (1987, July 20). The war between the generations. *Fortune,* pp. 78-80.

Hypothesizes that intergenerational wars can be expected as the baby boomers age and the burden of elderly care falls on a much smaller baby-bust population. Unless the Social Security and Medicare systems are redesigned, baby busters will need to turn over 40 percent of their income to support retired baby boomers. Suggested alternatives are to have people remain working until age seventy, give substantial tax breaks for those who fund their own retirement, and give tax breaks to wealthy people who subsidize poor retirees.

Mary Ellen Collins *is the president of People Power Consulting Service in Cincinnati, Ohio, and is a nationally known organizational consultant and trainer. Her company helps clients in business, manufacturing, health care, banking, universities, and schools to implement strategies for organizational effectiveness. Ms. Collins has developed and presented custom-designed educational workshops on the topics of management and organization development throughout the United States and Canada. She is a frequent keynote speaker and teaches at the university level in the fields of organizational behavior, management, and team building. She was selected as The 1991 Outstanding Adjunct Faculty member by her students. She is a member of several professional organizations, including the American Society for Training and Development, the Ohio Speakers Forum, and the American Management Association.*

MANAGING DIVERSITY IN THE WORKPLACE[1]

S. Kanu Kogod

INTRODUCTION: THE IMPACT OF DIVERSITY IN THE WORKPLACE

In 1987 the Hudson Institute released *Workforce 2000: Work & Workers for the Twenty-First Century* (Johnston & Packer, 1987), the now-famous study of the work force of the future, which was commissioned by the United States Department of Labor. This study offered predictions about changes that will occur in the demographic composition of the United States population and work force by the year 2000.

Among the startling projections were the following: White males will account for only 15 percent of the 25 million people who will join the work force between the years 1985 and 2000. The remaining 85 percent will consist of white females; immigrants; and minorities (of both genders) of black, Hispanic, and Asian origins. The Hispanic and Asian populations will each grow by 48 percent; the black population will grow by 28 percent; and the white population will grow by only 5.6 percent. In fact, it is projected that sometime in the next century non-Hispanic whites will lose their majority status in the United States.

A brief historical perspective helps to clarify these developments and their impact. Before World War I and after World War II, there were massive waves of immigration to the United States. These immigrants made up the great "melting pot" of the American culture; they worked toward assimilation and toward adopting mainstream American values. Now, however, as a result of the social and political changes of the Sixties and Seventies, things are different. The "New Americans," as the media have dubbed recent refugees, tend to hold onto their own languages and customs and try to maintain their distinct places within the overall American pattern.

It is important to note, though, that diversity is not an exclusively American issue. Just as the American work force is rapidly changing in all kinds of ways—in age mix, gender composition, racial background, cultural background, education, and physical ability—so are the work forces of many countries. Such changes are having and will continue to have a significant impact on organizational environments. In the past, when the employees of an organization represented much less diversity, there was less variety in the values that governed organizational operations and work performance. Now, however, because of increasing

[1] Adapted from *A Workshop for Managing Diversity in the Workplace* by S.K. Kogod, 1991, San Diego, CA: Pfeiffer & Company.

diversity, there are conflicting values among workers and, therefore, conflicting messages about how to do things. Changing demographics, along with economic factors and the high costs of turnover, have convinced organizations that they need to make efforts to retain employees, to develop them, and to promote from within. Thus, it is increasingly important for employees to learn to understand one another and to work together effectively and harmoniously.

HOW CULTURAL COLLISIONS DEVELOP

Culture is defined as a shared design for living. It is based on the values and practices of a *society,* a group of people who interact together over time. People absorb culture through the early process of socialization in the family, and then this process carries over to the ways in which they perceive themselves and the world. We all develop world views—simplified models of the world that help us make sense of all that we see, hear, and do.

We perceive our world views as making sense if they are consistent with our society's values and our abilities to anticipate and interpret the events we experience. Values, which vary from culture to culture and from person to person, are the standards that we use to determine whether something is "right" or "wrong."

At the beginning of any relationship, information is shared. Each person learns who the other is and what he or she wants. In a work setting, that information includes a definition of each person's role. This sharing of information occurs not only within and across work teams but also between a service provider and a customer. In the latter relationship, the shared information includes details about the product or service that the customer wants.

The degree to which information is shared and the amount of information shared vary greatly from relationship to relationship. Often people do not state their expectations of each other; sometimes they are not even aware that such expectations exist. But when these expectations are not met, collisions occur.

The greatest difficulty arises in a relationship when a person believes that "Only my culture makes sense, espouses the 'right' values, and represents the 'right' and logical way to behave." This mode of thinking is called *ethnocentrism.* When two ethnocentric people from different cultures interact, there is little chance that they will achieve an understanding of each other's world views. Common ethnocentric reactions to a differing world view are anger, shock, and amusement. The person whose expectations are not met may even attribute that failure to deliberate efforts on the part of the other person to disregard the injured person's values. When ethnocentric thinking pervades an organizational culture, the result can be exclusion of some, favoritism toward others, intragroup conflict, and unsatisfactory customer relations.

The outcome of a cultural collision may be any of the following:

- Termination of the interaction or the relationship;
- Isolation, meaning that one person avoids the other or the two people avoid each other;
- An insufficient sharing of information about expectations, which may lead to different or lowered expectations in future interactions; or

- Accommodation, in which one person strives to accommodate the other's expectations or both people accommodate.

If we are to manage diversity effectively, we must suspend ethnocentric judgments, begin to question why particular things are done, and strive toward negotiation or accommodation. The opposite of ethnocentrism is *cultural relativism,* the attempt to understand another's beliefs and behaviors in terms of that person's culture. The person who responds to interactions with cultural relativism rather than ethnocentrism is able to see alternatives and to negotiate with another person on the basis of respect for cultural differences.

In an organization the desired results of a cross-cultural encounter are synergy and pluralism combined with an appreciation of and contribution toward the company's goals and objectives. In order for these results to occur, people must be encouraged to honor multiple perspectives and to incorporate this approach into their quest to meet the fundamental needs of the organization.

THE HRD PROFESSIONAL'S ROLE IN MANAGING DIVERSITY

The human resource development (HRD) professional can help managers in their efforts to deal with diversity effectively. Acting in a consultative role, the HRD professional can assist them in analyzing and enhancing the organizational climate, creating a vision, determining strategies, and implementing action plans to turn their vision into reality.

Educating Managers About Diversity

Many organizations are beginning to recognize the impact of a diverse work force and are offering their managers tips on how to manage diversity:

- Understand that cultural differences exist.
- Acknowledge your own stereotypes and assumptions.
- Develop consciousness and acceptance of your own cultural background and style.
- Learn about other cultures.
- Be flexible; try to adapt to the style of the person with whom you are communicating.
- Provide employees who are different with what they need to succeed: access to information and meaningful relationships with people in power.
- Treat people equitably but not uniformly.
- Encourage constructive communication about differences.

As these tips point out, a manager can best deal with diversity by recognizing, identifying, and discussing differences. This approach represents a departure from Equal Employment Opportunity (EEO) programs, which denied differences and instead promoted the idea that acknowledging differences implied judgments of right and wrong, superiority and inferiority, normality and oddity. These programs were based on the assumption that openly identifying differences was equivalent to opening a Pandora's box of prejudice and paranoia. But, as one consultant said, echoing the new line of thought on the value of diversity, "We do nobody any favors by denying cultural differences." If managers seem skeptical, it is a good idea to explain that greater differentiation between people can actually break down the mind-set of prejudices. When we describe people in greater detail instead of less detail, we find more qualities in them to appreciate.

Managers also should be made aware that employees are often hesitant to make their individual perspectives known. Thus, it is important for managers to encourage people to express their unique identities. If this encouragement is not given, people may remain silent; this silence robs organizational members of the opportunity to develop valuable insights about one another that would enhance their effectiveness on the job and enrich their lives. Also, having access to multiple perspectives is essential to creative problem solving, strategic planning, and other critical organizational functions; and multiple perspectives can flourish only when curiosity about others is welcomed and the differences among people are honored.

The tips on managing diversity are not enough; they are much more easily talked about than acted on. It is this fact that has given rise to diversity training, which was developed to help managers cope with the personnel changes occurring in organizations.[2] Diversity training for managers is essential if an organization is to deal successfully with diversity. It is particularly important to provide a safe training climate in which managers can feel free to practice new skills and culture-sensitive behaviors. The training not only must help managers to understand the issues involved but also must enable them to apply that understanding to new situations that arise.

Analyzing and Enhancing the Organizational Climate

Diversity training can have little impact unless the organizational climate honors and supports cultural differences. In this kind of climate, people come to see that any communication—whether between employees or between an employee and a customer—is a multicultural event. When communication is understood and

[2] *A Workshop on Managing Diversity in the Workplace* by S. Kanu Kogod offers a complete workshop design for training managers. For additional information on this topic, refer to the following diversity products offered by Pfeiffer & Company: *Diversity Awareness Profile* (an instrument in both employee's and manager's versions), *Workforce America! Managing Employee Diversity as a Vital Resource,* and *Managing Diversity* Videocassette and Leader's Guide.

approached in this manner, the parties involved can investigate, define, and lay out each other's cultures like maps to new territories. The organizations that promote this view will not only provide powerful guidance for their employees but will also increase customer satisfaction.

An employee perceives the organizational climate as supporting cultural differences if he or she can answer "yes" to four questions:[3]

1. Do I have the time and tools to do my job?

2. Am I paid what I think I deserve?

3. Does the organization mean what it says about the importance of diversity?

4. Am I, as an employee, being treated in the same respectful manner in which the organization wants customers to be treated?

Every organization has a unique system of values and beliefs. These values and beliefs, which create a climate that employees perceive as either supportive or not supportive of diversity, are shaped by experience, historical tradition, competitive position, economic status, political circumstances, finances, and the work setting. The HRD professional can help managers to identify these forces and the barriers to managing diversity that characterize the organization.

For example, at Ricoh Company, Ltd.,[4] a Japanese organization, the corporate philosophy stresses quality while recognizing that people are the key to attaining it. The philosophy also expresses the organization's strategy: "Love your Neighbor, Love your Country, Love your Work."

At Ricoh quality means identifying problems and finding solutions. Everyone is responsible for quality, but top management is held accountable. It is taboo to say to a customer "That's not my problem," "That's not possible," or "That's not my fault." Following are the principles for quality that Ricoh stresses to its employees:

- "All people around you are your customers." (This statement emphasizes the "Love your Neighbor" aspect of the company's strategy as well as the value that Ricoh places on diversity.)
- "Quality cannot be built alone."
- "You own any problem that arises."

---

[3] These questions have been adapted from a presentation given by Ron Zemke in January, 1989, at the Best of America Conference sponsored by Lakewood Publications.

[4] The discussion of Ricoh's philosophy, strategy, and principles for quality is derived from an address given by Ricoh's president, Hiroshi Hamada, during The Quality Forum VII, a conference held in New York on October 1, 1991. The quotes are taken from Mr. Hamada's oral presentation.

Ricoh's president, Hiroshi Hamada, attributes the organization's success in linking philosophy and strategy with performance to a "transformation in human consciousness." It is this kind of transformation that the HRD professional can help an organization's management to devise and implement.

Creating a Vision, Determining Strategies, and Implementing Action Plans

Once the organizational climate has been analyzed and barriers identified, the next step is to help management create a vision for managing diversity in the organization—the way things could be in an ideal situation. Then the managers compare the way things *could be* with the way things *are* and assess the disparity between these two. Next the managers approach the issue from a problem-solving standpoint and determine what strategies to use to move the organization in the direction of the ideal.

It is a good idea to develop an action plan for each strategy, determining what specific tasks need to be done, who will do them and by when, who could provide help (for example, trainers, consultants, or internal experts on various subjects), what obstacles might stand in the way of proposed changes, and how to remove those obstacles or diminish their impact. This process yields a systematic plan to follow and increases the likelihood of success.

Managers, as the people with the greatest power in any organization, are the ones who must start the process of identifying and removing barriers as well as modeling the desired behavior with regard to diversity. Nonmanagerial employees cannot be expected to initiate this behavior.

The HRD professional needs to emphasize that the goal is to create a process—one that continually moves the organizational culture closer to welcoming multiple perspectives and tapping into the talents of all employees. As Roosevelt Thomas (1991, p. 10), the primary spokesperson for this new paradigm, states, "Managing diversity is a comprehensive managerial process for developing an environment that works for all employees."

When an organization is attempting to create such a process, its managers must understand that they can function either as powerful change agents or as barriers. Managers who use a facilitative approach are likely to be effective change agents; managers who use a controlling, directive approach are likely to be barriers.[5] Facilitative managers differ from their controlling counterparts in several ways that propel an organization toward an effective process for managing diversity:

1. They view both people and tasks as important to the organization. They find rewards in managing people as well as in accomplishing tasks.
2. They see employees as resources who can help to achieve business objectives, not just as tools to get the job done. Therefore, they work with

[5] See the article entitled "From Controlling to Facilitating: How to L.E.A.D." in this *Annual.*

employees, communicating openly and ensuring employee involvement in problem solving and in making decisions about how work is to be done.

3. They are comfortable with differences among people, with multiple perspectives, and with diverse work styles. Unlike controlling managers, they spend the time and effort required to listen to and evaluate points of view that are different from their own. They do not simply accept diversity as a reality that must be dealt with to avoid cultural collisions or lawsuits; they welcome it as a contributor to the organization's success.

4. They accept the fact that valuing and managing diversity constitute a long-term process and that it is not easy to determine at the outset how this process might contribute to the bottom line.

Once managers clearly understand the managerial behavior required to establish the desired process, they can progress to developing strategies. Strategies for addressing diversity may be aimed at any of three levels of the organization: system, task, or personal. Strategies at the *system* level include using culture brokers (external or internal consultants) who function as linking agents between cultural groups, developing and perpetuating slogans and stories about organizational heroes, enhancing language banks, creating incentives for managing diversity effectively, celebrating events that honor diversity, and instituting creative rewards and forms of recognition. Strategies at the *task* level include developing job aids that accommodate cultural differences[6] and implementing a system for envisioning results. Strategies at the *personal* level include such activities as developing and using procedures for negotiation and conflict resolution and conducting a brief interview with an employee from a culture that is different from one's own.

Implementing action plans for strategies requires time and patience, and the HRD professional can be an invaluable resource during this period. Non-managerial employees will need to be made aware of the organization's policies regarding diversity and the strategies that the managers have devised. They also may need specific training on diversity issues. Handouts like the one featured in Figure 1 can be a useful part of such training.

The HRD professional should let people know that he or she is willing to serve as a consultant, an arbitrator, or a mentor. It is also a good idea for the HRD professional to have resource materials available for those who need them: a list of diversity consultants and trainers as well as any reading materials and videos that can provide useful information and examples of how to handle different situations. Also, it is important for employees representing diverse cultures to have mentors or sponsors to guide them as they learn organizational norms. Consequently, the HRD practitioner may want to set up a mentoring program, making certain that employees from different cultures are linked with willing, savvy mentors.

---

[6] See the article entitled "Developing Successful Job Aids" in this *Annual*.

When someone from a different culture confronts you about a problem, communicating can be difficult. Following these suggestions may help you communicate more effectively in such a situation:

1. Listen.

- Actively listen to the other person. Paraphrase what you hear; then confirm that you heard correctly.
- Respond to *what* is being said, not *how* it is said.
- If the other person seems angry or frustrated, wait until the anger or frustration has been expressed before responding to the situation.
- Avoid an ethnocentric reaction (anger, shock, or laughter that might convey disapproval of the other person's expectations, phraseology, facial expression, gestures, and so on).
- Stay confident, relaxed, and open to all information.

2. Evaluate.

- Hold any reactions or judgments until you determine the cause of the problem. (Were your expectations or those of the other person violated? Was the problem caused by intrusion from sources outside the organization?)
- Ask open-ended questions (ones that cannot be answered with a simple "yes" or "no"). Answers to these questions will give you valuable information.

3. Negotiate and Accommodate.

- Agree with the other person's right to hold his or her opinion.
- Explain your perspective of the problem.
- Find out what the other person expects from you and/or the organization.
- Acknowledge similarities and differences in what you are able to provide and what the other person expects.
- Tell the other person what you are willing to do to correct the problem. Offer at least two options.
- Allow the other person to choose an option as long as the choice avoids harm to either of you or to the organization. In accommodating the other person's needs, go as far as you are willing to go and as far as the system will support you. If necessary, work to change the system.
- Commit to following through and providing a timely response.
- Thank the other person for letting you know about the problem and giving you and/or the organization a chance to correct it.

Figure 1. The Cultural Component of Problem Solving

CONCLUSION

Organizations that recognize the value of diversity and manage diversity effectively have realized these benefits:

- Diversity brings a variety of ideas and viewpoints to the organization—an advantage that is especially beneficial when creative problem solving is required.
- Diversity increases productivity and makes work fun and interesting.
- Employees are willing to take risks; they play to win rather than not to lose. As a result, creativity, leadership, and innovation are enhanced.
- Employees are empowered and have a sense of their potential in and value to the company.

Many if not most of us are facing or soon will face the opportunity—and the challenges—of meeting and working with people from different cultures. We and the organizations we work for can choose to see diversity in the workplace as a drawback or as a chance to grow. With training and practice, we can learn to listen to individuals from different cultures, to respond to them with cultural relativism rather than ethnocentrism, to negotiate, and to accommodate differences. Learning to use this response pattern is not easy, but HRD professionals can provide valuable assistance as organizational members strive to incorporate this pattern into their behavioral repertoire. All of us—HRD professionals and others—can work to transform our organizations into places where fresh perspectives are welcomed and where all employees feel free to express themselves, to test their assumptions, to take some risks, to forgive themselves when they make mistakes, and to see their mistakes as an opportunity to learn.

REFERENCES

Johnston, W.B., & Packer, A.E. (1987). *Workforce 2000: Work & workers for the twenty-first century.* Washington, DC: Hudson Institute.

Thomas, R.R. (1991). *Beyond race and gender.* New York: AMACOM.

S. Kanu Kogod, Ph.D., *is the founder and president of Bridges in Organizations, Inc., a consulting firm in Bethesda, Maryland, that addresses three key organizational issues: managing a multicultural environment, enhancing productive relations in the workplace, and improving customer service. She received her doctorate in sociocultural anthropology from the University of Florida and now applies her knowledge of anthropology to the management of diversity in organizations. In addition to her work as a consultant, she designs training and assessment programs and trains others in how to conduct diversity training. She is the author of* A Workshop on Managing Diversity in the Workplace *as well as several articles on cultural issues. In 1989 the Society of Applied Anthropology elected her as a Fellow for outstanding contributions to the field.*

TIME-BASED EVOLUTION AND FASTER CYCLE TIME[1]

Kenneth W. Herzog

If there were a universal "truth" applicable to business and industry across all organizational settings, it would be that organizations today encounter greater challenges than were encountered ten, five, or even one year ago. As a result, present-day organizations, more than ever before, must contend with Darwinian natural-selection mechanisms operating within their business environments. Thus, organizational evolution, like human and animal evolution, depends on continual adaptation to environmental influences. The demands of specific business environments are varied and sometimes complex, but they typically include the following:

- Increasing technological innovation;
- Decreasing availability of resources;
- Increasing customer demands for value-added elements of products and services; and
- Increasing competition in both the domestic and international marketplace.

The classic example of an organizational system sluggish in response to environmental-selection mechanisms is the American automobile industry. Once world-class leaders in automobile design and production, American manufacturers now frantically attempt to gain ground in a marketplace that they once dominated. There is evidence that some evolutionary progress and recovery are beginning to take place: for example, in the Saturn experiment by General Motors and partnership trends between American and Japanese automobile manufacturers. Nevertheless, a New York Times News Service article (1991) points out that during the first two quarters of 1991, Japanese automobile manufacturers increased their market share 4 percent over the same period in 1989. The increase, when added to existing market share, translates into nearly 30 percent of domestic passenger-automobile sales. American manufacturers do not enjoy such encouraging results.

The American steel industry is another classic example. Many believe that American steel—unlike automobile manufacturing—is, for all practical purposes,

[1] Based, in part, on "Faster Cycle Time," in J.W. Pfeiffer (Ed.), 1991, *Theories and Models in Applied Behavioral Science* (Vol. 4), San Diego, CA: Pfeiffer & Company.

nearly extinct. Similarly, consumer electronics, as an American industry, appears dangerously close to sharing the same fate. However, focusing an analysis entirely on manufacturing seriously underestimates the influence of evolutionary processes on nonmanufacturing sectors. For instance, savings and loan institutions, banks, and many other service-oriented industries just now are learning how much their vitality and survival depend on an ability to evolve relative to the natural-selection mechanisms operating in their environments.

The idea of adaptation is not new, as much of the human resource development (HRD) and organizational development (OD) literature has emphasized awareness of and adaptation to changing business environments for two decades. The hard reality is that neither technological innovation nor sensitized customer demand nor global competition is likely to decrease. Resources will not likely become more readily available. The hardest reality is that, like many animal species that are now extinct, organizations that do not evolve probably will fail to survive.

ORGANIZATIONS AS SYSTEMS

On the theoretical side, the concept of organizations as "systems" plays a major role in organizational evolution; that is, conceptualizing organizations as a continuing cycle of interrelated inputs, internal processes, and outputs functioning together in order to achieve a common purpose. Organizations are also open systems (Katz & Kahn, 1978) and therefore subject to environmental influence (see Figure 1). Most importantly, changes in any one aspect of the system necessarily cause changes in the other parts.

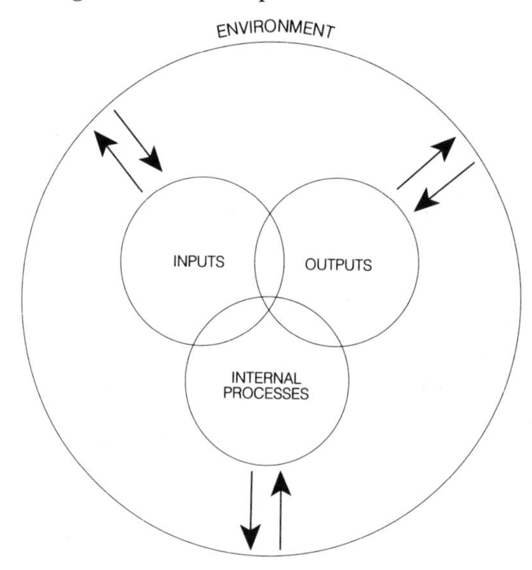

Figure 1. Organizations as Open Systems

For animal organisms, the environment is *the* source of oxygen, food, water, and other nutrient input. Without continued input the organism will not have the ability to sustain itself. Once nutrients are absorbed, biological and physiological processes transform nutrient input into outputs that increase the organism's likelihood of survival in its environment. Animal systems seek only nutrients that can be processed efficiently and produce species-survival outcomes. Evolution in the animal kingdom does not build in a need for excess.

Organizations share similar systemic attributes. For organizations, the environment is a source of customers, human resources, operating capital, raw materials, technology, and other nutrient input. Like animal organisms, without continued input of nutrients, organizations cannot sustain themselves. Similarly, once nutrients are absorbed, internal processes are activated to transform the nutrients into product and service outputs, which increase the likelihood of survival. However, unlike animal organisms, organizations tend to import excess nutrients and develop internal processes that functionally inhibit system efficiency and survival outcomes.

The universal truth within the world of animal systems is that environmental conditions change over time. Climates and habitats change, nutrients become more difficult to obtain, and competition for available resources increases accordingly. In response, animals alter the ways in which they seek and process inputs. The alterations occur through a series of naturally occurring genetic mutations within the organism. The mutations create changes in internal processing and nutrient-seeking behavior so that survival outcomes can continue. Genetic mutation is a survival-of-the-fittest natural-selection mechanism in which the "fittest" are transformed into organisms that are similar, yet more adaptive and appropriate for their environments. Natural selection is random and cannot be controlled by the organism itself.

Organizations also operate within environments that change over time. Technological nutrients continually increase in complexity and cost; raw materials, operating capital, and human resources become more difficult to obtain; and end users of organizational products and services increasingly demand higher-quality, value-added outputs. Further complicating the environmental picture, the number of organizations competing for the same customer attention in both the domestic and international marketplace continually increases. All of these factors create evolutionary demands for the organization to do more with less.

In response, organizations have learned that they too must alter the ways in which inputs are obtained and processed. The alterations occur through a series of internal mutations, which create changes in internal processing and behavior so that survival outcomes can continue. Organizational mutations are also part of environmental survival-of-the-fittest selection mechanisms, but here is where the comparison with animal organisms no longer holds. Unlike animal mutations, organizational mutations are not random; they are initiated through managerial action. Thus, organizational evolution is intentional and controlled through managerial decision processes and managerial behavior. Simply put, organizations can learn from animal evolution and, furthermore, can deliberately initiate action to generate evolutionary progress.

THE NEXT EVOLUTION

Present-day organizations represent the surviving fittest; in other words, those that have created intentional mutations within their internal processes so that organizational inputs can be efficiently transformed into customer-accepted outputs. However, being one of the fittest in the present evolutionary epoch does not ensure continued fitness as environmental conditions change. Consequently, the present fittest must proceed with a future awareness, because evolutionary processes will continue to select only the evolved fittest.

Evolution in general requires system behaviors that increase the likelihood of obtaining continued inputs. Characteristically, organizational evolution requires behaviors that produce product and service outputs acceptable to customers. Outputs accepted by and valued by customers return profit. Profit, in turn, increases the organization's ability to strengthen its customer base and to obtain the continued human resources, raw material, and technological nutrients needed for evolutionary progress. This pattern suggests that the surviving fittest, now and in the future, necessarily must evolve into customer-responsive organisms.

The evolutionary advantage enjoyed by customer-responsive organizations is well documented and has led some organizational anthropologists to predict that those first to respond to customer needs hold the highest probability of survival (Blackburn, 1990; Bower & Hout, 1988; Dumaine, 1989; Gupta & Wilemon, 1990; Meyer, 1990; Peters, 1989; Stalk & Hout, 1990; Uttal, 1987). Speed to market becomes even more critical, given the number of competitors—or predators—operating within the boundaries of a finite marketplace. Thus, speed to the marketplace through time-based management may very well be the next wave of organizational evolution.

FASTER CYCLE TIME

An organization that is first to reach customers with products and services has clear evolutionary advantages over its competitors in the same marketplace. Furthermore, the organization is likely to be perceived as innovative, responsive, and on the leading edge of evolutionary progress. Intangibles, such as good will, increase because of the higher value that customers place on organizational outputs. Market share and profit increase accordingly. Simply put, evolved, leading-edge organizations enjoy greater returns on outputs and, thus, greater ability to obtain nutrient inputs from their environment.

The evolutionary advantage enjoyed by first-to-market outputs is so strategically significant that, in nearly all cases, "the first entrant into a market typically dominates that market in both share and profit margins" (Meyer, 1990, p. 1). Similarly, Peters (1989) suggested that time-based management and speed to market are quickly becoming the fundamental determinant of competitive advantage or disadvantage. Organizational evolution into a time-based system can be facilitated through a process identified as *faster cycle time* (see Meyer, 1990; Pfeiffer, 1991).

Principles of Faster Cycle Time

Faster cycle time (FCT) is defined as an "ongoing ability to identify, satisfy, and be paid for meeting customer needs faster than anyone else" (Meyer, 1990, p. 1). The definition is intended to communicate the following six key points:

1. FCT is *continual* and *ongoing* and involves finding ways to constantly improve internal processing. Organizations that relax in a dynamic environment invite speedy evolutionary retardation.
2. FCT is concerned with *identifying* specific customer needs in order to be first with the ability to fulfill those needs.
3. FCT is concerned with *quality output and customer satisfaction,* which suggests that *high quality can never be sacrificed in order to speed products and services to market.*
4. FCT organizations deliver added value to customers and deserve to be *compensated adequately* for their contribution to increased customer satisfaction.
5. FCT is focused on *meeting customer needs.* Explicitly, this means that products and services that are not acceptable to customers are not acceptable to the organization.
6. FCT organizations develop and introduce products and services *faster than any competitor* in order to gain evolutionary advantages that lead to control of their markets.

In summary, faster cycle time is a time-based management process that highlights an organization's ability to quickly develop and bring its products and services to market. Yet, even though speed is emphasized, FCT moves beyond simple increases in the pace of work or simple replacement of people with machines and advanced technology. FCT requires *increases in the amount and speed of organizational learning* and compels systemic integration of new values, modified (mutated) organizational structures, and supporting reward systems to reinforce fundamental changes in the work process (internal processing).

KEY STEPS IN IMPLEMENTATION

As a part of organizational evolution (which is controllable), implementing FCT requires the elimination of unnecessary inputs and inhibiting process steps. Meyer (1990) outlines six fundamental principles or interconnected steps that must be in place and operational in order to ensure evolutionary success through faster cycle time. This section is devoted to a discussion of those steps.

1. Understanding the Customer's Definition of "Value Added"

Faster cycle time categorizes two classes of organizational work: that which creates output that is more valuable for end users (customers), and that which does not.

Value-added work is simply work the customer is willing to pay for. Predictably, value-added work increases revenue and, subsequently, profit. Thus, work that does not add value becomes a cost that reduces an organization's ability to obtain inputs needed for evolutionary progress. Faster cycle time is driven by an intensified *focus of organizational effort on work that adds value for the end customer and elimination of work that does not.*

Understandably, a value-added work focus is possible only after detailed definitions of what customers consider value-added have been developed. Customers are defined as "anyone willing to pay" for a product or service (Meyer, 1990). This definition differs from definitions found in other continual-improvement processes such as "total quality," in that "internal customers" are not recognized as part of the value-adding process. In time-based systems, the inclusion of "internal customers" skews explicit understanding of what is added value for the end users who actually pay for the added value. End users (customers) produce revenue, whereas internal customers produce cost and, hence, reduce profit.

Accordingly, the first step in FCT implementation is precise identification of end customers. Once identified, precision definitions of what is value added for the *customer* can be determined. Necessarily, information identifying what is value added for customers needs to come from customers. Any other source risks high levels of error. Then management defines the *value-added focus* of the organization, that is, its strategic direction and whether or not the organization is willing to commit sufficient resources to meet customer needs. A value-added focus results in *value-added propositions* (that is, specific statements by the organization that describe what is and what is not value added). Value-added propositions function as operational guidelines that unify the organization in accomplishing strategic value-added goals.

2. Focusing Organizational Work on What Adds Value for the End Customer

Managerial decisions on a strategic focus and the ensuing action to eliminate unnecessary inputs and processes can proceed only after customer-determined definitions of value-added elements are identified. Once identified, focusing on work that adds value can begin. An effective way to differentiate between work that adds value and work that does not is to create a map of the organization's *value-delivery system,* which includes everything required to complete the input/internal-processing/output cycle (see Figure 2).

The mapping process identifies critical inputs (including vendors and suppliers), critical internal processes and systems, and all major outputs. Effective maps include only the most important "how it is now" components of a system. Unnecessary detail should be eliminated to make identification of critical and important processes less confusing. System detail can always be added once the basic value-adding system is fully understood. The map must be realistic, not a vision of how things *should* be. The completed map should include all key players and stakeholders, key process steps, key tasks, and the amount of time required to complete each task.

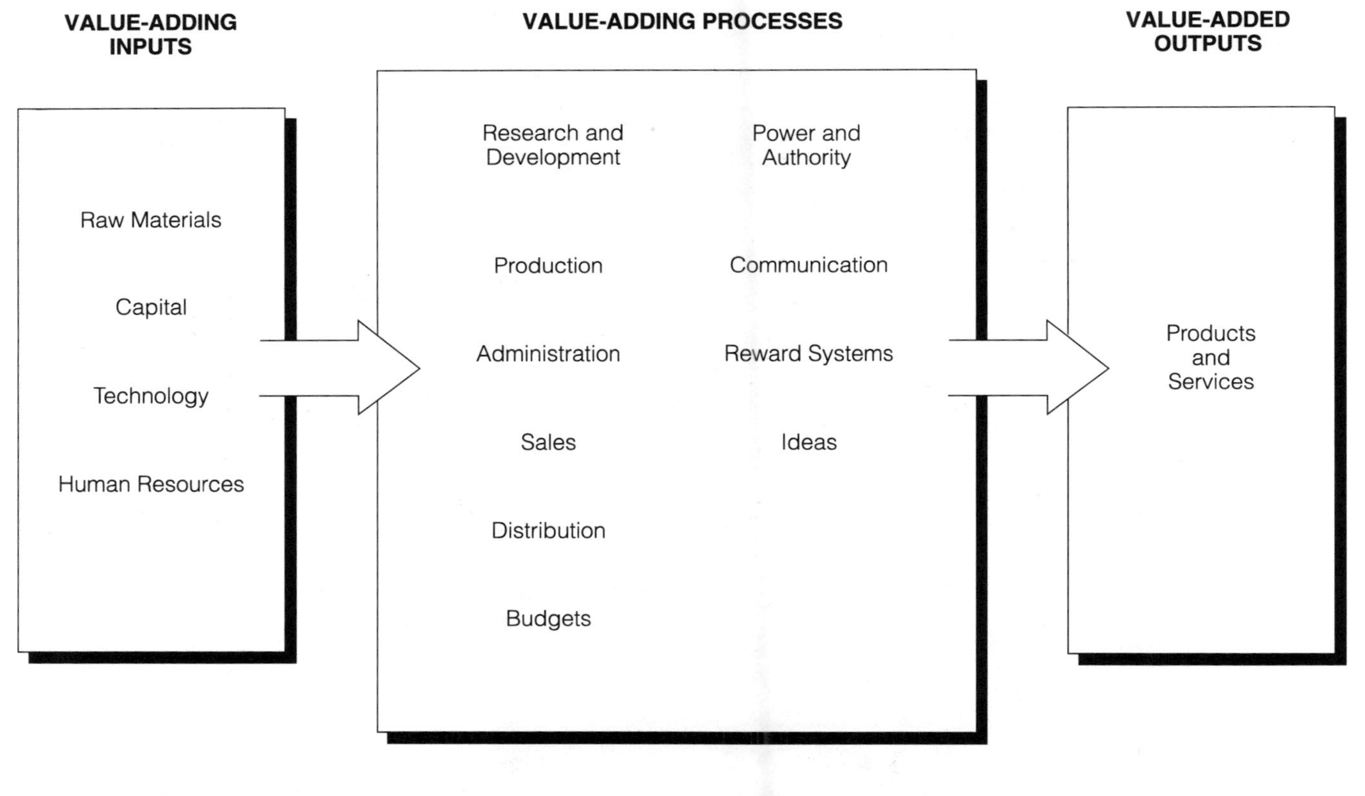

Figure 2. Example of Organizational Value-Delivery System

From "Faster Cycle Time" in J.W. Pfeiffer (Ed.), *Theories and Models in Applied Behavioral Science* (Vol. 4), p. 70, San Diego, CA: Pfeiffer & Company.

3. Restructuring the Organization

A well-developed map reveals all critical process steps and explicitly identifies value-added and nonvalue-added input/processing/output components. The information provides management with a clear picture of specific mutations required to focus on organizational work the customer is willing to pay for.

Flat hierarchical organizational structures and multifunctional work teams are essential for fast response to customers. By their very nature, centrally controlled, functionally differentiated, and hierarchically structured organizations do not respond well to customer needs. The fundamental reason for this failure is that such organizations tend to view customer concerns from rigid functional boundaries, making it extremely difficult to see the big picture of customer satisfaction. Fast response is next to impossible when function drives output. Fast response necessitates evolution into a multifunctional (cross-functional), team-based organizational structure; and this evolution requires shifts in the balance of power so that responsibility for implementing value-added propositions is shared among as many functions as feasible.

Multifunctional teams consist of both customers and representatives from each functional area whose work adds value to the end product or service. Customers, as team members, are essential in the continuous redefinition of *value added*. The team role is to support one another in value-added work, as defined by the team. According to Meyer, the evolution into team-based, cross-functional structure requires an *organizational architecture* that emphasizes values and supporting reward systems related to the following:

- Team charters rather than functional charters;
- Team goals rather than functional and individual goals;
- Team-member roles and responsibilities instead of functional roles and responsibilities;
- Team boundaries and limits rather than functional boundaries and limits;
- Team relationships with other teams, other functions, and organizational management;
- Team rewards; and
- Team-support requirements from functional areas.

4. Continuous Process Evolution

In contrast to functionally rigid architectures, multifunctional architecture utilizes and incorporates the knowledge, skills, and abilities from many different functional areas, all of which have expertise in varied elements of the organizational work process. Multifunctional cooperation, thus, affords the highest likelihood of overcoming tendencies toward excess and inefficient work processes, which inhibit fast response and result in evolutionary retardation.

Process means simply *how* work is accomplished within the organization. Continuous process improvements are notable evolutionary advantages. If internal processes are more efficient and effective and require less input, then speed to the marketplace and customer acceptance will increase correspondingly. The net effect is higher revenue, decreased operating costs, and higher earnings. Process improvements, therefore, must be pursued as enthusiastically as developing value-added products and services. Many organizations do not sufficiently attend to process for several reasons, including the following:

- Meaningful process improvement requires time, money, and additional resources;
- It can be difficult to implement;
- It requires high levels of cross-functional cooperation; and
- It is difficult to measure and show a return on investment.

Process evolution begins with dedicating whatever time, money, and resources are necessary for establishing process-improvement goals and developing meaningful process measures.

5. Setting Challenging Goals to Reduce Cycle Time and Publicly Measure Progress

Faster-cycle-time proponents suggest that meaningful process improvement is attainable through reductions in the time required to finish the *complete processing cycle,* that is, the amount of time necessary to transform inputs into customer-accepted outputs. Time-based strategy requires (or encourages) at least a 50-percent improvement as an initial goal for reductions in processing cycle time. If the goal were lower than 50 percent, employees could find many ways to tighten their belts and perhaps reach the goal without changing the process. The idea is to set challenging goals that require teams to move beyond simply increasing the pace of work and to find new paths for the process.

After challenging goals have been established and mutations determined, the focus shifts to measurement. If a process-cycle beginning and a process-cycle end can be defined, then what happens in between can be measured. Given that determining what to measure and what measures will be most meaningful is often subjective, it is important to select measures easily understood by the organization, its teams, and the industry in general. Measurement results then must be distributed or displayed to communicate clearly the progress toward improvement. Individuals, work teams, and organizations learn from and pay attention to what is measured.

6. Creating an Environment that Stimulates and Reinforces Continual Learning and Action

Meyer (1990, p. 13) defines organizational learning as the "creation of knowledge that is accessible and used throughout the entire organization to accomplish its mission." Organizational learning cannot take place until the people in the organization have access to information. Fast response and faster cycle time constitute a *competitive strategy* that must be *learned* throughout the whole organization.

Evolved organizations stimulate knowledge acquisition and learning as well as arouse innovation and creativity by asking the question *"so what?"* and by publishing the resulting information organization-wide. Without free-flowing information throughout all parts of the system, evolutionary progress in the entire system is severely inhibited. Learning organizations understand there is characteristically a period of "unlearning" and "letting go" of existing beliefs, policies, and power relationships. Accordingly, reward systems are structured in a manner that reinforces incremental progress and organizational ability to evolve through faster-cycle-time principles.

HUMAN RESOURCE DEVELOPMENT IMPLICATIONS

Organizational evolution does not occur randomly, nor does it occur as a result of chance. Evolution requires focused effort on the part of all organizational members. As organizations are, and always will be, products of their environments, new values and methods of work that "fit" into the business environment must be learned and integrated into the total organizational system. Accordingly, as speed to market becomes one of the more important determinants of successful evolution, the speed of organizational learning and the role of HRD in facilitating that learning become even more vital.

Over the past seventy years or so, *human resources,* as a functional specialty, has evolved. The vocabulary used for that functional identification has changed; for example, from "personnel" to "labor relations" to "employee relations" and finally to the present-day "human resources." The name changes alone indicate major evolutionary shifts in the focus of the human resource function. Appropriately, time-sensitive environments and time-based strategy require still further evolution. Freedman (1990) and Hackett (1988), among others, have suggested that the role of the HRD professional during the next evolution may very well be fivefold: keeper of stakeholder interests; negotiator and influencer; knowledge professional; futurist; and most importantly, catalyst and champion of change.

Keeper of stakeholder interests. As keeper of stakeholder interests, the HRD professional explicitly stresses the mission and economics of the organization and, thus, the interests of organizational management.

Negotiator and influencer. As negotiator and influencer, the HRD professional facilitates the communication of information and serves as a representative of employee interests.

Knowledge professional. As a knowledge professional, the HRD professional has technical expertise that is utilized specifically for support rather than for administration.

Futurist. As a futurist, the HRD professional is sensitive to external conditions and trends that influence the input/processing/output cycle.

Catalyst and champion of change. As a catalyst and champion of change, the HRD professional guides the organization in breaking down resistance to change and in breaking down the internal barriers inhibiting continuous learning and evolutionary progress.

Faster cycle time requires a *cultural change* whereby "business as usual" becomes transformed into a streamlined, time-sensitive, continuous-learning process. This transformation leads to ongoing evolutionary advantage only because continued learning becomes part of the organization's culture and value-delivery system. Human resource development, because of its penetrating involvement at all organizational levels, is in a unique position to greatly affect the outcome of organizational evolution.

REFERENCES

Blackburn, J.D. (1990). *Time-based competition: The next battleground in American manufacturing.* Homewood, IL: Dow Jones-Irwin.

Bower, J.L., & Hout, T.M. (1988, November-December). Fast-cycle capability for competitive power. *Harvard Business Review,* pp. 110-118.

Dumaine, B. (1989, February 13). How managers can succeed through speed. *Fortune,* pp. 54-59.

Faster cycle time. (1991). In J.W. Pfeiffer (Ed.), *Theories and models in applied behavioral science* (Vol. 4, pp. 65-70). San Diego, CA: Pfeiffer & Company.

Freedman, A. (1990). *The changing human resources function.* New York: The Conference Board.

Gupta, A.K., & Wilemon, D.L. (1990). Accelerating the development of technology-based new products. *California Management Review, 32*(2), 24-44.

Hackett, T.J. (1988, March). The real role of personnel managers. *Personnel Journal,* pp. 70-75.

Katz, D., & Kahn, R.L. (1978). *The social psychology of organizations* (2nd ed.). New York: John Wiley.

Meyer, C. (1990). *Six steps to becoming a fast cycle time competitor* (rev. 1.22). Los Altos, CA: Strategic Alignment Group.

New York Times News Service. (1991, September 4). Japan car makers come out on top in U.S. recession. *San Diego Union,* p. E-2.

Peters, T. (1989, June 12). Speed becomes a leading edge. *Fortune,* p. 12.

Stalk, G., Jr., & Hout, T.M. (1990). Redesign your organization for time-based management. *Planning Review, 18*(1), 4-9.

Uttal, B. (1987, March 2). Speeding new ideas to market. *Fortune,* pp. 62-64, 66.

Kenneth W. Herzog, Ph.D., *is a specialist in the areas of management and organization development. He received his doctorate in industrial/organizational psychology from United States International University, San Diego, California. Dr. Herzog is an adjunct professor of Business Management and Organizational Behavior at both The Union Institute and William Lyon University in San Diego. He is a contributing author for Pfeiffer & Company's* Theories and Models in Applied Behavioral Science *and for the American Society for Training and Development's (San Diego Chapter)* Training Trends.

USING PERSONALITY TYPOLOGY TO BUILD UNDERSTANDING

Toni La Motta

Understanding how others function is a first step in working with them. Organizations consist of people who differ from one another on almost every dimension possible. Diversity certainly is a challenge that is here to stay.

However, diversity also offers an opportunity to appreciate differences. In the face of constant change, organizations need the differing strengths of different types of people. Increasingly organizations are turning to human resource development (HRD) professionals to guide them in managing change and managing diversity.[1] The HRD professional then acts as a bridge between past and future technologies and as a facilitator between employees and managers and among various teams within an organization. As such, an HRD professional plays roles ranging from teacher to technician to prophet to psychologist.

In a dynamic environment, the most important and least understood HRD role may be that of psychologist. People react in many ways to changes around them; some adjust well, but others see change as threatening and react defensively. An effective way to diminish the defensiveness that occurs with change is to define roles clearly and to make personnel feel acknowledged and appreciated. Understanding theories of personality type can help an HRD professional in these endeavors.

This article begins with brief reviews of three related theories of personality typology: Jung, Myers and Briggs, and Keirsey and Bates. Jung's work formed the basis of the later work of Myers and Briggs; the work of Myers and Briggs, in turn, formed the basis of Keirsey and Bates' work. Next the article describes the four dimensions of personality that provide the structure for these three theories. These dimensions are extraverts/introverts, sensors/intuitors, thinkers/feelers, and judgers/perceivers. The article subsequently outlines Jung's functional types and then provides detailed explanations of the more widely recognized Myers-Briggs types and Keirsey and Bates temperaments.

The explanatory material is important to an understanding of the next section, the role of temperament and management style. Following that, four case studies of how personality typology can be used in an organizational setting are presented. Finally, the article describes action steps that can be taken by managers and HRD staff who want to use personality typology to enhance understanding in the workplace.

---

[1] See the article entitled "Managing Diversity in the Workplace" in this *Annual.*

HISTORICAL PERSPECTIVE ON PERSONALITY TYPOLOGIES

Jung's Theory of Type

Carl Gustav Jung was a Swiss psychiatrist whose theory of psychological types (Pfeiffer, 1991) helps people to recognize and to understand basic personality differences. In essence, this theory describes people's ranges of orientations to *perceiving* (sensing versus intuitive), *interpreting* (thinking versus feeling), and *responding* (extraversion versus introversion). By becoming aware of these basic differences, people can better understand others' motivations and behaviors and can expand tolerance and respect for those whose styles are different.

Jung recognized that people make clear choices from infancy on as to how they use their minds. Although each person has some of each kind of orientation, he or she generally favors one type over the other. Furthermore, types seem to be distributed randomly with regard to sex, class, level of education, and so on.

The Myers-Briggs Type Indicator

In the early 1940s, Isabel Briggs Myers and her mother, Katherine Briggs, began to explore ways to use Jung's theories to explain personality differences. With World War II as a backdrop for their work, the women saw peace in the world as the ultimate goal of understanding personality types. Their paper-and-pencil instrument for determining personality type became known as the *Myers-Briggs Type Indicator* (MBTI). The MBTI is based on a psychometric questionnaire whose results seem to determine accurately a person's viewpoint and style of behavior in all aspects of work and personal interaction. Use of the MBTI is extremely widespread; to date, several million Americans have taken it. The instrument also has been translated into Japanese, Spanish, and French, helping many others to understand and accept themselves and others.

Using Jung's theories as a starting point, Myers and Briggs designated three sets of letter pairs: E/I (extraversion/introversion), S/N (sensing/intuitive), and T/F (thinking/feeling). To these they added a fourth letter-pair set, J/P (judging/perceiving). The MBTI classifies each person in one of sixteen personality types, based on that person's preferences for one aspect from each of the four sets of letter pairs.

The Keirsey and Bates Sorter

David Keirsey and Marilyn Bates (1984), in their book *Please Understand Me,* use the same four dimensions that are found in the MBTI to outline four "temperaments." They define temperament to be "that which places a signature or thumbprint on each of one's actions, making it recognizably one's own" (Keirsey & Bates, 1984, p. 27). Temperament is based first on the S/N dimension; differences on this dimension are "the source of the most miscommunication, misunderstanding, vilification, defamation, and denigration" (Keirsey & Bates, 1984, p. 17). People with an S (sensing) preference gather information in concrete ways, based on facts in the here-and-now; temperament theory then subdivides them based on how they act on this information (judging or perceiving). People with an N (intuitive) preference gather information in abstract ways, based on intuition and possibilities; the temperament sorter then subdivides them based on how they make decisions about this information (thinking or feeling). Thus, according to the Keirsey and Bates Sorter, a person is characterized as SJ, SP, NT, or NF.

THE LETTER PAIRS

The dimensions used by Jung, by Myers and Briggs, and by Keirsey and Bates represent tendencies rather than absolute choices. In most situations, a person prefers one approach over another. A person who understands his or her own approach then can use this information to improve communication with others.

Extraverts and Introverts (E and I)

Jung identified two basic "attitude types," which describe the direction of a person's interest: extravert and introvert. In the context of personality typology, an extravert is a person whose energy source is the external world of people and things, and an introvert is a person whose energy source is the internal world of ideas.

An extravert generally appears friendly and easy to know; he or she tends to think aloud and to express emotions openly. An extravert often acts first and reflects later. In contrast, an introvert is most productive in private and tends to reflect first and act later. An introvert generally internalizes emotions and appears to be less self-revealing and to need a great deal of privacy. Contrary to popular notions, however, a healthy extravert may need time alone and a healthy introvert may have highly developed communication skills.

Sensors and Intuitors (S and N)

The S/N preference concerns the mental function of how a person takes in data from the outside world. The letter "S" is used for sensing, and the letter "N" is used to represent intuition.

A person is a sensor if he or she takes in information in parts, noticing fine details by means of the five senses. A sensor is a very practical individual who wants, trusts, and remembers facts. He or she is highly attuned to details and is usually very orderly and organized. For this person, learning is a linear process in which data are collected sequentially and facts are believed only when experience bears them out. A sensor values order and truth; often he or she is a hard worker who values perspiration more than inspiration. A sensor enjoys the present moment, takes directions easily, and may be most comfortable with tasks that are highly detailed and require repetition.

In contrast, a person is an intuitor if he or she perceives a situation in its entirety rather than piecemeal. An intuitor has a global perspective and is often described as living by a sixth sense. He or she is imaginative and is always anticipating future events. An intuitor looks primarily for relationships and patterns in the information taken in. He or she is an innovator who believes in and excels in hunches, visions, and dreams. An intuitor is adept at long-range planning and can recognize all the complexities in a given situation.

Taken to the extreme, the sensing function causes a person to miss the forest for the trees, and the intuitive function causes a person to miss the trees for the forest.

Thinkers and Feelers (T and F)

Once data have been collected, decisions often must be made, a process that is determined by one's T/F preference. The letter "T" represents thinking and the letter "F" represents feeling. Although this preference is based on how logic is used, thinking should not be equated with intelligence or intellectualism, nor should feelings be equated with emotion.

A thinker processes data in a formalized, linear fashion and can be described as logical. He or she uses an impersonal basis to make decisions in an exacting, structured, analytical manner. The thinker's actions are apt to be deliberate and based on cause and effect. A thinker is ruled by the intellect and will fight for principles; such a person is drawn to jobs that do not depend heavily on interpersonal dynamics.

In contrast, a feeler makes decisions based on a process that more closely reflects personal values or concerns for others. He or she looks at extenuating circumstances rather than rigid laws. A feeler often is artistic and sensitive to the opinions and values of others; consequently, he or she is best suited to a job that requires strong communication and interpersonal skills.

Judgers and Perceivers (J and P)

Jung's discussion of temperament actually dealt only with the S/N, T/F, and E/I preferences, emphasizing that each person has preferred styles of perceiving and judging that are best done in either the outer or inner world. Myers and Briggs built from Jung's theory and created a fourth pair of opposites for the MBTI, concerning the style in which a person lives life (J/P). The J/P preference represents the weight that each of the mental functions (S/N and T/F) is given. In general terms, this preference refers to lifestyle.

A judger prefers situations that are orderly and well planned, and the judging function is dominant in the decision-making dimension, regardless of whether the person is a thinker or a feeler. Such a person prefers a decided, settled path and tends to be neat and orderly. A judger must know priorities and works best when his or her attention is dedicated to one assignment. He or she likes to be prepared for any situation, runs life by making and adhering to lists, thrives on deadlines, and always sees a task through to the end. However, because of a strong desire for stability, a judger may find change troubling.

A perceiver, on the other hand, lives life in an open, fluid, and spontaneous fashion. The perceiving function is dominant in his or her actions, regardless of whether the person is a sensor or an intuitor. A perceiver sees life's possibilities and is always ready for the unexpected. He or she remains open to sudden changes and is comfortable with letting things happen by chance; this person adapts well to changing environments and usually enjoys being given a variety of tasks.

COMBINING ATTITUDE AND FUNCTION

Jungian Functional Types

Jung categorized people according to the psychological functions of thinking, feeling, sensation, and intuition; each of these functions then could be found in either extraverted or introverted individuals. In this way, Jung recognized eight functional types: extraverted sensing, extraverted intuitive, extraverted thinking, extraverted feeling, introverted sensing, introverted intuitive, introverted thinking, and introverted feeling. Complete descriptions of these eight functional types can be found in the article entitled "Jungian Typologies" in Volume 1 of *Theories and Models in Applied Behavioral Science* (Pfeiffer, 1991).

The Myers-Briggs Types

The sixteen four-letter type indicators that classify types in the Myers-Briggs Type Indicator (MBTI) consist of one letter representing a trait from each pair. Thus, the possible sixteen combinations are ISTJ, ESTJ, INTJ, ENTJ, ISTP, ESTP, INTP, ENTP, ISFJ, ESFJ, INFJ, ENFJ, ISFP, ESFP, INFP, and ENFP. Each of these types has certain characteristics and preferences that distinguish it from other types.

ISTJ (Introverted-Sensing-Thinking-Judging). The ISTJ type is dependable and decisive. Attention to detail, combined with dependability, draws a person of this type to careers in which he or she can work alone and can focus on results, objective thinking, and procedures.

ESTJ (Extraverted-Sensing-Thinking-Judging). People of this type perceive through their senses rather than through their intuition and can be described as practical and oriented toward facts. Because of their focus on visible, measurable results, this type is ideally suited to organizing and directing the production of products.

INTJ (Introverted-Intuitive-Thinking-Judging). INTJ types are naturally good at brainstorming and excel at turning theory into practice. They often choose careers that allow them to create and apply technology, and they often rise rapidly in an organization because of their abilities to focus on both the overall picture and the details of a situation.

ENTJ (Extraverted-Intuitive-Thinking-Judging). The ENTJ type uses intuition rather than sensing to explore possibilities and relationships between things. People of this type have a strong desire to lead and tend to rise quickly to upper-management levels.

ISTP (Introverted-Sensing-Thinking-Perceiving). An ISTP type excels in technical and scientific fields because he or she uses sensing and thinking to analyze and organize data. Not wasting time is a key value for a person of this type, who tends to become bored by tasks that are too routine or too open ended.

ESTP (Extraverted-Sensing-Thinking-Perceiving). The ESTP type makes decisions based on logic more than on feelings. Such a person prefers to learn as he or she goes along, as opposed to becoming familiar with an entire process in advance. An ESTP type has excellent entrepreneurial abilities but quickly tires of routine administrative details.

INTP (Introverted-Intuitive-Thinking-Perceiving). The INTP person uses intuition to explore possibilities, preferring new ideas and theories to facts. This person's love of problem solving means that he or she is well suited to research and other scholarly endeavors.

ENTP (Extraverted-Intuitive-Thinking-Perceiving). The ENTP type is attracted to work that allows the exercise of ingenuity. Such a person learns best by discussing and challenging and has little tolerance for tedious details.

ISFJ (Introverted-Sensing-Feeling-Judging). An ISFJ type combines an ability to use facts and data with sensitivity to others. Although uncomfortable in ambiguous situations, a person of this type is a hard worker and prefers work in which he or she can be of service to others, both within the organization and outside of it.

ESFJ (Extraverted-Sensing-Feeling-Judging). The ESFJ type is probably the most sociable of all types and thus is highly effective in dealing with others. He or she often leans toward a career that serves others, such as teaching or the ministry.

INFJ (Introverted-Intuitive-Feeling-Judging). The INFJ type has a natural gift for facilitating groups. Although interpersonal interactions are important to a person of this type, he or she can be comfortable with any work that allows opportunities to grow and to learn.

ENFJ (Extraverted-Intuitive-Feeling-Judging). An ENFJ person is a born leader who places highest priority on people. This preference, combined with his or her strong verbal-communication skills, makes the ENFJ type ideally suited for motivating others.

ISFP (Introverted-Sensing-Feeling-Perceiving). People whose type is ISFP excel at tasks that require long periods of concentration and have senses that are keenly tuned. They prefer to express themselves in concrete, nonverbal ways and are especially inclined toward the fine arts.

ESFP (Extraverted-Sensing-Feeling-Perceiving). An ESFP type uses sensing and feeling to live in the here-and-now and is most challenged by activities that are new and require some special effort. He or she prefers work that provides instant gratification, an opportunity to work with others, and avenues for learning and growing.

INFP (Introverted-Intuitive-Feeling-Perceiving). People of this type are best described as idealists; they value integrity, hard work, and concern for others. Although they are adaptable to most work situations, they are best suited for careers that involve service to others.

ENFP (Extraverted-Intuitive-Feeling-Perceiving). The ENFP type is most interested in finding new solutions to problems and is attracted to work that involves people. Such a person tends to be impatient with rules and procedures and serves better as a mentor for employees than as a boss.

Keirsey and Bates Temperaments

The Keirsey and Bates Sorter classifies people by *temperament* rather than by type. Based on Jungian definitions, the Sorter lists the four temperaments as sensing perceiver (SP), sensing judger (SJ), intuitive thinker (NT), or intuitive feeler (NF). Sensing perceivers and sensing judgers each make up between 35 and 40 percent of the population, while intuitive thinkers and intuitive feelers each constitute between 10 and 15 percent.

Sensing Perceiver (SP). An SP, or sensing perceiver, constantly seeks adventure and freedom and is open to whatever is new and changing. This person lives for the moment and makes an excellent negotiator. In a work setting, he or she may deal well with vendors and may be useful in keeping the staff abreast of new products and new releases. Such a person often is known as a troubleshooter who likes to resolve crises and to rally the support of others in solving a problem. Hot-line programs are often well served by people with SP temperaments.

Sensing Judger (SJ). A sensing judger (SJ) believes in rules, regulations, and rituals. He or she works best in a formalized, structured situation and often is well qualified to institute the structure that is needed in the workplace. A sensing judger would make a good librarian, inventory controller, scheduler, or administrator. He or she thrives on setting standards, whether in reference to resource selection or the day-to-day operating procedures of the department.

Intuitive Thinker (NT). A person who wants to understand, control, explain, and predict events is an intuitive thinker (NT). He or she is an intellectual purist and a self-motivated learner. An intuitive thinker can best serve an organization as a visionary and planner. He or she is a determined learner and will pursue something until it is mastered. An intuitive thinker makes an excellent system designer because of his or her conceptual ability and may be well suited to customer support because of a need to strive for resolution. Newsletter production may also be a good outlet for an intuitive thinker's skills.

Intuitive Feeler (NF). An intuitive feeler (NF) is enthusiastic and often has strong communication and interaction skills. Such a person often excels at public relations and can be effective as a liaison to other companies or departments. An intuitive feeler also often makes a good teacher, especially on the elementary level, because of his or her patience and understanding. Such a person is excellent at setting the atmosphere necessary for quality learning and training.

PERSONALITY TYPOLOGY AND MANAGEMENT STYLE

Because all temperament types bring their own strengths and weaknesses to the workplace, managers need to be aware of their own temperaments before they attempt to understand and lead the rest of the staff. Temperament, according to Keirsey and Bates (1984), is a prime determinant of management style. To use personality typing within a department, a manager must first look at the corporate culture in which the department exists, its particular mission, and the objectives of the available positions. He or she must consider whether the department is new, is seeking greater recognition, or is a mature group looking to improve or to maintain services.

Managers need to assess their own temperaments and personality styles and their inherent strengths and weaknesses before assessing the behavior exhibited by current or potential staff members. Most managers will need staff members with similar personalities to support them. However, opposite types are also needed to compensate for existing weaknesses. The best teams seem to be composed of people who have some personality differences but who are not total opposites. Differences can encourage group growth, while similarities can facilitate understanding and communication. When a team of complete opposites does exist, an understanding of type theory can go a long way toward alleviating disagreements and recognizing the need for team integration.

When looking for a clear vision of how to plan for the future, the manager should keep in mind that sensors are best at practical, detail tasks; that intuitors are best at creative, long-range tasks; that thinkers' skills are appropriate for analysis tasks; and that the skills of feelers are suited to interpersonal communications. A successful staff demands that all skills be used in the right place at the right time. A good manager will recognize the type of task that needs to be done and will assign the best and most appropriate talents to accomplish the job in harmony.

The Sensing-Judging (SJ) Manager

The SJ manager is a stabilizer or consolidator who excels at establishing policies, rules, schedules, and routines. Such a person is usually patient, thorough, and steady. An SJ manager will provide a sense of permanence that encourages industriousness and responsibility in a staff. A sensing-judging manager is a task master who feels that every person must earn his or her keep and therefore tends to be very reluctant to praise. Operational costs are carefully monitored, but true costs often are not. An SJ manager is impatient with delays, may decide issues too quickly, and often complicates matters by preserving rules that are unnecessary and by adapting slowly to change. On the other hand, this type of person has a strong understanding of policy and is a good decision maker. He or she runs meetings efficiently; is always punctual; and can absorb, remember, manipulate, and manage a great deal of detail—traits that certainly are useful to an organization.

The Sensing-Perceiving (SP) Manager

Unlike the SJ manager who sets up rules, regulations, and procedures, the SP manager excels at putting out fires. An SP manager has a good grasp of potential situations and is an excellent diplomat. The SP type is crisis oriented and makes decisions based on expediency; neither regulations nor interpersonal relations are so sacred that they cannot be negotiated by an SP manager. An SP manager is concerned with getting the job done and is very reluctant to pay attention to theory or abstractions. Such a person often makes commitments that he or she has difficulty carrying out when something comes up that is more current or more pressing. An SP manager can be unpredictable and, when not troubleshooting, can resist changes that are imposed by someone else. However, such a person adapts well when a situation changes, always seeming to be one step ahead. He or she is very practical and often sees breakdowns before they occur. Beginning or struggling organizations are ideally suited to the SP manager.

The Intuitive-Thinking (NT) Manager

An NT manager is the true architect of change, questioning everything and basing answers on proven laws and principles. Although he or she is not good at managing maintenance or consolidation projects, an intuitive-thinking manager excels at and takes pride in technical knowledge. An NT manager avoids crisis at all costs because everything must make sense to him or her. The NT manager may delegate the execution of organizational plans but afterward rarely feels that these plans were carried out satisfactorily. Such a person often has difficulty with interpersonal transactions because of his or her impatience and reluctance to show appreciation. A need to escalate standards continually results in the NT manager's feeling restless and unfulfilled. An NT manager sees the long- and short-term implications of a decision, can recognize the power base and the structure of an organization, and can make decisions based on impersonal choices. More than any other type, an intuitive thinker seems to have the vision to see all dimensions of a system, making him or her a very capable planner and constructor.

The Intuitive-Feeling (NF) Manager

A manager who is an intuitive feeler is probably inclined toward personnel management. He or she is committed to the personal progress of the staff, to seeing possibilities for others' growth, and to helping others to develop their potentials. An NF manager is democratic and encourages participation; in fact, he or she often is overly concerned with the staff's personal problems. Interpersonal relationships often drain the time and energy that an NF manager needs for his or her personal and professional life. However, an NF manager's ability to show appreciation can encourage staff; verbal fluency and enthusiasm make him or her an excellent spokesperson for an organization. An NF manager is often a good judge of the organizational climate; he or she shows great patience, despite a tendency to opt for stopgap solutions. Such a person can find himself or herself in conflict if the qualities of subordinates do not match the tasks required by the manager's superiors. In such situations, an NF manager can become frustrated at not being able to please all the people all the time; often, however, he or she learns to turn liabilities into assets.

PERSONALITY TYPOLOGY IN THE WORKPLACE

Personality typology can be used to classify a person's behavioral type in very general terms. Despite significant differences within each type, recognizable similarities are apparent. The purpose of studying types is not to judge others or to change their behavior, but rather to understand and to appreciate why people respond differently to the same stimuli. No preference is right or wrong; each has its own strengths and weaknesses. Effective decision making in the workplace can hinge on exploiting the strengths and minimizing the weaknesses of each type. For example, on a team project, an S (sensor) will note essential details and apply practicality. However, an N (intuitive) will exercise ingenuity, see the possibilities, and give a clear vision of the future. In addition, a T (thinker) will provide incisive analyses and an F (feeler) will supply the necessary interpersonal skills. Together all four will be effective in bringing the project to fruition.

Being typed, therefore, should not limit people but rather uncover their possibilities. Living or working with a person of the opposite type can generate friction, but understanding may help opposites to accept and to take advantage of each other's differences.

Case Study 1: Extraverted Feeler and Introverted Thinker

The following example illustrates how a manager and an employee used personality typology to resolve a conflict. The manager, Helen, showed a strong preference for extraversion and feeling; in contrast, the employee, Marie, tended toward introversion and thinking. When Helen would ask Marie how she felt about issues they had been discussing, Marie never expressed an opinion. Later, however, Marie would complain or express disagreement about the same issues to Helen or to another staff member. Once she understood the concept of personality types, Helen learned that the best way to encourage Marie's feedback in a positive manner was to ask Marie to consider the situation and to express her opinions within a few hours or days. This approach gave Marie the time she needed to sort through her ideas and to substantiate her viewpoint. Meanwhile, through typing, Marie began to understand Helen's need to verbalize and to monitor the environment around her.

Case Study 2: Training Extraverts and Introverts

In creating a training environment, a human resource development (HRD) professional must be aware that extraverts and introverts learn differently. For an extravert, concepts must follow experience; in other words, extraverts learn by example or trial and error. In contrast, an introvert wants to learn the theory or the concepts behind a lesson before trying to put them into practice.

For example, a trainer who teaches conflict-management skills to introverts might first familiarize them with theories of conflict and encourage them to read on the subject; then the trainer could conduct activities that involve group processes. A trainer teaching conflict-management skills to extraverts might need the opposite approach: Group experience would precede any written text or theory because extraverts learn best by trial and error and tend to have shorter attention spans.

The same consideration of E/I preference holds true for the working environment. Extraverts may experience a distracting loneliness when not in contact with people. They usually do not mind noise around the workplace, and some may even need noise (such as music) in order to work. The introvert, however, is more territorial. He or she may desire a defined space and may show a true need for privacy in the physical environment. Understanding and accommodating these needs and differences will foster the highest-possible productivity.

Case Study 3: A Perceiver and a Judger

Veronica, a perceiver, and Wayne, a judger, worked together on a project. Each time they met for strategic planning sessions, Wayne felt that nothing of value had been accomplished. However, Veronica felt satisfied that the sessions had unveiled many possibilities—but she also sensed Wayne's discomfort. Because they were aware of their differences on the J/P scale, they resolved the conflict by establishing a clearly defined agenda and setting strict time limits for each meeting; this satisfied the judger's needs. To satisfy the perceiver's needs, they agreed to explore as many areas as possible on a given topic and to reopen the topic at the next session to make sure that all the issues had been explored.

Case Study 4: Hiring Decisions That Reflect S/N Preferences

The way a manager interviews potential staff members may reveal his or her own sensing/intuitive preference. A sensing manager will be inclined to rely on résumés and proven experience, but an intuitive manager will be inclined to rely more on an actual interview and the applicant's potential. For example, an executive employment agent who wanted to hire an HRD manager for a major bank said that he wanted someone who had already started an HRD department successfully, preferably for a bank in the same state. This specificity indicates the agent's sensing mentality. When he was unable to fill the position according to his preference, he acceded to the bank's request for someone with the creative potential to deal with new situations and enough understanding of the HRD function to be able to create new programs—a more intuitive approach.

Because a work team needs a mix of types, managers and HRD professionals must not let their own S/N preference govern hiring decisions. For example, consider the following two approaches to learning a new computer program: (1) reading the manual and following the instructions closely, and (2) plunging into the task and looking up needed information only if it does not become obvious with use. Which approach is most successful? The answer depends on the learner. Sensors would rather use skills already learned, while intuitors prefer to develop new skills. To a sensing interviewer, an intuitor may appear to have his or her head in the clouds. Conversely, the intuitive interviewer may see the sensor as being too set in his or her ways and too materialistic. Both types have strengths and weaknesses, and both can be useful. Managers and HRD professionals who have good grasps of personality typing should be able to understand and work with both types, deploying them according to their strengths.

ACTION STEPS

The theories of personality typing that are discussed in this article must be implemented with great care and flexibility. The following checklist provides some general guidelines for managers and HRD professionals who wish to use personality-type testing to select and assign staff members:

- Read about personality-type theories (for basic bibliographic information, see Sample, 1984).
- Contact organizations that teach or use the theories.
- Assess the existing organizational climate to determine how the theories can best be used.
- Use the Myers-Briggs Type Indicator (MBTI) or a similar instrument to type members of the organization.
- Understand that a person's own personality type affects his or her perceptions of others.
- Help employees to understand type theory and encourage them to use this understanding to reduce conflicts.
- Consider type theory as one factor in selecting employees and in making assignments.
- Use typing to understand a person's potential and best work style, not to set limits.
- Stress that all personality types have strengths and orientations that can be invaluable to the organization.
- Use type theory to explain rather than to excuse.
- Celebrate differences.

REFERENCES

Keirsey, D., & Bates, M. (1984). *Please understand me.* Del Mar, CA: Gnosology Books Ltd.

Kroeger, O., & Thuesen, J.M. (1988). *Type talk: How to determine your personality type and change your life.* New York: Delacorte.

Pfeiffer, J.W. (Ed.). (1991). *Theories and models in applied behavioral science* (Volume 1). San Diego, CA: Pfeiffer & Company.

Sample, J.A. (1984). A bibliography of applications of the Myers-Briggs Type Indicator (MBTI) to management and organizational behavior. In J.W. Pfeiffer & L.D. Goodstein (Eds.), *The 1984 annual: Developing human resources* (pp. 145-152). San Diego, CA: Pfeiffer & Company.

Toni La Motta *is president of Toni La Motta International (TLI). A motivational keynote speaker, she conducts seminars for organizations on employee morale, team building, and customer service. Corporations use her expertise as a consultant on morale issues and reward and recognition plans. She is also an adjunct faculty member at National University in San Diego, California.*

MANAGING GREEN: DEFINING AN ORGANIZATION'S ENVIRONMENTAL ROLE

Marian K. Prokop

INTRODUCTION

Twenty years ago the United Nations Conference on the Human Environment was convened in Stockholm, Sweden, marking the start of the era of the environment. At that time, the conference was intended to make world leaders aware of environmental concerns. In contrast, a major United Nations Conference on Environment and Development will take place in Brazil in 1992. Its focus will be on the *economics* of environmental management. As Long (1991, p. 4) notes, "One can track the evolution of environmental concern over twenty years by watching it move from the back page of major newspapers to the front page, and now to the financial page."

A second change in focus between the two conferences is that the first focused on "tangible" forms of pollution (primarily air and water pollution); the second will encompass "intangible" forms of pollution (chemicals, radiation, and so on), as well as such topics as global warming, depletion of the ozone layer, deforestation, and pollution of the oceans.

Just as the shift in focus of the two conferences can be tracked, a change in the trends of environmental management can also be tracked. In the 1970s, governments sought improvements for pollution problems with regulation. Over time, governments have come to rely on market-based incentives, such as environmental taxes, deposit-refund plans, and tradable emission permits.

In the European Community, differences are readily apparent in how environmental concerns are handled. For example, Great Britain, as an island, has different pollution problems from those of the more densely populated Germany, which is situated in the center of Europe; this explains in part Germany's stricter environmental regulations and stronger green political party.

The twenty-four member countries of the Organization for Economic Cooperation and Development (OECD) represent 16 percent of the world's population, but their economies generate 76 percent of the world's trade and 50 percent of the world's energy use (Avérous, 1991). The OECD has taken an active role in five key areas: "the relationship between the economy and the environment; energy and the environment; clean technology; environmental health and safety; and cooperation with nonmember countries" (Long, 1991, p. 7).

Despite the progress made in some parts of the world, the outlook for the developing world is less optimistic. In most of the developing world, environmental concerns have been set aside in the face of population growth and debt problems. However, discovery of the hole in the ozone layer over Antarctica has pointed to the urgency of achieving global cooperation; the efforts of developed nations alone will be inadequate to address such global environmental threats.

This article describes the current trends in managing green and the reasons behind these trends. It outlines practical approaches to minimizing waste and maximizing resources and concludes with ways in which a human resource development (HRD) professional can assist an organization in defining its environmental role.

TRENDS IN MANAGING GREEN

"Going green" means that all parts of an organization must accept the organization's social and environmental responsibilities. Organizational decision making requires making choices from among various alternatives, each of which is more or less harmful to the world at large. For example, an organization committed to going green might decide to select suppliers based in part on each supplier's environmental responsiveness or to offer incentives to employees who carpool or telecommute (that is, work at home and communicate with the organization via computer modem). The organization might also decide to provide space for a recycling center to which employees and community residents could bring recyclable paper, glass, aluminum, and plastic.

In the past industry reacted to environmentalism; legislation mandated pollution control and hazardous-waste management. Now the trend is for environmentalism to stimulate innovation. Economic incentives offered by the government and pollution prevention strategies are key trends for the future.

Another trend is for companies to expand their environmental-management staffs (Deutsch, 1991). For example, at DuPont Company the number of environmental staff positions at its headquarters has increased from three to eleven in the past four years. At the International Business Machine Corporation (IBM), a vice president of environmental health and safety was appointed in 1990. At Ciba-Geigy environmental auditors work as an independent department that reports to the chief executive officer (CEO). At Polaroid Corporation environmental issues are incorporated into the management system by controlling the toxic waste that is generated, by researching new processes that are environmentally sound, and by monitoring the solid waste resulting from Polaroid products and packaging.

Traditionally the industrial sector had the most at stake in being environmentally responsible. Currently, however, the green movement has shifted to the consumer sector (Lublin, 1991). In the last few years more than twenty such companies have appointed environmental-policy officers, including Walt Disney Company; S.C. Johnson & Son, Inc.; Kraft General Foods; Dayton Hudson; Lever Brothers; and Colgate-Palmolive.

WHY COMPANIES ARE BEGINNING TO GO GREEN

McDonald's is a corporation that generates two million pounds of trash per day. In 1989 Fred Krupp, executive director of the Environmental Defense Fund, was called in as a consultant. McDonald's was facing declining sales and consumer pressure to eliminate its "clamshell" packaging. Krupp stressed that the company could not become a leader in environmental sensitivity by just giving money to environmental groups; instead, leadership required a change in operations. The Environmental Defense Fund and McDonald's set up a joint task force in 1990; the task force's report included more than forty recommendations, which, if adopted, could cut trash by three-fourths. Consumers will notice few changes because the majority of the trash at a McDonald's restaurant is generated behind the counter. For example, McDonald's opted to recycle all of its corrugated cardboard, which accounts for one-third of its trash output. In a parallel move, McDonald's required its suppliers to use boxes with at least 35-percent recycled content, thereby strengthening the demand for recycled corrugated boxes. In response to the costs of waste—actual costs and public-relations costs—McDonald's took the position that environmental responsibility was a role that the company could not afford to forego (Gifford, 1991).

This example illustrates the three incentives for businesses to "go green": marketing, social responsibility, and economic value.

Marketing. Consumers are beginning to respond to products that are environmentally responsible. One marketing firm reports that 89 percent of American consumers care about the environmental impact of products, and 78 percent will pay more for products that are "environmentally benign" (Bechtel & the editors of Rodale Press, 1990, p. 1).

In 1989 the Environmental Protection Agency identified IBM as a major emitter of chlorofluorocarbons, which deplete the ozone layer. In part to counteract the negative publicity, IBM committed to spending $100 million by the end of 1993 to correct the problem.

Social Responsibility. Investors are finding that how they evaluate investments needs to change. Choices made solely on the basis of financial return may neglect environmental costs, which will need to be borne somewhere. As Stevenson (1990, p. F13) notes, "The complete return on an investment includes not only the immediate financial reward, but also the financial and physical consequences to other people, the environment, and society."

Corporations also are finding that investing in socially responsible organizations makes good business sense. Ben & Jerry's and Patagonia are just two examples of companies that contribute substantial portions of pre-tax profits to green causes.

Economic Value. The savings from pollution control can be substantial. The 3M Company has incentive programs for employees to suggest pollution-control projects. In the past fourteen years, employees have created 2,700 projects that have saved the company more than $500 million (Jacobs, 1990).

Reducing waste alone can be profitable (Bechtel et al., 1990). In the past, AT&T spent $1 million per year to dispose of trash. With the advent of a recycling program, the company earns $365,000 per year selling recyclables. Similarly, a hospital in Allentown, Pennsylvania, saves $25,000 per year in hauling fees merely by separating cardboard from its trash.

PRACTICAL APPROACHES FOR MANAGING GREEN

All businesses have an impact on the environment. As Joel Makower, co-author of *50 Simple Things Your Business Can Do To Save the Earth,* says:

> To be in business is to be involved in a polluting activity, even if you're not in the manufacturing sector dealing with toxic ash and black smoke. Every company does two basic things: consume energy and resources and create waste. To "go green" reduces to two basic goals: reduce waste and maximize resources—both your investment, capital, and people and the land, water, and air. You can't help but get a better return in the long run. (Nixon, 1991, p. 11)

Practical approaches to managing green involve addressing the twin goals of minimizing waste and maximizing resources. The following sections outline suggestions for implementing these goals.

Goal 1: Minimize Waste

Minimizing waste consists of three steps: (1) reducing the amounts of materials used in an organization's operations, (2) reusing materials when feasible, and (3) recycling as many types of materials as possible.

Reducing the Materials Used

The Environmental Protection Agency estimates that the average American office worker generates as much as one and one-half pounds of paper waste per day. A simple way to alleviate this situation is to use voice-mail or electronic-mail (E-mail) messages instead of making copies of information for everyone in the organization. Another option is to route a single copy of information to a series of readers. Following are suggestions for further reducing the use of paper in an organization:

- Provide reusable cloth towels instead of paper towels in rest rooms;
- Replace frequent company-wide memos with a weekly newsletter;
- Supply ceramic mugs instead of styrofoam or paper cups for coffee;
- Use the smallest packing boxes possible;
- Reduce the size of product packages; and
- Use refillable packages.

Direct-mail marketers have special responsibilities in the area of reducing paper use. The Direct Marketing Association Task Force on Environmental Issues inspired a guidebook entitled *Keeping Your Company Green,* which includes a chapter on "green marketing" that makes the following recommendations (Bechtel et al., 1990):

- Use suppression files ("nixie" and "pander" files) in merge/purge operations to reduce the unwanted and undeliverable mail sent out;
- Purge files often and make use of the National Change of Address data bank;

- Mail fewer, more targeted pieces;
- Reduce the trim size of catalogs and mailings; and
- Try telemarketing.

Energy use is another area in which companies can conserve. On an average, lighting accounts for up to 40 percent of all the energy used in a commercial building. Therefore, a company might switch to compact fluorescent bulbs. The following calculations were made by Amory Lovins, research director of the Rocky Mountain Institute:

> A single 18-watt compact fluorescent light bulb produces the same light as a 75-watt incandescent bulb but lasts about 13 times as long. Over its lifetime, the new light bulb will slow global warming and reduce acid rain by avoiding emissions from a typical U.S. coal plant of one ton of CO_2 and about 20 pounds of SO_2 (sulfur dioxide).... The same fluorescent bulb will also save the cost of buying and installing a dozen ordinary bulbs (about $20); the cost of generating 570 kilowatt hours of electricity (about $20+ worth of fuel); and, during its lifetime, approximately $200-$300 worth of generating capacity. (Bechtel et al., 1990, pp. 46-47)

Businesses also can conserve energy by programing thermostats to automatically adjust the temperature when the building is empty; by wrapping water heaters with insulation and keeping them at 130 degrees; by encouraging car pooling—or, better yet, bicycle riding;[1] and by installing low-flush toilets and faucet aerators to lower water use.

Reusing Materials Whenever Possible

Many items can be recycled; however, using materials more than once before they are recycled is more environmentally responsible than recycling alone. Reusing, then, is the step between using and recycling; following are some ideas for reusing materials:

- Write or print on both sides of a sheet of paper;
- Reuse folders, notebooks, envelopes, and so on;
- Make scratch pads from scrap paper;
- Refill laser-printer toner cartridges;
- Re-ink printer ribbons;
- Reuse packing boxes; and
- Use old newspapers or shredded computer paper for packing materials.

---

[1] While encouraging bicycle riding to conserve energy, employers also can take the opportunity to encourage the protection of human resources by stressing the importance of riders' wearing bike helmets and observing proper safety precautions.

Recycling Materials

Every ton of recycled paper means saving seventeen trees; 4,100 kilowatts of energy; and 7,000 gallons of water. It also keeps sixty pounds of pollution out of the air and three cubic yards of trash out of landfills. Similarly, the energy saved by recycling one glass bottle can light a 100-watt light bulb for four hours, and recycling one aluminum can will save enough energy to operate a television for three hours (Bechtel et al., 1990).

Recycling is now mandatory in nine states, and legislation is pending to make it mandatory in twenty-two more states. In response to the Resource Conservation and Recovery Act, the United States Government Printing Office requires a minimum of 50 percent recycled fiber in all its printed products. Even the *Encyclopaedia Brittanica* is printed on recycled paper. But producing products made of recycled materials requires a constant supply of recycled materials. Companies can support recycling in the following ways:

- Switch to toilet tissue, paper towels, and copy paper made from recycled materials;
- Use wooden stir sticks for coffee instead of nonbiodegradable plastic stir sticks;
- Buy recycled paper from a wholesaler who is committed to developing new recycled products;
- Replace polystyrene peanuts—which contain ozone-depleting chlorofluorocarbons (CFCs)—with alternatives that are made without CFCs;
- Use recycled boxes for shipping;
- Appoint someone to supervise in-house recycling;
- Put two wastebaskets at each desk, one for recyclables and the other for nonrecyclables;
- Buy a silver-recovery filter system for darkroom chemicals;
- Recycle used fluorescent light tubes; and
- Recycle the wood in damaged shipping pallets.

Goal 2: Maximize Resources

Maximizing resources has to do with making the best possible use of all of the resources available to a company, including its investments, capital, people, land, water, and air. The means that organizations employ to maximize resources are as varied as the organizations themselves. One common element in each of the approaches is a recognition on the part of the organization of its responsibilities and a commitment to uphold them.

Investment, Capital, and People. Corporate America has spent $850 billion on pollution cleanup in the past twenty years—with $72 billion spent in 1990 alone (Boroughs & Carpenter, 1991). The balance between the business community and environmentalists is shifting; businesses are beginning to find that prevention is less costly than treatment. Some environmentalists compare pollution prevention to wellness programs (Sheets, 1990, p. 46): "It is not only the moral and ethical thing to do; it makes sense on a dollars-and-cents basis."

Similarly, people are a company's greatest resource; conserving human resources goes hand-in-hand with conserving other resources. Companies maximize these human resources by a variety of means, including encouraging community volunteerism, sponsoring corporate wellness programs, and providing opportunities for personal and professional growth.

Land, Water, and Air. "Design for disassembly" is an offshoot of the reduce/reuse/recycle movement. The phrase refers to items whose component parts can be coded and recycled by professional recyclers. One example is BMW, whose Z1 sports car boasts a metal frame and plastic bumpers, doors, and panels, all coded for recycling (Groves, 1991).

While designing for disassembly is a complex approach to maximizing resources, simpler approaches abound. For example, Lakewood Publications recently planted 15,000 trees in its home state of Minnesota as a step toward replenishing the trees used to publish its magazines, newsletters, and books. Trees not only provide the raw material for paper but also absorb carbon dioxide in the atmosphere, a key step in reversing global warming. For Lakewood, tree planting is one step in a long-term approach to environmental responsibility.

A company can maximize resources in many ways, ranging from buying unbleached coffee filters (to bypass the dioxin production that results from the bleaching process) to halting the testing of products on animals to detoxifying products by eliminating chlorine-bleached paper, plastic outer wraps, and the use of heavy metals in inks (Bechtel et al., 1990). Another approach could be for the company to endorse the Valdez Principles.

THE VALDEZ PRINCIPLES

The Coalition for Environmentally Responsible Economies (CERES) was founded in 1988 "to devise and implement strategies for influencing the environment through capital allocation" (CERES, 1991, p. 2). Its membership includes such groups as the National Audubon Society, the Sierra Club, the United States Public Interest Research Group, and the AFL-CIO Industrial Union Department. On September 7, 1989, CERES released a set of ten guiding principles, called "The Valdez Principles," named in response to the environmental disaster created by the *Exxon Valdez*. Corporations that wish to publicly affirm their commitment to environmentally sound business practices may choose to adopt the Valdez Principles (Figure 1).

As of August, 1991, twenty-nine companies had endorsed the Valdez Principles. In addition, several *Fortune* 500 companies are considering a partnership with CERES around the principles. The Valdez Principles illustrate the potential for voluntary corporate self-governance in environmental responsibility.

The Valdez Principles*

By adopting these Principles, we publicly affirm our belief that corporations and their shareholders have a direct responsibility for the environment. We believe that corporations must conduct their business as responsible stewards of the environment and seek profits only in a manner that leaves the Earth healthy and safe. We believe that corporations must not compromise the ability of future generations to sustain their needs.

We recognize this to be a long-term commitment to update our practices continually in light of advances in technology and new understandings in health and environmental science. We intend to make consistent, measurable progress in implementing these Principles and to apply them wherever we operate throughout the world.

1. ***Protection of the Biosphere.*** We will minimize and strive to eliminate the release of any pollutant that may cause environmental damage to the air, water, or earth, or its inhabitants. We will safeguard habitats in rivers, lakes, wetlands, coastal zones, and oceans and will minimize contributing to the greenhouse effect, depletion of the ozone layer, acid rain, or smog.

2. ***Sustainable Use of Natural Resources.*** We will make sustainable use of renewable natural resources, such as water, soils, and forests. We will conserve nonrenewable natural resources through efficient use and careful planning. We will protect wildlife habitat, open spaces, and wilderness, while preserving biodiversity.

3. ***Reduction and Disposal of Waste.*** We will minimize the creation of waste, especially hazardous waste, and wherever possible recycle materials. We will dispose of all wastes through safe and responsible methods.

4. ***Wise Use of Energy.*** We will make every effort to use environmentally safe and sustainable energy sources to meet our needs. We will invest in approved energy efficiency and conservation in our operations. We will maximize the energy efficiency of products we produce and sell.

5. ***Risk Reduction.*** We will minimize the environmental, health, and safety risks to our employees and the communities in which we operate by employing safe technologies and operating procedures and by being constantly prepared for emergencies.

6. ***Marketing of Safe Products and Services.*** We will sell products or services that minimize adverse environmental impacts and that are safe as consumers commonly use them. We will inform customers of the environmental impacts of our products or services.

7. ***Damage Compensation.*** We will take responsibility for any harm we cause to the environment by making every effort to fully restore the environment and to compensate those persons who are adversely affected.

8. ***Disclosure.*** We will disclose to our employees and to the public incidents relating to our operations that cause environmental harm or pose health or safety hazards. We will disclose potential environmental, health or safety hazards posed by our operations, and we will not take any action against employees who report any condition that creates a danger to the environment or poses health and safety hazards.

9. ***Environmental Directors and Managers.*** We will commit management resources to implement the Valdez Principles, to monitor and report upon our implementation efforts, and to sustain a process to ensure that the Board of Directors and Chief Executive Officer are kept informed of and are fully responsible for all environmental matters. We will establish a Committee of the Board of Directors with responsibility for environmental affairs. At least one member of the Board of Directors will be a person qualified to represent environmental interests to come before the company.

10. ***Assessment and Annual Audit.*** We will conduct and make public an annual self-evaluation of our progress in implementing these Principles and in complying with applicable laws and regulations throughout our worldwide operations. We will work toward the timely creation of independent environmental audit procedures which we will complete annually and make available to the public.

---

*From *The CERES Guide to the Valdez Principles* (pp. 4-5) by CERES, Inc., 1991, Boston: Author. Copyright © 1991 by CERES, Inc. Reprinted by permission.

CONCLUSION

Human resource development (HRD) practitioners are in unique positions to facilitate the transformation to managing green. To start, HRD staff can model behaviors that minimize waste and make efficient use of resources. The next step might be to route a copy of this article to managers to educate them on environmental issues and to encourage them to consider the organization's environmental policy. Subsequently HRD professionals can urge top management to consider whether environmental responsibility should be a part of a company's values and mission statements. By incorporating environmental responsibility into these statements and then publicizing the statements throughout the organization, top management can demonstrate its environmental commitment to employees.

Once the organization's position on environmental responsibility has been delineated, HRD professionals can arrange and/or conduct company-wide training on how to implement activities that are environmentally responsible. One important facet of the training should be to solicit ideas from employees and then to use as many of their ideas as feasible. This earns the employees' commitment and honors their contributions. As an offshoot of the training, the organization can publicize—both internally and externally—what it is doing to fulfill its responsibilities to the environment.

Throughout this process, HRD professionals need to emphasize that environmental concerns and economic concerns are interdependent. As William Reilly, administrator of the Environmental Protection Agency, notes:

> Environmental protection is a sound economic investment.... The star corporate performers of the 1990s will be the companies that are ahead of the environmental power curve. Their customers, employees, stockholders, and boards will increasingly demand a positive environmental performance—not only out of concern for the environment, but also because pollution is a sign of poor management, waste, and inefficiency. (Reilly, 1990, p. B4)

The "no-growth" initiatives of the 1970s have been replaced by calls for "sustainable development," in which economic growth is measured in terms of quality and quantity. "Economics" and "ecology" have the same Greek root, *oikos,* meaning "household" and "everything in its proper place" (Long, 1991, p. 7). The challenge for the 1990s is to integrate the two concepts once again through defining the organization's environmental role.

REFERENCES

Avérous, C. (1991, February/March). An uneven track record on the environment. *The OECD Observer,* pp. 8-13.

Bechtel, S., & the editors of Rodale Press. (1990). *Keeping your company green.* Emmaus, PA: Rodale Press.

Boroughs, D., & Carpenter, B. (1991, March 25). Cleaning up the environment. *U.S. News & World Report,* pp. 45-52.

CERES, Inc. (1991). *The CERES guide to the Valdez Principles.* Boston: Author.

Deutsch, C. (1991, March 3). Giving the environment teeth. *The New York Times,* p. F29.

Gifford, B. (1991, August 19). The greening of the golden arches. *The San Diego Union,* pp. C-2, C-4.

Groves, M. (1991, April 20). Companies spot gold in the "green" movement. *Los Angeles Times,* pp. D1, D4.

Jacobs, D.L. (1990, September 2). Business takes on a green hue: Alliances with environmental groups seek to reduce waste. *The New York Times,* p. F25.

Long, B.L. (1991, February/March). Managing the environment. *The OECD Observer,* pp. 4-7.

Lublin, J.S. (1991, March 5). "Green" executives find their mission isn't a natural part of corporate culture. *The Wall Street Journal,* pp. B1, B4.

Nixon, W. (1991, July 25). The recycling game. *Publishers Weekly,* pp. 11-14.

Reilly, W. (1990, April 22). A world in our hands: Forget the doomsayers—environmental action means both progress and profits. *The Washington Post,* pp. B1, B4.

Sheets, K.R. (1990, February 19). Business's green revolution. *U.S. News & World Report,* pp. 45-46, 48.

Stevenson, G. (1990, March 25). The complete return on investment. *The New York Times,* p. F13.

***Marian K. Prokop** is an editor for Pfeiffer & Company in San Diego, California. Ms. Prokop previously worked as a writer/trainer for migrant education programs in New York and California. She has been a contributor to the* Annuals *and is one of the co-authors of* Pfeiffer's Official Frequent Flyer Guide, *co-published by Pfeiffer & Company, Bonus Books, and Frequent Publications in 1989.*

GUIDELINES FOR CONTRIBUTORS TO PFEIFFER & COMPANY PUBLICATIONS

In 1991 our guidelines for contributors were revised and expanded to include more helpful information to authors who are interested in submitting manuscripts to Pfeiffer & Company. Although these guidelines are available on request from our Editorial Department, we wanted to make this information available as soon as possible in order to reaffirm our interest in receiving submissions both of *Annual* pieces and of other manuscripts. Therefore we are reprinting the guidelines here for our readers.

GENERAL STATEMENT OF PUBLISHING POLICIES AND INTERESTS OF PFEIFFER & COMPANY

Copyright Policy

Authors who are submitting material to Pfeiffer & Company should be aware of our copyright policy for the *Annuals* and certain other books. These publications are copyrighted, but any material published in them that is not copyrighted by others may be freely reproduced for *educational/training activities* (up to a maximum of one hundred copies per year) without prior written permission. Pfeiffer & Company does, however, require that appropriate credit appear on all reproductions, including the title of the piece, author, name of source publication, editor/author of source, and date of publication. Systematic or large-scale reproduction or distribution (more than one hundred copies)—or inclusion of items in publications for sale—may be done only with *prior written permission.*

The *Annual* Series

We are interested in receiving professional development papers (theory along with practical application); instruments (paper-and-pencil inventories, rating scales, and other feedback tools); and structured experiences for possible publication in the *Annual* series. These materials should be immediately useful to practicing professionals in the field of human resource development (HRD). (The *Annual* is not designed to accommodate statistical research; we recommend that such papers be sent to any of the excellent journals in the field.)

Before undertaking a writing project intended for this publication, authors are advised to study recent *Annuals* and to inquire about the current need for materials on a particular topic.

Materials intended for the *Annuals* and questions about *Annual* submissions should be directed to the *Annual* Editor, Pfeiffer & Company.

Book Manuscripts

We are interested in reviewing book-length manuscripts, complete training or instrumentation packages, and other publications that are practical, useful, and appropriate to Pfeiffer & Company's broadly based, human resource development market. Authors of such manuscripts should enclose a specific proposal that includes a table of contents; two sample chapters; and a statement of the intended use, intended audience and market, and unique strengths or aspects of the proposed publication. (For detailed instructions about preparing materials for submission, refer to the following pages.)

Manuscripts for book-length publications and questions about book-length submissions should be directed to the Acquisitions Editor, Pfeiffer & Company.

SPECIFICATIONS FOR THE *ANNUAL* SERIES

Structured Experiences

Structured experiences are intended to be specific, practical tools for the HRD practitioner, describing complete, experiential learning experiences. The following major divisions should be included, in order:

- *Goals:* one or several—the objectives of the activity, which will be met by means of the process and discussions.
- *Group Size:* total group or number of subgroups, if any, and minimum and maximum sizes of subgroups.
- *Time Required:* actual time needed for the entire experience, including introduction, activity, and processing discussions.
- *Materials:* a listing of any forms or work sheets needed—with exact titles indicated—and any special equipment or materials such as blank paper, pencils, scissors, clipboards, and newsprint flip charts.
- *Physical Setting:* size and number of rooms; arrangement of chairs and tables, if any; seating requirements; and so on.
- *Process:* the step-by-step sequence that is necessary to complete the experience successfully, indicating what the facilitator does and what the participants do and ending with a discussion to help the participants to process and integrate their learnings. See "The Experiential Learning Cycle" in the *Reference Guide to Handbooks and Annuals* (1992 edition) or the "Introduction to the Structured Experiences Section" in *The 1983 Annual: Developing Human Resources.*
- *Variations:* possible alterations or adaptations of the process.

All work sheets, role-play instructions, and other materials to be handed out to participants should be included with the structured experience. Work sheets and other handouts should be typed or printed on separate sheets of paper following the description of the activity (as listed above). Do not incorporate as handouts any previously published University Associates/Pfeiffer & Company material (instruments, work sheets, and so on).

If a structured experience calls for the use of a lecturette, the content of that lecturette must be provided in the form of a handout.

A detailed discussion of developing and preparing a structured experience can be found in the "Introduction to the Structured Experiences Section" of the 1974 *Annual*, in the "Introduction to Structured Experiences" of the *Reference Guide to Handbooks and Annuals* (1990 edition), and in *Using Structured Experiences in Human Resource Development*, book one in the University Associates Training Technologies series.

Contributors of structured experiences should bear in mind that these materials will be reproduced for training purposes by users of the *Annual*.

If an activity is accepted for publication, the author must be willing to sign over the copyright to Pfeiffer & Company.

Instruments

The Instrumentation section of the *Annuals* contains paper-and-pencil survey-feedback devices such as inventories, rating scales, questionnaires, and so on, that are designed to be used for training purposes by group facilitators and may be reproduced for such uses. Thus, we at Pfeiffer & Company are looking for instruments that provide immediate, practical feedback to participants to help further their learning in a particular area. We do not publish instruments for research, psychodiagnostic, or therapeutic purposes, although many of the ones that we do publish have been used for research in previous versions and have solid reliability and validity statistics to back up their usefulness. We also do not publish computer-scored instruments in the *Annuals*.

Instruments submitted for the *Annuals* should not be overly complex and should be easy to score (preferably by the respondents themselves).

All instruments should contain the following elements:

1. An *introduction* containing the theoretical and technical rationale for the instrument and the background necessary to use it effectively.

2. A *description* of the instrument form and scoring sheet and of the interpretation sheet, if any.

3. Discussion of how to *administer* the instrument, including general introduction, instructions, and time expectations.

4. Brief discussion of how best to *present* to the participants the theory behind the instrument. (Note that the theory generally is not presented until *after* the respondents have completed the instrument form.)

5. The best way to have the participants *predict* how they will score in terms of the instrument's dimensions.

6. A description of the *scoring process* (that is, how to fill out the scoring sheet).

7. How to help the participants to *interpret* their scores, including an explanation of how to fill out the interpretation or profile sheet, if one exists.
8. Which data generated by the instrument are likely to be appropriate for *posting* (if posting individual scores is not appropriate, group or subgroup data frequently can be posted) and how best to facilitate a discussion to process and integrate the participants' learnings. This may include forming subgroups to compare scores, legitimizing differences, and integrating the feedback derived from the instrument with the participants' self-images, jobs, and so on.
9. Other *suggested uses* for the instrument.
10. Data about *reliability and validity* of the instrument.
11. Starting on a separate page, the *instrument form,* beginning with instructions to the respondent.
12. On a separate page, the *scoring sheet,* including instructions for completing it.
13. On a separate page, the *interpretation or profile sheet* (if any), including instructions for completing it and interpreting the data.

For further information about devising and presenting instruments, see the "Introduction to the Instrumentation Section" of the 1980, 1981, and 1983 *Annuals;* the "Introduction to Instruments" in the *Reference Guide to Handbooks and Annuals* (1990 edition); and *Using Instruments in Human Resource Development,* book two in the University Associates Training Technologies series.

If an instrument is accepted for publication, the author must be willing to sign over the copyright to Pfeiffer & Company.

Professional Development Section

Professional Development Papers

Professional development papers (called "theory and practice papers" in the older *Annuals)* are intended to provide theoretical background as well as information about new techniques, models, and research applications for HRD professionals. They should be directed toward the further professional development of the trainer or consultant and should have a *practical* focus.

The length of a professional development paper generally is from fifteen to forty-five typed, double-spaced pages, which will appear as seven to twenty-two typeset, printed pages. Frequent headings and subheadings are recommended to indicate the paper's divisions and content.

As for all submissions, the best guide to subjects appropriate for this section is a survey of the current HRD literature and the contents of recent *Annuals.*

Specifications for typing manuscripts for the *Annual* are the same as those for all of Pfeiffer & Company's publications and can be found under "General Specifications for Submitting Manuscripts" later in this article. Attention is directed to the specifications for quotations, reference citations in the text, and reference lists or bibliographies.

If an article is accepted for publication, the author must be willing to sign over the copyright to Pfeiffer & Company.

Lecturettes

Lecturettes are brief, simply worded statements of theoretical positions. They are intended for the use of the facilitator who wishes to introduce theory or background information to a group. Because facilitators may choose to deliver these papers orally or to use them as handouts, the topic of a lecturette should be presented clearly, simply, and directly, with emphasis on ease of delivery. A lecturette should be written from an objective point of view.

The length of a lecturette generally is from two to ten typed, double-spaced pages, which will appear as one to five typeset, printed pages. (We try to restrict lecturettes within structured experiences to four double-spaced pages or two typeset, printed pages.)

The use of frequent headings and subheadings in the text is helpful to indicate organization, divisions, and emphasis of the content.

Specifications for quotations, reference citations in the text, and reference listings or bibliographies are delineated in the following section, "General Specifications for Submitting Manuscripts."

If a lecturette is accepted for publication, the author must be willing to sign over the copyright to Pfeiffer & Company.

GENERAL SPECIFICATIONS FOR SUBMITTING MANUSCRIPTS

If at all possible, authors should submit their manuscripts on IBM-compatible disks. WordPerfect 5.1 format is preferable, but ASCII format also is acceptable. A disk should be accompanied by *two* printed copies of the manuscript.

All copy should be *typed or printed double-spaced,* on white, 8½" x 11" paper. Computer-printed manuscripts are acceptable if printed double-spaced with a fresh, *black* ribbon (not gray) and with fully formed, *letter-quality* characters. Manuscripts that are not legible will not be considered for publication. Non-justified text is strongly preferred.

Please include a large self-addressed, sufficiently stamped envelope if you wish to have your manuscript returned.

The proposed title and author's name should be typed alone on the first page. If there is more than one author, the names should appear in the order of significance of their contributions, with the senior author or contributor listed first. The author's last name should be typed in the upper-right corner of each page. Pages should be numbered consecutively in the upper-right corner.

Ideal margins are as follows: left margin, 1 inch; right margin, 1 inch; top margin, 1.5 inches; and bottom margin, 1 inch.

All heads and subheads should be typed flush with the left margin. Major heads dividing sections of the manuscript should be typed in all uppercase letters. Secondary or subheads should be typed with initial capital letters only. Headings should not be underlined. Each heading should be preceded and followed by an extra double space. Please omit any specifications as to fonts, type size, and so on.

Paragraphs should not be indented with tabs (that is, the first word of the paragraph should be typed flush left). Use an extra double space between paragraphs.

Words should not be hyphenated at the end of a line.

Computer files should be spell checked, if possible, before submission.

Each figure, chart, table, graph, or other illustration should be typed or drawn on a separate page, double spaced, and should be inserted at the appropriate point in the text (on the page following the first mention of it). If possible, any graphic work other than type (such as grids, maps, and drawings) should be done in India ink on heavy white paper, suitable for reproduction. Tables (numerical grids, columns and rows, and so on) should be numbered consecutively and distinguished from figures. Figures (such as illustrations or depictions of processes) also should be numbered consecutively. Both figures and tables should be titled.

Footnotes should be either typed at the bottom of the page on which the footnote number appears or listed consecutively on a subsequent page.

Please note that a reference citation should be included *in the text* for every quotation, to indicate any work on which the current text is based, or for any work that is referred to in the text.

Reference citations in the text should include the names of all authors and the date of publication, following the APA format (as given in the *Publication Manual of the American Psychological Association,* third edition, 1983). This book may be obtained from the American Psychological Association, P.O. Box 2710, Hyattsville, MD 20784, (202) 955-7600. Copies are $19.50 each, with a $2.00 shipping and handling charge per order.

A complete reference listing must be supplied for each reference noted in the text. The reference list or bibliography must be in alphabetical order and typed on a separate sheet or sheets at the end of the manuscript. Each reference/bibliographical listing should be *accurate and complete* and should follow the format prescribed by the APA *Publication Manual.*

If it is decided that your book will have an index, use a yellow marker on one copy of your manuscript to highlight the terms that you want indexed. Highlight only *substantive mentions* of a desired term, that is, references to the term that discuss it in some detail and are not simply cursory mentions of the term or name.

As always, the purpose of Pfeiffer & Company's *Annual* series is to serve as a clearinghouse of ideas and activities for and by HRD professionals. Therefore, the *Annual* staff encourages readers to submit material for consideration. Contributors with questions may telephone Pfeiffer & Company's Editorial Department at (619) 578-5900 with any questions about suitability of material, submission procedures, and so on.

CONTRIBUTORS

Terri Burchett
Organization and Management Development Specialist
Tucson Medical Center
Education Services
P.O. Box 42195
Tucson, AZ 85733
(602) 324-5081

Gerry Carline
Training and Development Associates
1223 Maybery
Moose Jaw, Saskatchewan S6H 6X7
Canada
(306) 692-2703

Douglas A. Cohen
AT&T Bell Laboratories
Room 1D-634
101 JFK Parkway
Short Hills, NJ 07078
(201) 564-2955

Mary Ellen Collins
People Power Consulting Service
7667 Hopkins Road
Maineville, OH 45039
(513) 683-9234

Patrick Doyle
Principal
High Impact Training Services
RR2 Perth Road Village
Ontario, Canada K0H 2L0
(613) 353-6517

Jeannette Gautier-Downes
Jeannette Gautier-Downes and Associates
2656 Montrose Place
Santa Barbara, CA 93105
(805) 682-8824

Gary Gemmill, Ph.D.
Professor of Organizational Behavior
School of Management
Syracuse University
Syracuse, NY 13244-2130
(315) 443-2601

Leonard D. Goodstein, Ph.D.
1737 S Street, NW
Washington, DC 20009
(202) 234-8613

Anthony M. Gregory
Senior Partner
Civun
Usishkin 2.8 A
Ramat Hasharon, Israel
(972) 3-5404217

Kenneth W. Herzog, Ph.D.
8395 Westmore Road, #3
San Diego, CA 92126
(619) 578-6380

Bonnie Jameson
Consultant
1024 Underhills Road
Oakland, CA 94610
(415) 832-2597

Janice R. Joplin
Graduate Teaching Associate
Department of Management, Box 19467
University of Texas at Arlington
Arlington, TX 76019
(817) 795-8737

S. Kanu Kogod, Ph.D.
President
Bridges in Organizations, Inc.
9118 Redwood Avenue
Bethesda, MD 20817
(301) 469-6008

Kathleen Kreis, Ed.D.
Director of English
Buffalo Public Schools
730 City Hall
Buffalo, NY 14202
(716) 842-3193

Toni La Motta
President
Toni La Motta International (TLI)
3997 Camino Lindo
San Diego, CA 92122
(619) 587-2106

Patrick Leone, Ph.D.
Manager, Management Development
IDS Financial Services
T/12—Unit 965
IDS Tower 10
Minneapolis, MN 55440
(612) 342-8592

Josephine Lobasz-Mavromatis
Associate Professor
Institute of Public Service
International
University of Connecticut
1800 Asylum Avenue
West Hartford, CT 06117
(203) 241-4924

Robert William Lucas
Senior Trainer
American Automobile Association
1000 AAA Drive
Heathrow, FL 32746-5063
(407) 444-7520

Debra L. Nelson, Ph.D.
Associate Professor of Management
Management Department
College of Business Administration
Oklahoma State University
Stillwater, OK 74078
(405) 744-5106

Carol Nolde
Developmental Senior Editor
Pfeiffer & Company
8517 Production Avenue
San Diego, CA 92121
(619) 578-5900

Udai Pareek, Ph.D.
Chairman, Scientific Advisory
Committee
Indian Institute of
Health Management Research
1 Prabhu Marg
Jaipur 302011
India
(141) 550700
Telex 365-2655
Fax 41-141-550119

Marian K. Prokop
Editor
Pfeiffer & Company
8517 Production Avenue
San Diego, CA 92121
(619) 578-5900

James Campbell Quick, Ph.D.
Professor of Organizational Behavior
Department of Management,
Box 19467
University of Texas at Arlington
Arlington, TX 76019
(817) 496-0567

Jonathan D. Quick, M.D.
Adjunct Associate Professor
Department of Management,
Box 19467
University of Texas at Arlington
Arlington, TX 76019
(817) 496-0567

Gaylord Reagan, Ph.D.
Human Resource Manager
Weyerhaeuser Paper Company
7517 F Street
Omaha, NE 68127
(402) 331-5100

Fran Rees
President
Rees & Associates
2302 W. Lompoc Circle
Mesa, AZ 85202
(602) 491-3620

Allison Rossett, Ed.D.
Professor of Educational Technology
Department of Educational Technology
San Diego State University
San Diego, CA 92182-0311
(619) 594-6088

Marc B. Sokol, Ph.D.
AT&T Bell Laboratories
Room 1L-524
101 JFK Parkway
Short Hills, NJ 07078
(201) 564-4402

Gary Wagenheim
Assistant Professor
Organizational Leadership
and Supervision
School of Technology
Purdue University
1420 Knoy Hall of Technology
West Lafayette, IN 47907-1420
(317) 494-5613

Wm. Randolph Warley, Ph.D.
Assistant Professor
Business and Human Services
University College
Mercer University
Tift College Drive
Forsyth, GA 31029
(912) 994-3001

Jerry Zabel
High Impact Training Services
RR2 Perth Road Village
Ontario, Canada K0H 2L0
(613) 353-6517